HEROIC
CONSERVATISM

HEROIC
CONSERVATISM

*Why Republicans Need
to Embrace America's Ideals
(And Why They Deserve to Fail
If They Don't)*

MICHAEL J. GERSON

HarperOne
A Division of HarperCollinsPublishers

The Council on Foreign Relations is an independent, nonpartisan membership organization, think tank, and publisher dedicated to being a resource for its members, government officials, business executives, journalists, educators and students, civic and religious leaders, and other interested citizens in order to help them better understand the world and the foreign-policy choices facing the United States and other countries. Founded in 1921, the Council takes no institutional positions on matters of policy. The Council carries out its mission by maintaining a diverse membership; convening meetings; supporting a Studies Program that fosters independent research; publishing *Foreign Affairs,* the preeminent journal on international affairs and U.S. foreign policy; sponsoring Independent Task Forces; and providing up-to-date information and analysis about world events and American foreign policy on its Web site, CFR.org.

The Council takes no institutional position on policy issues and has no affiliation with the U.S. Government. All statements of fact and expressions of opinion contained in its publications are the sole responsibility of the author or authors.

HarperCollins Web site: http://www.harpercollins.com
HarperCollins®, ®, and HarperOne™ are
trademarks of HarperCollins Publishers

FIRST EDITION

Library of Congress Cataloging-in-Publication Data is available.

ISBN: 978-0-06-134950-8

07 08 09 10 11 RRD(H) 10 9 8 7 6 5 4 3 2 1

To my wonderful, long-suffering family.

Contents

Acknowledgments

I deeply appreciate the help and wisdom of all my friends and former colleagues who read and commented on the manuscript of this book. I am grateful to Neal Kozodoy for his careful review of several chapters, and to Roger Hertog for his kindness and support. I'm especially thankful for the counsel and friendship of Pete Wehner, the most relentlessly principled man in Washington. On leaving the White House, I was fortunate to find Josh Kvernen, who has ably fulfilled every unreasonable research request. I am grateful to Richard Haass, Gary Samore, and the Council on Foreign Relations for giving me a welcoming new home. Bob Barnett has been kind and patient in helping me construct a life beyond government. And I am thankful to my editor Mickey Maudlin and the very professional team at HarperOne.

Above all, I owe a debt to my colleagues in the speechwriting department of the White House—writers, researchers, support staff—who did exceptional work under impossible circumstances. I am thankful for the memory of Jen Reilly, who showed me the meaning of faith and maturity. And I will always be grateful to John McConnell and Matt Scully—the finest of men.

Chapter 1

Heroic Conservatism

Sometimes in government the most dramatic and noble events come disguised as endless meetings, what might be called the banality of goodness.

The president sat as usual in his blue-and-yellow striped chair at the right of the fireplace in the Oval Office. Much of his senior staff gathered on couches and chairs around the coffee table. The topic for this "policy time" on the afternoon of November 18, 2002 was a proposal that had been kept carefully hidden from much of the government: an emergency plan to provide AIDS treatment and prevention to Africans on a massive scale. Four months before, Deputy Chief of Staff Josh Bolten had given instructions to experts at the National Institutes of Health to "think big." The plan under discussion, crafted by a brilliant NIH researcher named Mark Dybul, was designed to reach two million people with lifesaving drugs, prevent seven million new infections, and provide compassionate care to ten million AIDS victims and the orphans they leave behind. It would be the largest health initiative to combat a single disease in history.

As the plan was developed, only a few people were brought in on the secret. The small team at NIH working on the project had been instructed by the White House to talk to no one. At early stages, not even the Secretary of Health and Human Services, Tommy Thompson, or the National Security Advisor, Condoleezza Rice, had been informed. Bolten, his staff, researchers at the National Institutes of Health, and I were engaged in a humanitarian conspiracy, to prevent an ambitious plan from being watered down or bogged down in the normal, inertial processes of government.

The plan was not only ambitious; it was controversial. Smaller attempts to ramp up AIDS treatment in Africa had accomplished little. In Botswana, a three-year effort had resulted in only two hundred people on AIDS drugs. When eventually informed about the final NIH plan, officials at the Office of Management and Budget and some officials at the National Security Council were highly skeptical. At fifteen billion dollars over five years, the plan cost too much. The infrastructure to deliver drugs did not exist. This kind of foreign-aid spending had never been done successfully before; why would this be an exception? The Centers for Disease Control, smarting at not being consulted, dismissed the approach as "half-baked."

In the Oval Office, the president focused on the details of implementation in a businesslike manner, attempting to poke holes in the proposal. "It doesn't matter how good the goal is if it doesn't work. Will this work?" The policy experts responded by describing an innovative network model, which would deliver drugs through layers of satellite medical centers, even by motorcycle to distant villages. Unlike past foreign-aid programs, the plan would set specific goals, and tie money to performance. At least we would know if it worked or it didn't.

This emphasis on the treatment of AIDS in the developing world was the great risk and originality of the plan. Global health experts, to that point, had generally put their hope in prevention. People with AIDS were considered already lost, extending their lives a costly, uncertain venture, and a poor investment. On this issue, during the meeting, Condoleezza Rice showed a rare flash of emotion: "My mother," she said, "was diagnosed with cancer when I was a teenager. She got treatment, and lived until I was thirty. You bet those years meant something to me—and they would mean something to every African child whose mother lives to take care of them."

The discussion of detail had given way, for me, to a sense of history. During the twentieth century, in other government meetings, in other rooms in Berlin, Moscow, and Beijing, political decisions were calmly debated and made that resulted in genocide and the deaths of millions. Now, in a room where I sat, a decision was pending that could save the lives of millions. It was a vivid reminder of the reach and influence of America: the futures of men, women, and children in African slums and remote villages who would never know our names might depend on the words spoken in the Oval Office that day. President Bush went around the room, asking for conclusions. Most supported the plan; the keepers of the budget opposed. At the last, he came to me. "Gerson, what do you think?"

"If we can do this, and we don't," I said, "it will be a source of shame." As the meeting broke up in a solemn quiet, the president cheerfully mocked, "That's Gerson being Gerson!"

Six weeks later, President Bush took his motorcade up Pennsylvania Avenue to deliver the State of the Union, a serious speech, ending with a long indictment against the dictator of Iraq: "Trusting in the sanity and restraint of Saddam Hussein is not a strategy, and it is not an option." No one expected Africa or AIDS to make an appearance. Among the White House staff, there had been a determined, last-minute attempt to remove the proposal. ("Americans don't want to hear about giving money to foreigners; they care about kitchen-table issues that affect their families.") But the president kept it in, and spoke these words:

Today, on the continent of Africa, nearly thirty million people have the AIDS virus—including three million children under the age of fifteen. There are whole countries in Africa where more than one-third of the adult population carries the infection. More than four million require immediate drug treatment. Yet across that continent, only 50,000 AIDS victims—only 50,000—are receiving the medicine they need.

Because the AIDS diagnosis is considered a death sentence, many do not seek treatment. Almost all who do are turned away. A doctor in rural South Africa describes his frustration. He says, "We have no medicines. Many hospitals tell people, you've got AIDS, we can't help you. Go home and die." In an age of miraculous medicines, no person should have to hear those words.

Ladies and gentlemen, seldom has history offered a greater opportunity to do so much for so many.... To meet a severe and urgent crisis abroad, tonight I propose the Emergency Plan for AIDS Relief—a work of mercy beyond all current international efforts to help the people of Africa.... I ask the Congress to commit $15 billion over the next five years, including nearly $10 billion in new money, to turn the tide against AIDS in the most afflicted nations of Africa and the Caribbean."

In my time at the White House, these were not the most eloquent words I helped write for the president of the United States, but they were the most satisfying.

Less than three years later, outside Kampala, Uganda, my Jeep neared the end of a long dirt road, where I was met by an escort of two dozen women who sang and danced in front of my car for a quarter of a mile to a squatter's camp called the Ajoli quarter. At a small clinic, I met Rose, a Ugandan nurse who runs an AIDS ministry called Meeting Point International, supported in part by the President's Emergency Plan for AIDS Relief.

The Ajoli quarter is the home of striking contrasts. The village is really a densely populated slum, with mud houses and open sewers. A great tide of central Africa's problems and horrors has lapped up on the side of this steep Ugandan hill. Ninety percent of the residents are women or children, refugees from up north, where a brutal, cultish rebel group called the Lord's Resistance Army killed large numbers of the men. Many of the women are HIV positive, and have terrible stories of suffering. A young woman I met had been abducted by the LRA along with other members of her village. She calmly described their first night's "welcoming meal," in which one of the villagers was killed, and the rest were forced to eat him, to instill a proper fear.

Many of the younger boys had been kidnapped by the LRA and trained as soldiers—forced, as Rose said, to do "terrible things," such as cannibalism, and murdering neighbors in their home village so they could never return. One of the former child soldiers I met was maybe sixteen or seventeen years old. When the leader of the LRA, a messianic madman named Joseph Kony, visited his prisoners, all were forced to prostrate themselves—but this young man looked up in curiosity, and they took out one of his eyes as punishment.

But in this place of gathered suffering, I found a concentrated joy. About five hundred people greeted me with the strange and cheerful trilling typical of the region. A group of female dancers, in native skirts and bright orange tops, and a band of young male drummers in pink shorts and yellow shirts, did a raucous performance—and even when Rose tried to get them to stop, they went on with song after song. The performance was loud, slightly suggestive, and somehow holy, an act of defiance against violence and death and fear and despair. It felt like angels bringing happy, rowdy music to the gates of hell—and the gates of hell will not prevail against it.

At the center of it all is Rose, a Christian, slightly plump Ugandan nurse who began using her own money to pay for school fees for former child soldiers, and for AIDS drugs for refugees—at that point she had about two hundred people on treatment. With outside support, she has opened a little clinic and a day-care center. She pays for taxis to get people to the hospital and goes there every Tuesday so her patients can see a friendly face. She organizes soccer games to demonstrate that women on AIDS treatment can become strong once again. And she encourages music and dance to fight the clinical depression many people with AIDS face. Rose does all this with a spirit of cheer that makes a slum feel like a celebration. They call her "Aunty Rose," and everyone gets greeted and touched like her oldest friend. "They are not defeated by the sickness, poverty, and death," she says of the refugees she serves. "They have a dignity and a value. They are children of God. What I give is because I love them."

One woman's story at Meeting Point is typical. Her husband infected her with HIV, and when she refused to abort their child, he left her. Her son eventually became sick and thin from HIV and TB. "The teacher insulted my youngest as a 'skeleton,' and threw a book at the boy. Whenever he was at the gate of the school, the children called him 'skeleton' again. He cried the whole night through. I didn't know if he would die or I would die first." Eventually, friends urged her to go to Meeting Point. At first, she says, "I thought I was in the wrong place. People were dancing, not miserable like me. I didn't know in the whole world there was someone who would show me love." Then, "They started to bring AIDS drugs for that boy. Almost immediately his condition changed, and he is happy and back in school. Now I fear nothing." Now on AIDS treatment herself, she volunteers to help other HIV-positive women. "The one they wanted to bury is the one who is going to assist them," she says. "We are here. We are kicking."

The generosity of the poor turns out to be more impressive than anything we give them. At the center of the Ajoli quarter, a short walk through the red dirt streets, is a steep-walled, open-pit mine. Brush is pushed against the walls and set on fire, to remove water from the rock and cause it to crumble, leaving a permanent haze in the air. The women of the village support themselves by breaking rocks from the pit into gravel with small metal hammers. Each has her own pile she adds to for several hours a day. After Hurricane Katrina on America's Gulf Coast, these women, many of them HIV positive, somehow collected $1,000 and sent it to the American embassy to help with relief efforts. When I thanked them on behalf of our government, I have never seen a group of people more proud of themselves. "We are the donors now," I was told.

Near the end of the welcoming ceremony, one of the HIV-positive women gave me a piece of folded legal-sized paper, soiled with red clay. It read:

> We [are the] patients and children of Meeting Point International. We want to express ourselves that we are the richest in the world. We are not poor. Kony came to free us and instead he cut our mouth, eyes and ears. Politicians came and gave us promises—we remained poor, sick, without hope. Some people came without any promises, stayed with us and loved us. That is why we are here. We are free. We want also to love others truly.

I came to that slum expecting to feel pity. Instead, I felt awe for people who are rich and free. Their final song, performed by women in purple dresses they had made themselves, was sadder than the ones before it. The chorus went: "Life is so sweet, but very short indeed." Because of a political decision made seven thousand miles away, at least some of those lives were lengthened. And that means something. Because even in the haze of that mine, even in the shadow of death, life is so very valuable, so very sweet.

In that Oval Office meeting, and in the slums outside Kampala, I saw one of the high points of political idealism in modern history: an American president, out of moral and religious motivations, pledging billions to save the lives of non-citizens, with no claim to American help other than their humanity. It had a profound effect on me. Before meeting men, women, and children rescued from death in Uganda, Namibia, South Africa, Kenya, and Mozambique, my appreciation of the power of government to do good had been largely theoretical. But here was the living, dancing evidence of what ambitious, moral, effective government can accomplish. Here was an example of what America can do and be in the world. And even if I were tempted, these experiences would not allow me to be cynical about politics.

Critics dismiss this as an aberration—an isolated act of compassion by a president normally obsessed by force and war. It is not an aberration. It is one expression—maybe the least controversial expression—of the organizing principle of the Bush era: an idealism of amazing historical ambition. President Bush's religiously informed moralism, his impatience with political "small ball," his indifference to establishment criticism, have combined to produce far-reaching changes in domestic and foreign policy; far-reaching changes in Republican Party ideology. Opponents may call those changes unwise, or poorly executed. It is difficult to call them inconsequential.

In the aftermath of the attacks of September 11, 2001, President Bush did not merely pursue a popular fight against al-Qaeda terrorists. He conceived of a foreign-policy project as grand and difficult as the Cold War. He set out to remove dangerous, terror-sponsoring regimes in Afghanistan and Iraq, and replace them with governments favorable to the War on Terror. He determined to undermine the appeal of radical Islam by promoting democracy and human rights in the Middle East and other disputed parts of Africa and Asia. He has launched initiatives on disease and development to provide hopeful alternatives to bitterness and violence, increasing foreign assistance faster than any time since the Marshall Plan. And he has expressed these shifts in a frank moral language of right and wrong, good and evil. The stated, moral goal of his second inaugural, "the end of tyranny in our world," is the most ambitious presidential statement on foreign policy since President Woodrow Wilson pledged to "make the world safe for democracy"—and it went beyond that pledge.

The domestic ambitions of the Bush era have been limited by competing international emergencies. But they have still included a major reform of the federal role in education; the addition of a massive prescription-drug benefit to Medicare; and the use of government to support the work of faith-based charities. Republicans who feel that the ideology of Barry Goldwater—the ideology of minimal government—has been assaulted are correct. And this has been accompanied by a strong reassertion of the central place of religion in our common life—not just as a source of comfort in times of tragedy, but also as a foundation for claims of universal human rights and dignity.

In more than five years as a speechwriter and policy advisor to President Bush, I took a hand in both defining and explaining these changes. The president, unlike many of his predecessors, consistently used major speeches to put his personal imprint on policy, to force changes within his own administration, and to set his doctrines in rhetorical stone, requiring future presidents to deal with them. The goals of the Bush presidency can be found in the text, not in the subtext—in the words he chose to use, not in maneuvering behind the scenes. In this process, he came to rely on me to help collect and express his intuitions. And I know that these ambitions were not merely rhetorical. They were intended as major departures from precedent. They were intended to inaugurate an era of idealism.

But as the Bush era comes to a close, a backlash has built. Many Americans have found the ambitions of the last few years exhausting; the costs higher than predicted; the promised successes delayed and distant. Cynicism, not idealism, is the order of the day. Is it credible to talk about the spread of democracy as Iraq divides into warring, sectarian camps? Or to stand for human rights after the pictures from Abu Ghraib? Isn't the world too complicated and sensitive to slight for an American president to talk confidently about "good" and "evil"? Is government too discredited after the failures of Hurricane Katrina to address problems of poverty and racial division? Wouldn't America be better off accepting our limits and lowering our sights?

After recent exertions, this attitude is predictable, even understandable. It is also dangerous. A retreat from idealism and ambition, at this point in our history, would be a disaster for Republicans, for conservatives, and for America.

This book is not an exhaustive history of the Bush years; that is a subject that will occupy many thicker volumes. I have a different purpose: to argue for idealism in a weary time. After five eventful years in the West Wing, I am convinced that the bold use of government to serve human rights and dignity is not only a good thing, but a necessary thing. I believe the security of our country depends on idealism abroad—the promotion of liberty and hope as the alternatives to hatred and bitterness. I believe the unity of our country depends on idealism at home—a determination to care for the weak and vulnerable, and to heal racial divisions by the expansion of opportunity. And I believe my party, the Republican Party, must carry this message of idealism and courage to a tired nation in a pivotal moment, or face a severe judgment of history.

There is no doubt that the times are weary. The backlash against idealism can be found in both American political parties.

Some Democrats, unbalanced by hatred of President Bush, have turned against the confident promotion of freedom in the world. At the time of the 2006 State of the Union address, a group of Democratic and liberal activists organized a viewing party to react to the speech. Every time President Bush used the words *freedom* or *terror,* or *weapons of mass destruction,* the organizers would ring a bell, and the crowd would laugh. In portions of the Democratic Party, just a few years after 9/11, terrorism is a source of humor, derided as a Republican myth, and the word *freedom* has become a laugh line.

On foreign policy, many Democrats do not know what they are doing, because they do not know what they are undoing. In order to undermine the current president, they are carelessly throwing away the tradition of President John F. Kennedy, who said that "the rights of man come not from the generosity of the state, but from the hand of God." They are abandoning the tradition of Franklin Roosevelt, who argued: "We will accept only a world consecrated to freedom of speeches and expression—freedom of every person to worship God in his own way—freedom from want—and freedom from terrorism. Is such a world impossible of attainment? [The] Magna Carta, the Declaration of Independence, the Constitution of the United States, the Emancipation Proclamation and every other milestone of human progress—all were ideals which seemed impossible of attainment—yet they were attained."

What can liberalism possibly mean apart from idealism in the cause of liberty? But that idealism is seldom a Democratic theme today. Some Democrats—there are notable exceptions—are left in a position of opposition without alternatives, of anger without hope, of criticism without idealism. And by offering no solutions of their own to the combination of Islamic radicalism and proliferation, they are asking Americans to passively accept a mortal threat.

The one issue where many Democratic leaders embrace an absolute commitment to liberty is abortion—but, in this case, they define liberty as the right of the strong to control and end the lives of the weak. And this has more to do with power and autonomy than compassion and the protection of human rights. During the 1999 congressional debate on partial-birth abortion—a procedure that violently ends lives during birth—Democratic Senator Barbara Boxer was pressed on the Senate floor to say she would oppose the medical killing of children *after* birth. She refused to commit, saying that children only deserve legal protection "when you bring your baby home."

This frank defense of infanticide is the unconditional surrender of an older, better Democratic tradition. "The moral test of a government," said Senator Hubert Humphrey in 1976, "is how it treats those who are in the dawn of life, the children; those who are in the twilight of life, the aged; and those who are in the shadow of life, the sick, the needy, and the handicapped." It requires a long and difficult search today to find that kind of moral idealism in the party of Hubert Humphrey.

And above all, many Democratic leaders have become resolutely secular. Its chairman, former Vermont Governor Howard Dean, asserts, "My religion doesn't inform my public policy." Democratic activist George Soros complains, "The separation of church and state, the bedrock of our democracy, is clearly undermined by having a born-again president"—effectively adding a new constitutional test for that office: a candidate must not only be born in America, he must only be born once. But it wasn't long ago that the three-time Democratic nominee for president, William Jennings Bryan, was also the most prominent evangelical Christian in America—and no one saw a contradiction. Bryan called his support for progressive causes—from women's rights, to safe working conditions, to progressive taxation—"applied Christianity."

In fact, a rigid secularization would remove one of the main sources of social justice in American history—throwing away another inheritance that Democrats do not seem to value. In our history, religion has often been the carrier of conscience, the source of idealism and reform. It was religious faith that motivated abolitionists through decades of campaigning against slavery; that led young African American girls to risk abuse by sitting at segregated lunch counters; that put foot in front of foot toward police with truncheons on the Edmund Pettus Bridge in Selma, Alabama. Religion, for these Americans, taught objective standards of social justice, not merely personal standards of piety. In general, they believed all individuals had rights because those rights had an Author; that the endowment of this Creator was the source of human worth and the basis for human equality; and that these God-given rights deserved the protection of law. They were confident in the rightness of their cause—and in a Providence that eventually honors personal sacrifice in just causes, in this life or the next.

Among the main thinkers of modern liberalism, this resentment of traditional religion runs even deeper. For influential academics such as the late Richard Rorty of Stanford, the first purpose of education, and the prerequisite for liberal democracy, is to remove a religiously based belief in absolute right and wrong. The goal of teaching is to "arrange things so that students who enter as bigoted, homophobic, religious fundamentalists will leave college with views much like our own." Parents should be warned that "we are going to go right on trying to discredit you in the eyes of your children, trying to strip your fundamentalist religious community of dignity, trying to make your views seem silly rather than discussable." While religion may survive in some form—perhaps as "a religion of literature" that replaces Scripture—any kind of moral judgment must give way to the accepting, relativistic values of democracy. For many liberal thinkers, traditional religious beliefs are a threat to tolerance as the basis for public policy. Ethical relativism is the only answer to moral arrogance.

There is no doubt that religion can be the source of a false and intolerant political certainty. It is a mistake to believe there is a single biblical or moral view on issues like tax policy or missile defense. These are prudential matters, to be debated on their merits. On policy issues, there is often, as the saying goes, truth in my opponent's error, and error in my own truth.

But this is different from asserting that truth itself is unreachable or relative. A philosophy of systematic skepticism and doubt has direct consequences for individuals and for a nation. If moral standards don't exist for others, it is infinitely harder to impose any standards on ourselves—infinitely more difficult to fight the natural pull of selfish interest. Men and women are left without a compass, without a core, and often turn to the lonely pursuit of self. Who would want to call young people to a life of skepticism? What heroes would this creed create? Teaching tolerance to the young is essential. Yet tolerance, at its best, is a morally mandated respect for the lives and opinions of others, not neutrality between just and unjust, noble and base, good and evil.

And there are consequences for our political life, as well. If there are no truths we can know with certainty, there are no self-evident truths of the Declaration of Independence. Our national commitment to human dignity becomes one option among many. The deepest teachings of our conscience may be right ... they may be wrong ... they may be a construct of our culture ... they may result from the chemistry of our brain. This view has many sophisticated advocates, but most heroes of conscience in American history could not be counted among them. "We are not wrong," said Dr. Martin Luther King Jr. "If we are wrong, the Constitution of the United States is wrong. If we are wrong, God Almighty is wrong. If we are wrong, Jesus of Nazareth was merely a utopian dreamer that never came down to earth. If we are wrong, justice is a lie, love has no meaning."

Interest, not justice, is the natural state of society. Justice is an achievement, always won through sacrifice. And that sacrifice is a result of our duties, not our doubts.

A backlash against idealism, in different forms, can also be found in the Republican Party. We are seeing a trend toward foreign-policy "realism," which is deeply skeptical other countries can sustain democracy. Old foreign-policy hands such as former National Security Advisor Brent Scowcroft argue that the promotion of liberty in the Middle East has disturbed "fifty years of peace." He urges support for "stability" because elections are too risky. The "bad guys," he says, "are always better organized."

But "fifty years of peace" has seen several wars of aggression against Israel; and the region's supposed "stability" produced the hijackers of 9/11. The Middle East's mixture of tyranny, radicalism, and stagnation is not only toxic, it is explosive, resulting in the mass murder of American citizens on American soil. The status quo in the Middle East is not stable or sustainable. Whatever the complications that come from Iraq, they do not change the fundamental reality we face: unless change comes to the Middle East, it will continue to produce ideologies and people who kill our citizens; and the scale of that killing will increase as technology advances. We will have spreading freedom, or we will have spreading violence. The traditional responses of foreign-policy realism—the more effective management of favorable dictators—is the application of a band-aid to a cancer.

Many Republicans are also questioning activism and idealism on the domestic agenda, arguing that President Bush's "big government conservatism" is the reason for recent political setbacks. One conservative commentator, after the Republicans lost the House and Senate in 2006, talked of this silver lining: "At least compassionate conservatism is dead." Now is the time, the argument goes, to get back to the real business of conservatism: cutting government.

I saw this governing vision—really a vision to reject governing—at work in the aftermath of Hurricane Katrina. The disaster revealed a kind of poverty that mocks our pledge to be "one nation." In attempting to deliver benefits to victims, the administration found men and women who had never had a bank account, families entirely disconnected from the mainstream economy. A problem so clearly rooted in governmentally enforced oppression—generations of slavery and segregation—demanded an active response by government, to encourage economic empowerment and social mobility.

Yet the response of many Republicans on Capitol Hill and in Washington think tanks was to use the disaster as an excuse for reducing spending. Some Republican leaders proposed to offset the costs of Katrina by cutting the Medicare prescription-drug benefit for seniors. By this odd logic, the repair of levees should be funded by taking drugs from old people. And there was worse. At one post-Katrina meeting with White House officials, a conservative think-tank sage urged: "The president needs to give up something *he* wants. Why not the AIDS program for Africa?" The argument here is stunning: that the best way for conservatives to prove their ideological purity is to let African children die.

This is different from a belief in limited government—a conviction that all conservatives share. It is a disdain for government itself, and a brutal indifference to the consequences of indiscriminately eliminating it. For Republicans headed toward important elections, this kind of crude anti-government message would be a political disaster. Campaigning on the evils of government while opponents talk of health care and education will seem, and be, small-minded, cold, and uninspired. And the question will naturally arise: "Why do you want to be captain of this ship when your goal is to run it onto the rocks?"

The moral stakes for the party are even higher. What does anti-government conservatism offer to urban neighborhoods where violence is common and families are rare? Nothing. What hope does it provide to children in foreign lands dying of diseases that can be treated or prevented for the cost of American spare change? No hope. What achievement would it contribute to the racial healing and unity of our country? No achievement at all. If Republicans run in future elections with a simplistic anti-government message, ignoring the poor, the addicted, and children at risk, they will lose, and they will deserve to lose.

•   •   •

This is an odd and dangerous historical moment. Both political parties are exhausted and timid at just the wrong time—the very time when history is increasing its demands.

Over five years in the White House, I witnessed the arrival of a series of historical challenges, any one of which would strain the energy and creativity of an administration or a generation. I saw the beginnings of a global war on a clear, September day—a war in which any lapse of vigilance, on any future day, could bring more funerals and ruins and fear. Yet some Democrats have chosen this time to deny that America is in a war at all. During his campaign for president, Senator John Kerry preferred to call it "primarily an intelligence and law-enforcement operation." It is the modern equivalent of running for office on the slogan: "Forget Pearl Harbor."

I saw the unprecedented natural disaster of Katrina reveal a continuing form of brutal, economic segregation that will continue to discredit our ideals until it is overcome. I visited regions in Africa where millions are drowning in a sea of disease and violence—at a time when only America has the resources and national calling to help on the scale of the need. Yet some Republicans have chosen this time to call for a return to the narrow bounds of a minimal government.

I saw acts of liberation in Afghanistan and Iraq as noble as any in our history—and the rise of enemies who are using the tools of murder to reverse those verdicts, and turn those nations into battlefields. I saw autocrats in Iran learn to fear the momentum of democracy—then regroup and seek a nuclear prop for their power, raising the prospect of nightmares beyond imagining. Yet some foreign-policy realists, of every ideological background, have chosen this moment to call for retrenchment and retreat.

This is a strange way to prepare Americans for difficult, necessary tasks—like using liquor and luxury to train an athlete; or inculcating fear and caution in a commando; or replacing the call of a trumpet in battle with a kazoo. Weariness and doubt can be found and fed in any nation. But these mental attitudes do nothing to alter our historical challenges. Giving in to these tendencies, in our circumstance, is not "realism"; it is a surrender to sentiment at the expense of our values and our interests. Americans may be tired, but history doesn't care.

This kind of historical moment is difficult, but not unprecedented. In the middle years of the Civil War, the North suffered a series of humiliating defeats at the hands of a numerically inferior enemy. A peace movement gained momentum. President Lincoln fell into deep depression. One observer wrote: "Even Lincoln himself has gone down at last. Nobody believes in him any more." "We are now on the brink of destruction," concluded Lincoln. "It appears to me the Almighty is against us, and I can hardly see a ray of hope." Discouragement, in these circumstances, seemed reasonable—but a loss of nerve would have left a different country.

President Lincoln's response was an act of idealism that dramatically increased the stakes of the war. Upstairs at the Executive Mansion, he took a document out of his tall hat and said to his cabinet: "I have prepared a small paper of much significance. I have said nothing to anyone, but I have made a promise to myself and my Maker. I am now going to fulfill that promise." With a firm hand, he signed the Emancipation Proclamation. Later, he called it "the great event of the nineteenth century" and added, "It is a momentous thing to be the instrument, under Providence, of the liberation of a race."

The beginnings of the Cold War offer a similar example. Exhausted by more than 400,000 deaths in World War II, Americans suddenly faced an expanding, aggressive Soviet empire. The early stages of European reconstruction failed badly, leading to a winter of malnutrition. In 1946 and 1947, communists won 48 percent of the vote in Italy, 46 percent in France. President Truman feared the loss of Greece and Turkey to communist pressure, the collapse of Italy, the Russian occupation of the Mediterranean coast, and the fall of the Iron Curtain on "Bordeaux,

Calais, Antwerp and The Hague." It was, he later said, "hell and high water every day." Discouragement seemed reasonable—but a loss of nerve would have shifted the early course of the Cold War, and resulted in a different world.

In these circumstances, President Harry Truman committed a tired nation to the defense of Greece and Turkey, declaring it "the policy of the United States to support free peoples who are resisting attempted subjugation by armed minorities or by outside pressures." He approved the Marshall Plan, to revive the failing reconstruction of Western Europe. When West Berlin was cut off in a blockade by Soviet forces, he declared, "We stay in Berlin, period." American and Allied military planes flew more than 270,000 fights over the course of a year to deliver food, coal, and other supplies to a lonely, frightened city. And after a surprise invasion of South Korea from the north, Truman committed America to a bloody, unpopular, necessary, eventually stalemated Asian war, which cost Truman his popularity. "I remembered," he said, "how each time the democracies failed to act it encouraged the aggressors to keep going ahead."

There are other examples. Lyndon Johnson, a southern president from a segregated state, witnessed the beating of protesters at Selma, Alabama, and called for a joint session. The entire Virginia and Mississippi delegations boycotted, but seventy million Americans watched on television as Johnson proposed an ambitious Civil Rights Act. He told the hushed Congress: "At times history and fate meet at a single time in a single place to shape a turning point in man's unending search for freedom. So it was last week in Selma, Alabama.

"Should we defeat every enemy," he continued, "and should we double our wealth and conquer the stars, and still be unequal to this issue, then we will have failed as a people and as a nation. For, with a country as with a person, 'What is a man profited if he shall gain the whole world and lose his own soul?'"

President Ronald Reagan repudiated a tired policy of détente, and determined to seek victory, not a stalemate, in the Cold War. And he symbolized this shift by calling the Soviet government an "evil empire." The dissident Natan Sharansky recalls: "Tapping on walls and talking through toilets, word of Reagan's 'provocation' quickly spread through the prison. The dissidents were ecstatic. Finally, the leader of the free world had spoken a truth—a truth that burned inside the heart of each and every one of us."

In each of these cases, objections were raised: Emancipation was divisive and would undermine the war effort, which should be directed to preserving the union, not ending slavery. Moving quickly on civil rights would result in a backlash and trample on the principle of free association. Calling the Soviet Union "evil" was provocative, simplistic, and counterproductive.

Yet in each of these cases, the critics are remembered in footnotes. Those who called America to moral ideals and duties have proven to be more realistic in their assessment of America's true, long-term interests. Particularly in dark moments of doubt and uncertainty, a stubborn, confident idealism has often illuminated an unsuspected path, shown a better way. Far from being impractical or unrealistic, it often has broken a spell of discouragement and resulted in achievements beyond the dreams of realism. In these historical tests, Americans learned, or should have learned, some lessons. America is ultimately stronger when it is faithful to its ideals, even at a cost. Our nation, over time, is more secure when our values advance in the world. And sometimes in history, the greatest need is simple courage in a good cause.

Asserting high ideals always opens up a gap between rhetoric and reality, which makes it easy to criticize idealistic leaders as hypocrites. The Declaration of Independence is an empty promise, because its author and many who signed it owned slaves. Roosevelt's Four Freedoms are hypocritical, because America entered into an alliance with Stalin against Hitler. The goal of ending tyranny in our world is a fraud, because we maintain relations with Saudi Arabia. But this argument itself is dreamy and unrealistic. Leadership in politics often consists of maintaining ideals in the midst of inconsistency. G. K. Chesterton wrote of Abraham Lincoln: "He loved to repeat that slavery was intolerable while he tolerated it, and to prove that something ought to be done while it was impossible to do it…. But, for all that, this inconsistency beat the politicians at their own game, and this abstracted logic proved most practical after all. For, when the chance did come to do something, there was no doubt about the thing to be done. The thunderbolt fell from the clear heights of heaven."

This is the irreplaceable contribution of idealism: When the chance comes to do something, it leaves no doubt about the thing to be done. It holds the great ideals as a sacred trust, to be drawn upon in saner, more hopeful days. And sometimes, even in a tired time, even when the arguments against idealism have piled up in mountains, a thunderbolt can fall from the clear heights of heaven. Suddenly, against all the expectations of realism, the Emancipation Proclamation is signed, a death camp is liberated, the Civil Rights Act is passed, a hated wall falls, a dissident is elected president, an African child cold with death comes back to life.

We have begun our own large, uncertain historical project—a struggle against totalitarian perversions of Islam, a conflict elevated to the highest historical stakes by the spread of destructive technology. We face the central, continuing challenge of American history: to overcome the racial divisions that scarred our founding. And we have entered our own moment of doubt and uncertainty about the course ahead.

The upcoming political season is likely to be polarized and shrill. But it will have this virtue: the arguments will not be minor or small. Politicians will be debating the role of America in the world: Should we persist or retreat in the Middle East? Promote democracy or a narrower version of stability? Confront Iran, or engage Iran? And the arguments of the new season will also concern the role of government in our society: Is it time for cuts, or new exertions? Will conservatism return to a philosophy of "government is the problem" and "leave us alone"?

Beneath all these arguments is a single debate—now the main controversy of American politics—between idealism and cynicism, between ambition and retrenchment, between conviction and doubt.

I believe, as at other historical moments of testing, that America needs a renewal of courage and idealism in the cause of human dignity. This approach, in my view, must be conservative. The defense and fulfillment of American values such as liberty, tolerance, and equality requires moral and religious confidence in those values, and a commitment to preserve the institutions that shape them. I am a conservative, because I believe in the accumulated wisdom of humanity—a kind of democracy that gives a vote to the dead—expressed in the institutions and moral ideals we inherit from the past. When those ideals and institutions are casually discarded in the cause of personal liberation, the result is usually personal suffering and social decay. We cannot prosper as a "cut-flower civilization"—separated from our sustaining roots.

But this preference for the old and settled, at key historical moments, is radically incomplete. It is a fact of history that many conservatives opposed the abolition of slavery as a form of radicalism, and preferred the settled cultural traditions of the South. Many opposed government-mandated improvements in working conditions in the nineteenth century, fearful of interference in the market. Many opposed the civil-rights movement in the twentieth century as disruptive and revolutionary. In the absence of moral and religious convictions about human dignity, conservatism can become a tired and cynical defense of the status quo. In these cases, the habit of conservatism, disconnected from a moral vision of human rights, became a source of injustice—as it can become today.

The care of our times requires something more: a belief that the interests of America are served by the hope and progress of people in other lands, and a sense of urgency in the cause of social justice at home. This kind of daring and activism is very different from the world-weary conservatism of Europe, with its distrust of philosophic abstraction, its disdain for religious enthusiasm, its belief that tradition trumps moral conviction. This approach challenges a Republican orthodoxy that is often unmoved by poverty and unwelcoming to the immigrant. And it broadens beyond the narrow passions of the Religious Right, recognizing that the Scriptures put far more emphasis on serving the poor and defenseless than on judging the behavior of our neighbors.

What we need is a heroic conservatism: a commitment to changeless ideals—which, when confidently applied, are a force for revolutionary change in our nation and the world. For me, the roots of a heroic conservatism are found in Abraham Lincoln, who was willing to risk bloody war rather than abandon the universal moral claims at the heart of the American experiment. Those roots are found in the tradition of Christian reflection on politics and government, embodied in Roman Catholic social teaching: a conservative respect for the institutions of family and community, paired with a radical, uncompromising concern for the poor and weak. The roots of heroic conservatism are also found in America's long history of religiously inspired reform movements—the work of morally passionate malcontents who pushed for abolition, insisted on the reform of prisons and mental hospitals, and led the struggle for women's rights and civil rights.

This is an eclectic vision, but a very American one. All these strains of political thought are united by a moral conviction: that every human being has a worth independent of their background or accomplishments; that the least have the same value as the great. This belief, in America, can seem commonplace. It is actually the most revolutionary principle in human history: unleashed in Judaism, carried by Christianity, affirmed by the American Founding, contested by violence across the world. Its claims are universal, and thus inherently missionary. Every ideology that opposes it should fail. Every ruler who assaults it should fall. Every person who affirms it for themselves will be offended when it is denied to others.

How should this principle be applied in our time? What would a politics look like that consistently put the demands of human dignity—the conviction that everyone is a child of God—at its center? Beyond the millions dying of AIDS, what acts of compassion and justice would we owe to the betrayed and hopeless children of America's inner cities? To the Egyptian dissident imprisoned on trumped-up charges? To the refugee fleeing genocide in Sudan? To the severely handicapped child, dismissed as a worthless burden?

In the pages that follow, I will address those questions. But I will begin by looking at the lessons and cautions of my time in government—a period in which idealism has been asserted and debated in unprecedented ways. It is not, needless to say, a story of unqualified success. Politics is never the story of utopia achieved. It is always the story of flawed men and women with high ideals, rushed toward thousands of decisions they cannot fully understand. And some of those decisions are invariably mistaken.

Yet, given our historical challenges, an adolescent disillusionment is an unaffordable luxury. It is easy for idealism to slip into arrogance—a sense of superiority to a world that never achieves our own standards of purity. But this is a misunderstanding of politics and of life. No one said the great causes would be easy. History proves the opposite. Many reformers and heroes of conscience subsist for their whole lives on promises of change they never see fulfilled. Many generations die in chains before one generation breaks them. Setbacks should neither surprise nor discourage us. And it would be a pathetic kind of idealism that allowed those setbacks to undermine our commitments to justice and liberty.

In the White House, I was sometimes discouraged and frustrated, but never disillusioned. In bitter political campaigns, in a White House at war, in visits with dissidents, in tense foreign capitals, in remote African villages, I have seen reasons for hope instead of cynicism—and the emerging outlines of a better kind of politics, waiting to be born.

Chapter 2

Remaking Republicanism

I arrived at the JW Marriott Hotel in downtown Washington, DC, on an April morning in 1999, hardly expecting a life-changing conversation. A few days before, an assistant to Governor George W. Bush had called my office at *U.S. News and World Report*, asking for some samples of my writing. An old political acquaintance of mine had evidently mentioned my name to Bush, but I had never met the governor of Texas, or even spoken to him. I had seen him in person only once, on a campaign swing in Texas during the waning days of the Dole campaign in 1996. He had impressed me that day by his considerate brevity, allowing a tired Senator Dole to shorten the event and get some rest. In contrast, Governor Pete Wilson of California, earlier that day, had given a long-winded speech, mainly about himself, while Dole wilted in the California sun.

Governor Bush was not yet a declared candidate for president, but he was already being treated as the Republican front-runner, tracked by a pack of journalists and photographers. He was in Washington to attend a meeting of the National Governors' Association. I assumed he was also beginning to look for campaign help, and would be talking to a number of prospects on a long list.

Escorted past the Texas Rangers that guarded the governor, I entered an outer room of the Bush suite, where Karl Rove paced and talked with manic energy into a cell phone. Between calls he introduced himself. As we talked, it became clear that he had mistaken me for Mark Gerson, a fine conservative writer who was not me, or even a relative. He seemed slightly disappointed I had not written Mark Gerson's recent book on neoconservatism, which he had read, and went back to his cell phone.

Called into the suite, I shook hands with the governor and Karen Hughes, his spokeswoman and close advisor. Bush's manner was both welcoming, and slightly impatient. After motioning me to sit down, he began with disorienting bluntness: "This isn't an interview. I've read your stuff. I want you to write my announcement speech, my convention speech, and my inaugural address. And I want you to move to Austin right away."

Politics is often the realm of subtle signals, in which hints and body language often matter as much as words. It was immediately clear to me that Governor Bush did not operate in this way. Trying to avoid a direct answer to his direct offer, I steered the conversation to my views of what a campaign might look like. I was concerned the Republican Party lacked a domestic message, that we had little to offer to the poor and addicts and children in trouble. But I was convinced that with a little creativity on education and welfare reform, we could compete with the tired, perfunctory agenda of the Democrats, and change the image of the Republican Party in the process. Bush leaned in toward me, a typical gesture to show his intensity, and said: "I lived through the 1960s. I saw cities on fire because of divisions in our country. And I never want to see that happen again." Thinking back from years later, the reference strikes me as uncanny. We had been destined to see cities on fire, for a very different reason.

Gathering my thoughts while we talked, I ended the conversation by raising two conditions. First, I wanted to be a formal part of the policy process in the campaign. I knew it was much harder to write about proposals if I wasn't a participant in the debates that produced them. Second, I wasn't going to abandon my children, then aged three and one, by working until nine o'clock every night, seeing them on weekends like a divorced parent. I knew that every campaign, at some point, becomes a whirling chaos that ruins the best intentions, but I was going to try to have a normal family life. He indicated that neither would be a problem.

As I left the hotel, I was impressed by what I had seen. His confidence was contagious; though not yet a candidate, he was thinking about his inaugural. He was youthful, likable, and enthusiastic. The kind of unreserved (and, as yet, undeserved) confidence he showed in me was flattering; there is nothing more flattering than trust. And his thoughts on race and poverty ran parallel to my own. It was just the right appeal for me—and even more appealing because it seemed to lack all calculation. I left the meeting wondering if he was even capable of calculation.

I am less sure what he saw in me. Certainly nervousness. I have always been uncomfortable with small talk, and subject to a debilitating shyness. He probably saw a certain seriousness and moral intensity, which family and friends have sometimes pointed out to me, mainly to make fun of. Overall, it could not have been an impressive first encounter.

I come from a typically varied, American background. One grandfather was a New Yorker, from a family of German Jews, with intellectual interests and vague religious commitments. My other grandfather was a Nazarene minister from the hills and hollows of Kentucky, called to faith by an audible voice while wandering in the woods—a tall, impressive man who played the guitar and ministered to a circuit of rural churches. I was raised in Presbyterian churches that held to a cold but serious Calvinism, more focused on intellectual rigor than emotional expression or liturgical beauty. I suspect that all these traditions have left their imprint.

Religion was taken seriously in our home, and for that reason President Jimmy Carter, a Baptist deacon and Sunday school teacher, was liked and respected. His forthright claim to be "born again" generated considerable loyalty from evangelicals, and considerable controversy among others. One liberal theologian, Albert Outler, commented at the time that evangelicals "want a society ruled by those who know what the Word of God is. The technical name for that is 'theocracy,' and their Napoleon, whether he likes it or not, is Jimmy Carter." It was perhaps the only time Jimmy Carter has been compared to Napoleon, and the promised American theocracy did not arrive with his election. But that has not stopped the charge from being made again and again about other religious politicians in the decades since.

For me, Jimmy Carter was not a theocratic hope, but an antidote to the moral bankruptcy of Nixonian republicanism—its cynical manipulation of power and its amoral foreign policy. Carter's promise of clean government and the promotion of human rights struck a chord. I read and reread his autobiography, *Why Not the Best?*, distributed campaign material, and debated on his behalf during an assembly at my Christian high school. I waited for hours at the St. Louis riverfront to shake his hand when he toured down the Mississippi on the riverboat *Delta Queen*. Like a first romantic infatuation, a first political infatuation is usually remembered with fondness and embarrassment. And my openness to the Democratic Party was not to last long.

Jimmy Carter had been publicly ambivalent about the issue of abortion, vaguely supporting the right to choose, but opposing federal funding. The Democratic platform on which he ran reflected this ambivalence, recognizing the "religious and ethical nature of the concerns which many American have on the subject of abortion." But by 1984, the platform defined abortion a "fundamental right," and any sign of ambivalence, or moral seriousness, was gone. At the same time, attacks on religious conservatives became a surefire applause line in Democratic speeches. As a candidate in 1984, Senator Walter Mondale talked of "radical preachers" and "extremists who control the Republican Party." Adding insult to ignorance, he warned they could "unleash an orgy of religious intolerance in our land." The Democratic Party had set out actively to alienate people like me, and it succeeded.

I ended up at Wheaton College in Wheaton, Illinois, studying theology. The behavioral expectations were high: no drinking or dancing, neither much of a sacrifice in my case. The faculty was theologically orthodox, but politically diverse—some were pro-choice on abortion, many were Democrats. None would have called themselves fundamentalists. Wheaton evangelicalism, in many ways, was defined in opposition to the narrow fundamentalism of, say, Bob Jones University—more intellectually open, more culturally engaged, less politically predictable. And the history of Wheaton College fed into that way of thinking. The school had been founded before the Civil War by an ardent abolitionist, and it educated African Americans and women before that was generally done. I combined an appreciation of this socially conscious evangelicalism with a growing respect for Roman Catholic thinkers and examples, particularly John Paul II, who joined his social conservatism with a passionate concern for the poor and weak. I volunteered for the 1984 Reagan campaign in Illinois, decisively leaving the Democratic camp. And between Greek and Bible classes, I wrote a column for the school newspaper.

College journalism is useful, if only to eventually measure your progress beyond those early, cringe-making efforts. In my case, Charles Colson got hold of one of my columns on Mother Teresa, and asked to meet me at the O'Hare Airport Hilton, shortly before my graduation. Colson had been a high-level White House official in the Nixon administration; was jailed on Watergate-related charges; and founded a prison ministry upon his release. Apart from my family, he would become the single most influential person in my life.

I had been accepted at Fuller Theological Seminary in California for graduate studies. But after our discussion, Chuck asked me to put my academic plans on hold, move to northern Virginia (where his ministry was headquartered), and help him with a book and other research and writing projects. My expectations of him had been conditioned by depictions in the Watergate books—hard-charging, ambitious, loyal to a fault, but with a considerable mean streak. In person, I found him deeply considerate, supportive of my stumbling efforts, and determined to promote my career. This exceptional life will always be my primary example of the transforming power of faith. Prison and disgrace has left Chuck stripped of arrogance and self-serving ambition, which allowed an amazing organizational and inspirational talent to be used for nobler purposes. The ministry he built, Prison Fellowship Ministries, was (and remains) one of the most important social-reform movements of our time, offering a second chance to hated and invisible men and women in our society. Many of the former prisoners I met at Prison Fellowship—people sometimes guilty of terrible crimes—were more serious and mature Christians than I could ever hope to be. And this success demonstrates the unique contribution of faith-based organizations: while government attempts at rehabilitation uniformly fail, Prison Fellowship manages to turn convicts into moral examples.

The pull of politics remained strong for me. When a Congressman named Dan Coats was selected to serve out Vice President Dan Quayle's unexpired term in the Senate, Chuck sent a letter of introduction. Dan Coats was a graduate of Wheaton College, a serious evangelical, and a man of good reputation. I also found him to be a rare, maybe unique, example of genuine humility at the highest levels of politics—a virtue politics does little to encourage or reward. Senator Coats had also been profoundly influenced by seeing the social contributions of faith-based groups—in his case, the compassion and professionalism of Gospel Mission outreach to the homeless. Following the Republican revolution of

1994, we were both convinced that a message of cutting government wouldn't be enough to sustain the party. As his policy director and speechwriter, I helped to craft a series of legislative proposals to promote the work of faith-based institutions—from homeless shelters to maternity group homes—through grants, vouchers, and tax incentives for charitable giving. Then we went door to door trying to sell the approach to Republican leaders. The reception from Newt Gingrich and others was polite and dismissive—the proposals were treated like the enthusiasms of a slightly eccentric relative. And when the moment came for Republicans to show their priorities, they insisted on a government shutdown, including the closing of the Washington Monument and other tourist sites. These actions proved deeply unpopular, confirmed an image of Republican radicalism, and strengthened President Bill Clinton at a key moment.

With an election in sight, I felt ready for a presidential campaign. As I surveyed the prospects, I knew I would work for Democratic Governor Bob Casey of Pennsylvania, a holdout in his party who remained resolutely pro-life, pro-family, and pro-poor. "By embracing abortion," he argued, "the Democratic party is abandoning the principle that made it great: its basic commitment to protecting the weakest and most vulnerable members of the human family." Casey called the absolutist pro-choice position a manifestation of the "Cult of the Imperial Self." And he thought that Republican libertarianism—the elevation of personal and economic freedom over other values like compassion and community—was a different application of the same Social Darwinist impulse. "This," he said, "is how the Cult of the Imperial Self manifests itself in Republican circles." I could have easily worked for such a man, but serious health problems prevented his candidacy.

Instead, I left Capitol Hill to work for former Congressman Jack Kemp, who called himself a "bleeding-heart conservative" and was pondering a 1996 presidential run. Several successive generations of young people were attracted to Jack for the same reasons. He is hopeful, relentlessly upbeat, and deeply committed to social inclusion. He is completely uncynical, and involved in politics because he believes in ideas. He has never personalized debates, and never made a personal enemy that I know of. He is the closest thing the Republican Party offers to the cheerful idealism of Hubert Humphrey, but when the moment of choice arrived, he decided not to run, for reasons known only to himself.

In the end, I was asked to work as a junior speechwriter on Senator Bob Dole's campaign, starting at the San Diego convention. It was a marvelous, memorable example of how a campaign should not be run. The staff was rent by rivalries. The campaign had no discernable domestic policy. Instead of dealing with education or welfare, or anything having to do with the lives and struggles of human beings, Senator Dole talked about the Tenth Amendment to the Constitution, which he carried in his suit pocket and produced during his stump speech. This is the portion of the Constitution that reserves powers not specifically given to the federal government for the states—an important principle of limited government, but hardly a compelling message. And luck, in the end, wasn't with Senator Dole, a factor not to be underestimated in presidential politics. Late in the campaign, I worked on what I thought was a subtle and effective speech, calling attention to President Clinton's character, or lack of it. Immediately after the speech was delivered, Dole leaned on a loose rail on the stage and fell to the ground on his back. The image on the front page of every newspaper the next day showed his face in a painful grimace that made him seem ancient, fragile, and unthinkable as president.

As a candidate, Senator Dole had many of the drawbacks of the World War II generation—all the reticence and brittleness that came from unfair suffering. As a man, he also had all of that generation's virtues—its courage, resilience, and large conception of America's purpose in the world. He is hard to like and easy to respect, and I came to respect him greatly. At the very end of the campaign, when the outcome was all but certain, I was on the plane when he embarked on ninety-six hours of nonstop campaigning in nineteen states, bringing him close to exhaustion and collapse. It was a brave and selfless act, which gave a last-minute boost to Republican prospects, and probably saved a number of congressional seats. A few weeks after his concession, he summoned me to his nearly deserted presidential campaign office near Union Station in Washington. All that was left of a government-in-waiting were a few assistants, a number of half-filled boxes, and his dog wandering in and out of the office. He described to me a recent bout with shingles in painful detail. It was a reminder of the pitiless side of politics, which had quickly moved on to other obsessions. But it was typical of Senator Dole's toughness that he quickly moved on to a fulfilling new life.

My own path took a turn when, after the election, I was approached by the national editor of *U.S. News and World Report* to take a leave of absence from Capitol Hill (where I had returned) and write a cover story for the magazine. Soon after it appeared, I was offered a position as a senior editor. Having little else to occupy my ambitions, I took the job, but wondered how a conservative would be received in the world of journalism. I need not have worried. Over two years, I was assigned fascinating stories, was treated with kindness, and made some close friends, including Gloria Borger, who acted as my guide, protector, and Jewish mother (though hardly motherly in her youthful beauty). The main story of that period was the impeachment of President Bill Clinton. When it became clear from physical evidence that the president had lied about his affair, the mainly liberal journalists up and down the hall turned strongly against him, convinced that resignation was appropriate and inevitable. But I watched as Clinton was saved by the American people, who refused to abandon him—a tribute to his skill, perseverance, and shamelessness.

In the spring of 1999, I was asked to go to Texas to cover the announcement of Governor Bush's exploratory committee. After the initial call from the governor's office asking for writing samples, I told my editors that wouldn't be possible. Precisely because I had not sought Governor Bush's offer, accepting it seemed obviously right, or at least unavoidable. Soon afterward, I was on a plane to Austin, as a participant in events I had expected to cover as a journalist. On that trip, I jotted down for myself on a yellow legal pad two objects that I felt were worth pursuing: first, "the recovery of American rhetoric"; second, "giving Republicans a message of social justice."

When I arrived in Austin, the Bush campaign was being run out of Karl Rove's cramped political consulting firm, but really out of Karl Rove's spacious mind. Karl is the most unusual political operative I have ever met, so exceptional he doesn't really belong in that category. His knowledge of American history would put many historians to shame; when we have met with historians together, I have seen him point out factual errors in their books. This knowledge of history is matched by a love for its romance; he visits its shrines and collects its scraps (carefully archived pictures of McKinley's funeral, ballots from the 1860 election). Karl has a relentlessly curious mind, which digs down several layers in policy debates and retains a shocking level of detail. He also has a relentless sense of humor—bringing pies to critics in the press, brushing dandruff off my shoulder, using diminutive nicknames like "Mikie"—which is both disarming and controlling. This cruise-director manner may well be a reaction to his own innate shyness; he once told me, "I used to be a geek like you, but I got over it."

Karen Hughes was the closest to the president of this small group—an imposing, strong-willed, former television journalist. She brought no agenda to the campaign other than the governor's success, and he appreciated it. She could be difficult and opinionated, but never devious. And she had a knack for knowing the public mind and the governor's instincts. Karl was valuable because he thought in ways that no one else did. Karen was valuable because she thought in ways that everyone else did, which is often the key to being an effective communicator.

Josh Bolten, who came to Austin from the financial world in London about the time I came from Washington, was a quieter, self-effacing contrast to the more vivid Texans. He was more comfortable wielding influence indirectly, but his professionalism and competence made that influence considerable. And the policy process he organized as policy director was perhaps the most exceptional element of the Bush campaign. He brought in a parade of experts to Austin for a series of half-day policy briefings, on issues from Social Security solvency, to tax policy, to defense transformation, to education reform. These were like advanced academic seminars for the governor and his staff, and they laid the groundwork for the issues we'd raise in the campaign and the agenda we'd pursue in the first term. One evening after dinner at the governor's mansion, a poised and formal academic named Condoleezza Rice, along with other defense-policy experts, spent hours going through the possible scenarios on North Korea. How far would an invasion from the North initially get? How quickly could America get additional troops into the region? How long would victory take? How much of Seoul would be destroyed? How many civilians and soldiers were likely to die? I went to sleep that night with difficulty, sobered by the duties we were seeking.

My first adjustment in Austin was stylistic. The governor spoke with a folksy bluntness in a Texas idiom. My speechwriting influences were mainly from the golden age of American speechwriting in the 1960s—speeches by leaders who favored the highly crafted, rhythmic use of language. President John F. Kennedy: "Now the trumpet summons us again—not as a call to bear arms, though arms we need—not as a call to battle, though embattled we are—but as a call to bear the burden of a long twilight struggle." Senator Robert Kennedy: "Let us dedicate ourselves to what the Greeks wrote so many years ago: to tame the savageness of man and make gentle the life of this world." Dr. Martin

Luther King Jr.: "If physical death is the price that I must pay to free my white brothers and sisters from a permanent death of the spirit, then nothing can be more redemptive."

The main focus of this style is on the words themselves—how they sound together, build in emotion through repetition, and string together in biblically inspired cadences—rather than on image and story. This is very different from either the misty-eyed sentimentalism of Reagan, or the spare directness of West Texas. I was concerned that my words would be viewed like the tuxedo the governor hated to wear—formal and uncomfortable. And I had reason to worry. Not long after I arrived, I was called into Karen's office and told that people had concerns about the fit, and that I was very much on probation. Once, in a foreign-policy speech, I managed to insert one of my favorite quotes by Pericles—and even I had to admit, when delivered, it didn't sound very Bush-like.

I made a sincere, but only partially successful effort to adjust. Before the campaign began in earnest, the governor was regularly addressing audiences brought to the governor's mansion from around the country, in a sort of front-porch campaign. I tape-recorded those sessions, had them transcribed, and began to form the ideas into an announcement speech—using the governor's favorite ideas, but putting them into a more formal structure, and adding some phrases of my own. Some, like "the soft bigotry of low expectations," stuck in his mind and entered his repertoire. We went over these announcement remarks in regular lunches at the mansion, an investment of the governor's personal time that helped me immensely, and showed how seriously he took the words that would define his campaign. Eventually, we developed a productive give-and-take. As long as the structure of speeches was rigidly logical, and most of the language was direct and active, he would accept an element of elevation—and even, over time, came to demand it.

My best early decision was to hire two writers who would share the burden, and eventually share some of the most intense days of my life. John McConnell, whom I knew from the Dole campaign, is, with scientific certainty, the nicest human being on earth—a man who has never had a former friend. He also has a talent for the perfectly appropriate, crystalline phrase. Matt Scully, who worked for Governor Bob Casey of Pennsylvania, is an elegant writer with a gentle manner—a manner that hides a ferocious commitment to the defense of the weak, particularly animals. No one I know writes more convincingly about the need for a culture of life and mercy, because no one feels those causes more deeply themselves. For seven years these two speechwriters would be my friends and partners, and hardly a cross word ever passed between us.

My second adjustment in Austin was more personal. I found that I had little in common with the governor. He was athletic, outgoing, likable—and I was none of those things. He had a penchant for crude humor that made me uncomfortable; not blasphemous language, but the vulgarity of the locker room. After one policy session at the mansion, everyone had gone but me, and the governor had some time before his next appointment. He asked me, "Do you want to hang out a little while?" With rudeness that now seems crazed, I replied, "Not really." He put his arm around me and said: "No, you don't do that, do you?"

But over the months, I came to like Governor Bush both as a person and a politician. He is, above all, a man without a mask. Interest, frustration, disdain, or sadness come unfiltered to his expressive face. Many politicians, including men like Ronald Reagan and Bill Clinton, brought a set of acting skills to politics that they could turn on in any meeting or before any audience. Governor Bush lacked those skills, making his boredom or impatience obvious when he would rather be elsewhere. But this gave him a different appeal. When emotionally engaged, his authenticity is compelling. His personal honesty is nearly compulsive. He cries easily, a trait he says he gets from his father. And many of the times I have seen him tear up, he has been talking about his father, to whom he sometimes refers as "the sweet guy."

This emotional nature makes Bush keenly aware of the feelings of others—a kind of emotional intelligence that picks up when people are not feeling valued or included. One early policy meeting at the mansion concerned humanitarian interventions: when does America use military force in areas tangential to its direct interests? Dick Cheney, Condi Rice, and half a dozen other distinguished defense experts were conducting an intense discussion, while I was in a chair against the wall, feeling very much out of place. I was not even sure Governor Bush was aware I was in the room. But he interrupted the discussion, leaned back in his chair, and said: "I'll tell you what I really want to know. I want to know what Mike Gerson thinks about all of this." The other participants were doubtlessly confused, and I said little of interest, but it was something I didn't forget.

In daily encounters, Bush is possessed by a restless, nervous energy. Sometimes during a private lunch he will watch television, walk around the room, and suddenly call on the intercom for baseball scores. He eats at the pace of a pie-eating contest, often finishing dessert before others are halfway through their meal. His response to this level of energy is an obsession with discipline and self-mastery—as though he realizes his appetitive side must be carefully tamed. So he goes to bed early, exercises with intensity and regularity, and insists on orderly, punctual meetings. For Governor Bush, self-discipline served as a substitute for ambition. He viewed it as unseemly to crave success, having only disdain for politicians who have calculated their path to the presidency since the age of ten. But he viewed it as possible to deserve success through self-mastery.

His manner, as I got to know him, was a curious mixture of self-assurance and humility. He had a physical strut that matched an aggressive confidence in his own judgments, particularly his immediate judgments of people (which could be unfairly harsh). But in policy meetings he could be an attentive and respectful listener. Unlike many politicians, he did not view such discussions as an opportunity to assert dominance or impress the other participants. His questions were basic and pertinent—the kind of questions I might have asked if I hadn't felt self-conscious about being seen as uninformed. And I saw this lack of pretension in a personal way. At one press availability at the mansion with the whole traveling press corps, he introduced me as the "man who is working on the convention speech." It is difficult to imagine Richard Nixon or even Ronald Reagan introducing his speechwriter to the press—the pretensions of politics would not have allowed it.

I found the governor to be motivated by a deep anti-elitism. This was not an anti-intellectualism—he clearly respected the academic experts who came to Austin for policy sessions. But he had an unhidden disdain for any kind of class consciousness, and for people like Steve Forbes (his primary opponent from the Forbes family) and Vice President Al Gore, whom he viewed as elitists. There are always two paths for privileged sons of the prominent: to join the club, or to get the offer and conspicuously turn it down. There is a kind of pride in either option. But by turning it down, George Bush developed a populist pride, not an aristocratic one. Other presidents, such as Richard Nixon, deeply resented not being invited by the "best families." Bush had seen the best families, and was not very impressed. By natural inclination, and by conscious revolt, he fully inhabited the myth of Texas, which he had seen as a barefooted boy in Midland—the response of community to sandstorms and adversity; the entrepreneurship of the oil field; a certain hopeful quality of the open sky.

This anti-elitism had political consequences, particularly on social policy. At one front-porch session at the governor's mansion, a well-dressed and clearly liberal Republican woman asked a question hostile to the teaching of abstinence. Isn't this strategy unrealistic and judgmental? Governor Bush reacted with barely concealed contempt. Abstinence for young people is the only sure way to avoid pregnancy, the only sure method to avoid disease, and these cultural attitudes that blurred the line between right and wrong were going to have to change.

In Bush's view, the cultural confusion of elites was undermining the moral values that allowed normal people to live successful lives.

On the issue of abortion, the governor was conservative, but not inflexible. Early in the policy process, a former Reagan advisor named Martin Anderson came to Austin, arguing that the governor should push for a change in the Republican platform on this issue. The plank, he argued, was too absolutist, not even allowing the exceptions for rape and incest the governor supported. In fact, the platform was purposely silent on rape and incest, and a platform fight would have been bruising and pointless. The governor dismissed Anderson's proposal out of hand; the platform was not changed. Yet Governor Bush did make changes of tone and approach on this issue. He did not believe that restrictions on abortion were likely to come quickly, in sudden leaps like a constitutional amendment. Legal changes would need to be preceded by social and cultural changes—the persuasion of more and more people to accept a culture of life—and this progress was likely to be incremental. It was a sophisticated, Lincolnian view of social change: set out a clear ideal—in this case, a society in which unborn children are "welcomed in life and protected in law"—but proceed by increments, building consensus and limiting the practice at its edges.

On issues beyond culture, however, Governor Bush's instincts were entirely different. In policy discussions on education, welfare, and Social Security, we were exploring the active use of the federal government to force the pace of reform and empower individuals with choices and resources. We were focused on outcomes for individuals—African American children in failed schools, and addicts in need of treatment—not just procedures, like Senator Dole's attempted revival of the Tenth Amendment; on effective government, not on cutting government. And the governor consistently pushed his policy team to "think big"; his most damning characterization of any proposal was, "This is small ball." A variety of personal and political factors—Bush's energy, self-assurance, and indifference to the opinions of establishment Republicans—combined to create an unexpected ideological ambition. A governor only four years from his first successful election not only wanted to run the Republican Party, but to remake it—an exhilarating prospect for me. Long before I arrived in Austin, Governor Bush had signaled this ideological ambition by talking about "compassionate conservatism"—modifying the term "conservatism" because it was somehow incomplete. Now we had to define compassionate conservatism for the party and the country—and the skepticism and resentment it provoked became the main issue of the primaries.

Our first political opportunity in the campaign came when a number of Republican primary opponents attempted to prove their conservatism by attacking the idea of compassion. Former Vice President Dan Quayle ordered his staff "to never, ever utter the words 'compassionate conservatism,'" which he called a "silly and insulting" slogan. Lamar Alexander referred to the phrase as "weasel words." Steve Forbes called it "mealy mouthed rhetoric and poll-tested clichés." It was an odd spectacle—a crop of Republican candidates attacking a Christian virtue, like running for president as the anti-love candidate, on a "down-with-kindness" ticket. And it provided a wide political opening.

Governor Bush was scheduled to be in Cedar Rapids, Iowa, on June 12, 1999 for an early, testing-the-waters campaign event. It was decided to make this his surprise presidential announcement. Against a backdrop of tractors and hay bales, Bush gave the speech we had been working on for weeks at the mansion. "The purpose of prosperity," he said, "is to leave no one out ... to leave no one behind. I'm running because my party must match a conservative mind with a compassionate heart." Taking aim at the critics, he continued: "I know this approach has been criticized. But why? Is compassion beneath us? Is mercy below us? Should our party be led by someone who boasts of a hard heart? I know Republicans—across the country—are generous of heart. I am confident the American people view compassion as a noble calling. The calling of a nation where the strong are just and the weak are valued. I am proud to be a compassionate conservative. I welcome the label. And on this ground I'll take my stand."

Compassionate conservatism was still more of a phrase than a philosophy. Over the next several weeks, Governor Bush gave a series of detailed policy addresses to fill out his beliefs. In the process, he established a pattern, which was continued when he became president. He used major speeches to push his own policy process for new ideas; to clarify his thinking as he edited; to announce his commitments in serious detail; and to drive the news of the day. This may sound unexceptional. It is actually rare. Many candidates and presidents make news more indirectly through leaks, briefings, and surrogates. Governor Bush believed that leaks and preliminary briefings stole his thunder. For him, the speech was the thing—the instrument he could directly shape and control. And for a speechwriter with policy interests, this was an opportunity for influence.

Governor Bush began to fill out the meaning of compassionate conservatism in his first policy speech of the campaign, given on July 22, 1999, in Indianapolis—a speech that came to be known as "The Duty of Hope." It started with the recognition that America has deep and persistent social problems in the shadow of our prosperity. "For many people, this other society of addiction and abandonment and stolen childhood is a distant land, another world. But it is America. And these are not strangers, they are citizens, Americans, our brothers and sisters." These problems call for loving concern and action. "Often when a life is broken, it can only be rebuilt by another caring, concerned human being. Someone whose actions say: 'I love you. I believe in you; I'm in your corner.'" This recognition requires a "bold new approach" from government. "In every instance," Governor Bush declared, "where my administration sees a responsibility to help people, we will look first to faith-based organizations, charities, and community groups." And the speech went on to detail a number of proposals to support groups mentoring the children of prisoners, providing after-school programs, and engaging in drug treatment.

While making these proposals, Governor Bush flatly rejected the "destructive" view "that if government would only get out of our way, all our problems would be solved"—a vision with "no higher goal, no nobler purpose, than leave us alone." Here we were using a symbol to send a signal. The libertarian activist Grover Norquist had proposed to define conservatism as the "leave us alone" coalition—a movement united by the desire to get government off our backs. Governor Bush replied that there are "some things that government should be doing—like Medicare for poor children. Government can't be replaced by charities—but it can welcome them as partners, not resent them as rivals."

The peroration of the speech summarized much of what I believe about politics: "Americans will never write the epitaph of idealism. It emerges from our nature as a people, with a vision of the common good, beyond profit and loss. Our national character shines in our compassion. We are a nation of rugged individuals. But we are also the country of the second chance, tied together by bonds of friendship and community and solidarity.... I know the reputation of our government has been tainted by scandal and cynicism. But the American government is not the enemy of the American people. At times it is wasteful and grasping. But we must correct it, not disdain it.... In this campaign, I bring a message to my own party. We must apply our conservative and free-market ideas to the job of helping real human beings—because any ideology, no matter how right in theory, is sterile and empty without that goal."

This was intended as an ambitious reformulation of Republican ideology. Libertarian indifference to the poor was contrasted against the "common good" and "solidarity," specifically Roman Catholic themes of social justice that had influenced me and many other compassionate conservatives. Governor Bush, an evangelical Protestant, was already, perhaps, the most Catholic-sounding presidential candidate in American history (since candidates such as John F. Kennedy had gone to great lengths to avoid sounding like Catholics at all).

Reaction to the speech varied widely. Professor John DiIulio of the University of Pennsylvania called it "the most significant reformulation of what government should do and how it should do it by any leading candidate for president since Woodrow Wilson." Ed Crane, of the libertarian CATO Institute, said the speech epitomized "Bill Clinton's impact on the American polity," and sounded like it was written by someone "moonlighting for Hillary Rodham Clinton." But the controversy was just beginning.

A few months later, in late September of 1999, House Republicans proposed to balance the fiscal books by tinkering with the Earned Income Tax Credit, an anti-poverty measure that encourages work. At a campaign stop in San Jose, California, Governor Bush spontaneously denounced the plan, saying that conservatives should not "balance the budget on the backs of the poor." A week later, he delivered a speech at the Manhattan Institute in New York, defending a strong federal role in education, to require regular testing in reading and math, and to impose accountability on schools that persistently failed to increase those scores. At that speech, Governor Bush continued his revision of the Republican message: "Too often, on social issues, my party has painted an image of America slouching toward Gomorrah.... Too often my party has focused on the national economy, to the exclusion of all else—speaking a sterile language of rates and numbers, of CBO this and GNP that.... Too often my party has confused the need for limited government with a disdain for government itself. But this is not an option for conservatives.... Our Founders rejected cynicism, and cultivated a noble love of country. That love is undermined by sprawling, arrogant, aimless government. It is restored by focused and effective and energetic government."

Conservative activist Phyllis Schlafly shot back: "Bush's two calculated and spiteful attacks on Republican members of Congress reveal a man who is neither compassionate nor conservative." Paul Weyrich of the Free Congress Foundation added: "Other politicians who have declared war on the conservative movement—like Nelson Rockefeller, for example—found out the hard way that this was a serious mistake." Judge Robert Bork, who had written the book *Slouching Toward Gomorrah,* said that "evidently Bush thinks conservatives are another species altogether."

The reference at the Manhattan Institute to the title of Bork's book had been entirely my idea. It was intended as another signal: the governor was a cultural conservative, but not the kind of cultural pessimist who believed that America was in terminal moral decline. But this symbol backfired in ways that exposed the governor to unnecessary criticism. Robert Bork is a prickly cultural pessimist. But he is also one of the most sympathetic figures in the conservative movement, unfairly smeared in his Supreme Court confirmation battle. Using him as a foil was a mistake, provoking outrage from serious writers such as Charles Krauthammer, who accused Bush of "triangulating off Robert Bork" and "slouching toward the center."

There are few feelings in politics worse than provoking criticism for your candidate by your own poor judgment. After a Robert Novak column appeared attacking me by name, I went to bed that night with the sick feeling that comes from being both foolish and exposed. Governor Bush called my home after I had gone to sleep, leaving a long, reassuring message on my answering machine. He woke me up with another call at 6 a.m., to make sure I wasn't feeling too upset. "This kind of thing happens to me all the time," he told me. "You can't let it get to you." He had (accurately) diagnosed that this incident would undermine a fragile self-confidence. And his phone call was the kind of act that not only builds confidence, but loyalty.

Not long afterward, the Council for National Policy—a who's who of conservative leaders—came to Texas for their annual meeting. Karl invited many of the most prominent to the governor's mansion in Austin, to meet Bush in person. At the reception, Karl grabbed my arm, pulled me over to conservative activist Paul Weyrich, and cheerfully introduced me as "the one who savaged Judge Bork"—just the kind of awkward moment Karl enjoys. For months I had been setting ideological fires, and deserved to be singed.

The best political minds, however, recognized the shift that was taking place. After the 2000 election, during the transition, President-elect Bush met and talked to President Clinton at the White House. Clinton specifically mentioned the Duty of Hope speech Bush had given in Indianapolis as a sign his campaign was serious.

Candidate Bush cemented his front-runner status through phenomenal fund-raising—$36 million in the first six months of 1999, a record that discouraged rivals and caused several to leave the contest. But no presidential campaign can succeed on money alone. The result of a primary contest is determined in key moments of testing and personal revelation, which display a candidate's crippling flaws, or unexpected virtues. For Governor Bush, there were several of these moments.

The first came in the Iowa Republican debate in December of 1999. The moderator, John Bachman, asked all the candidates to talk about a political philosopher or thinker who had influenced them. "Governor Bush—a philosopher-thinker and why." Bush responded without hesitation: "Christ, because He changed my heart." Bachman continued, "I think the viewers would like to know more on how He's changed your heart." Governor Bush looked slightly uncomfortable. "Well, if they don't know, it's going to be hard to explain. When you turn your heart and your life over to Christ, when you accept Christ as Savior, it changes your heart. It changes your life. And that's what happened to me."

I had been involved in the debate preparations, and this response was not planned in advance. The answer emerged because Christian faith lies close to the surface of Bush's identity, and has genuinely influenced his political thinking. The reaction of some commentators was sneering. "Jesus may be many things," said one, "but he isn't a political philosopher." Of course, Jesus of Nazareth was not merely a political philosopher. But it is simple ignorance to discount His influence in the history of Western political thought. His teachings on the dignity and worth of the individual, the priority of conscience, limits on the power of the state ("render unto Caesar what is Caesar's, and unto God what is God's"), the inherent value of women and children, all stood in contrast to Greek and Roman political thinking, and eventually modified and eclipsed them. When pressed for reasons he promotes democracy, or fights AIDS, President Bush will often say, "Because we should love our neighbors as ourselves." That quote from Jesus would have been a common response throughout Western and American political history—and it would be hard to imagine that history without it.

Though Bush's response in the debate was not politically calculated, it had rippling political effects. Many evangelicals saw a national political figure who was not evasive or defensive about his deepest beliefs. Another southern governor, like Jimmy Carter, had spoken the language of faith with obvious authenticity. This began a strong, lasting relationship with religious voters, and bound people like me personally to the candidate. I did not believe he was somehow chosen by God, but I was impressed he had chosen to talk about God in public.

Others looked at the same response and saw a national political figure who was, according to Maureen Dowd, "guilty of either cynicism or exhibitionism." This represents a deep misunderstanding of the man and his background. When George Bush was asked by his friend Don Evans to come to a Bible study in 1985, he became part of a movement known as small-group evangelicalism. Several friends (usually all men or all women) meet regularly to read scripture, share their personal struggles, and pray together. These are also known as accountability groups, because the members are supposed to hold each other responsible for progress in Christian discipleship. These meetings tend to be personal, not political—focused on marital challenges, personal decisions, or job pressures, not abortion, gay rights, or the teaching of evolution. The approach is generally therapeutic, not judgmental, an atmosphere of "sharing," empathy, and transparency. The emphasis is on emotions, not intellectual doctrines. Bible study generally does not concentrate on "what this means in the Greek," but rather on "what this means in my life." These groups tend to be ecumenical, not theologically exclusive, often including "seekers" who would not call themselves Christians at all. More rigid critics sometimes accuse the small-group movement of "theological fuzziness." But by avoiding divisive doctrinal and political debates, and emphasizing an inclusive, personal Christianity, small-group evangelicalism has reached many who feel uncomfortable in a pew—including a fun-loving, hard-drinking oil man from Midland, Texas.

It would be natural for a Christian of this background to say Jesus was his favorite philosopher. But when a student at a South Carolina forum not long afterward suggested that God had chosen Bush to lead America, it was also natural for Bush to respond: "I've got a personal faith, but far be it from me to tell you this is God's will. I don't get to put words in God's mouth, and neither do you."

The essence of this type of evangelicalism was revealed at another event, which went largely unnoticed by the press. In January of 2000, right before the Iowa caucuses, Bush traveled about thirty minutes outside Des Moines to a rural drug-treatment facility called Teen Challenge, where he listened to the moving stories of young addicts who were recovering with the help of faith. Then Governor Bush, stripped of his normal confident manner, spoke emotionally about his struggles with alcohol. He traced his decision to quit drinking to Billy Graham, who "planted a seed in my heart. It wasn't Billy. He was the messenger." "I'm on a walk," he quietly told the teens and their families. "And it's a never-ending walk as far as I'm concerned. I understand. I do. I used to drink too much and I quit drinking.... I want you to know that your life's walk is shared by a lot of other people, even some who wear suits."

This the language of the Bible-study group—transparent, empathic, personal, humble. It is certainly not the harsh judgmentalism of the fundamentalist caricature. The evangelical concept of grace requires humility—a deep recognition of personal sin, and a dependence on a loving and forgiving God. And for George Bush, this conviction of sin and forgiveness acts as a counterweight to his natural self-assurance, essentially taming an arrogant streak. This experience of grace served to humanize the candidate, as it had humanized the man. Bush was a believable Christian because he was a believable sinner. His faith lacked any taint of self-righteousness.

His experience of redemption was personal, but it has a direct effect on George Bush's political beliefs. He is convinced that societies are capable of hopeful change because individuals are capable of hopeful change, based on his own experience. That transformation, in his view, is often (though not exclusively) rooted in faith. And as governor, he set out to support faith-based institutions—Teen Challenge helping young addicts, Prison Fellowship reaching prisoners—that have good track records of transforming lives. This approach is different from a certain kind of conservatism, which views human nature as fixed and fallen, and government as the management of chaos through the imposition of impartial rules. George Bush believes that social reform and moral improvement is possible, because he believes that individual reformation is possible. And while government cannot directly create this reformation, it can promote institutions that do.

Governor Bush also saw, in his own story, a symbol of the choice before the Baby Boom generation. Some, he believed, had experienced that generation's excesses but eventually learned its lessons—reasserting the importance of self-discipline, moral rules, and family commitments. Others, like Bill Clinton (nearly the same age as Bush), had ignored those lessons. In nearly every campaign speech, even when it wasn't part of the written text, he would insert: "My first goal is to usher in a 'responsibility era.' An era that stands in stark contrast to the last few decades, when the culture has clearly said: 'If it feels good, do it. If you've got a problem, blame someone else.' Some people think it is inappropriate to draw a moral line. Not me. For our children to have the lives we want for them, they must learn to say yes to responsibility, yes to family, yes to honesty and work. I have seen our culture change once in my lifetime, so I know it can change again."

Another revealing moment of the campaign—a moment that tied me closer to the candidate—came at a town meeting in South Carolina in February of 2000. Bush had adopted the town-hall format because his campaign events had begun to feel stilted and scripted, and he was good at folksy interaction with the audience. On that day, however, an audience member pressed Bush to support draconian anti-immigration measures. And Bush bristled: "Family values don't stop at the Rio Grande River," he responded. "If you're a mother and father with hungry children, you're going to put food on the table. That's reality. That's called love."

There could be no political benefit in emotionally defending illegal immigrants in South Carolina immediately before a decisive Republican primary. This response came from long-standing beliefs about immigration: that immigrants contribute more to America than they take; that enforcement alone will not stop illegal immigration; that economic opportunity on the Mexican side of the border is the only eventual answer. But the intensity of Bush's answer in South Carolina indicated something more: a strong tendency to individualize policy debates. His personal interactions with Mexican immigrants had shaped his policy views. He talks about an immigrant who worked at his childhood home in Midland: "She loved me. She chewed me out. She tried to shape me up. And I came to love her like a second mom."

This kind of personalism could be seen in other ways. He defended his tax cuts for their good effects on the "single mom who is a waitress." He promised to create a prescription-drug benefit in Medicare because seniors faced the choice of buying drugs or buying food. His faith-based proposals were driven, in part, by meeting a troubled teen who asked him, "So what do you think of me?" There is a danger in using specific, individual cases to dictate government policy; it is possible to develop vast inefficiencies for the benefit of a few. But this personalism is also a natural extension of Christian faith, which is essentially individualistic and humanistic. The measure of social justice is the welfare of individuals, not the interests of the majority, or the working out of impersonal political goals like socialist equality or absolute human autonomy and choice. Individuals are eternal, valuable, and ultimately more important than any ideology of the right or left.

A final revealing moment of the primary campaign was his reaction to defeat in New Hampshire in February of 2000. I had traveled with the candidate on a swing through Iowa and New Hampshire not long before. In Iowa, all his considerable charm and tired jokes worked; the crowds were large, warm, and responsive. In New Hampshire, the same folksy, Texan charm fell entirely flat; crowds were sparse, applause lines went unnoticed, many voters carried notebooks they filled out with suspicious intensity. It felt like campaigning on the moon. Americans across the country may watch the same television programs, and shop at the same cloned superstores, but regionalism is not dead in American politics—Texas remains a tough sell in New Hampshire.

But a loss to Senator McCain by nineteen points was not expected. And the effects rippled out quickly. In South Carolina, a necessary primary win for the governor, the poll numbers fell twenty-five points in twenty-four hours. In Austin, I had lunch with Policy Director Josh Bolten, and estimated that our chances of getting the nomination were now about fifty-fifty; he thought they remained a little higher. In New Hampshire, as the votes came in, media advisor Stuart Stevens began to pack his bags, telling strategist Mark McKinnon, "We're fired. You don't lose New Hampshire by nineteen points and keep your job." All the key campaign people soon got a call to gather in Governor Bush's hotel room. Laura Bush and Bush's old friend Don Evans were already there. Mark expected the candidate to be livid. Instead, Bush said: "First, it doesn't look good. I think you all did a fantastic job. The responsibility rests on my shoulders, and I'm sorry I let you down. But we need to walk out of here with our heads held high. People will see how we respond. Times of adversity are a test—and we're going to meet this test." Mark remembers that "everyone in that room felt relieved of a burden of guilt." And that night, Governor Bush's concession speech was upbeat and delivered entirely without self-pity.

This was a lesson in loyalty. Even after winning the New Hampshire primary, Ronald Reagan abruptly fired advisor John Sears. In politics, this is hardly unusual. Bush operated differently. His quick, instinctual judgments of people could be harsh, but once those judgments were made, they were very difficult to shift. Particularly in times of testing, Bush views himself as a "team builder"—shoring up the confidence of the players by showing confidence in them. This is a virtue. At times when I was at the center of some controversy, I have benefited from this loyalty. But as with most leaders, the best attributes can become weaknesses. The flip side of loyalty and team building can be a tolerance for failure, as when, in the aftermath of a stumbling Katrina response, the president commended the head of federal emergency management for doing "a heck of a job." Sometimes the team needs to be rallied. Sometimes the lineup needs to be changed.

But at this stage of the campaign, the president's loyalty sent a signal. For months after the New Hampshire loss, during the ups and downs of the primary season, the Republican establishment of Washington—the former officials, and lobbyists, and party operatives—insisted that the faltering Bush campaign needed "adult guidance." The listing ship would only be righted if a real expert—someone like themselves—were sent to Austin to take charge. In late April, Governor Bush finally responded to this drumbeat—by appointing Don Evans, his close friend of thirty years and Bible-study partner, as campaign chairman. It demonstrated an aggressive contempt for the conventional wisdom of political elites. And it was a statement that he would come to Washington, if he came at all, on his own terms.

The primary battle against Senator McCain was eventually won in state-by-state, hand-to-hand combat. But now, heading into our convention in Philadelphia, we faced an even more difficult task: to argue for change in a time of peace and prosperity. The Bush campaign was walking against a stiff headwind of good news: unemployment stood at 4 percent, inflation was low, the budget was in balance, the international picture seemed relatively stable. But the governor counted a few advantages: a vague public disgust about the low moral standards of the Clinton years; a feeling that President Clinton had wasted his political capital on small-scale proposals like school uniforms; and a growing recognition that Vice President Gore's political skills contrasted poorly with Clinton's. The vice president was running a cautious campaign, trying to avoid Clinton's ethical taint by keeping him at a distance, while warning that any change in political direction would be "risky" for the country. It is always tempting for an incumbent to run a campaign based on risk-aversion, but it seldom works, because Americans, conditioned by examples like Reagan and Kennedy, expect a certain boldness of vision and leadership in a president.

In June, Karl Rove arranged for me to take off some time by myself at the senior Bush's presidential library at Texas A&M, so I could begin to write the governor's convention speech. I stayed in the former president's apartment there, furnished in the Federal style of the White House, with a large presidential seal in the marble floor at the entrance—an island of formality amid the Waffle Houses and cattle pens of College Station, Texas. For seven days, I read past convention speeches, pulled together an outline, and began to work on phrases. There is no speech with higher stakes in American politics. Other speeches, such as an inaugural, have more historical gravity. But a failed convention speech can make writing an inaugural speech unnecessary. More people will see the candidate during the hour that closes a convention than at any other time during the campaign. The political consequences of success or failure are immediate and measurable. And the best convention speeches are a mix of soaring vision, tough political shots, effective humor, and personal self-disclosure—a balance that is difficult to achieve.

After returning from College Station, and producing a draft along with my colleagues John McConnell and Matt Scully, I traveled to Kennebunkport, Maine, to go over the convention speech with the governor. The Bush family home sits with impressive prominence on the rocky shore, the house light filled, welcoming, and casual. On the porch overlooking the Atlantic, I met President Bush and Barbara Bush for the first time. The former president's manner was kind and vague. When Governor Bush told his mother I was working on the convention speech, she said: "Then we'll know who to blame."

During the speech review process with Karen, Karl, and the governor, some of the tougher anti-Gore lines were removed. Governor Bush was always skeptical of what he perceived to be harsh negativity. He did not want to say of Clinton and Gore, for example: "They came in together, now let us see them off together." This line, and others like it, were placed into Dick Cheney's convention speech, which Matt and John were working on—and the vice presidential nominee didn't have the slightest hesitance to deliver them. As Cheney's speech approached, Andy Card, in charge of running the Philadelphia convention, procured a copy, and felt it was too negative. He sent edits to Cheney that would have toned the remarks down. Days passed, and the vice presidential nominee's only response was silence. On the evening of the speech, to a raucous reception, he delivered the speech word for word, as written.

Governor Bush had never before occupied so large a national stage. On the day of the speech, advisor Mark McKinnon was charged with "staffing" Bush—making sure his suit and tie looked good, getting him anything he needed. Mark, assuming the governor would be nervous and apprehensive, didn't engage him in conversation. In the suite, Mark heard music, which at first he thought was the radio. It was actually Governor Bush, whistling "Go Tell It on the Mountain." When Mark asked him why he seemed so relaxed, Bush told him: "I am so confident in the words of the speech; that it is an accurate, pure reflection of who I am. I am confident that I will be accepted or rejected on the basis of what I am." That is, perhaps, the most satisfying achievement of a speechwriter.

The convention speech was a summary of everything that had come before. It began with a tribute to his father. "My father was the last president of a great generation. A generation of Americans who stormed beaches, liberated concentration camps, and delivered us from evil." The spotlight then shifted to the Baby Boom generation. "Now the question comes to the sons and daughters of this achievement: what is asked of us?" Instead of questioning the existence of American prosperity, the governor argued that its promise was being wasted. "Never has the promise of prosperity been so vivid. But times of plenty, like times of crisis, are tests of American character. Prosperity can be a good in our hands—used to build and better our country. Or it can be a drug in our system—dulling our sense of urgency, of empathy, of duty."

The speech praised President Clinton for his tremendous personal skills—an implicit contrast to Vice President Al Gore, who lacked them—but then used Clinton as the symbol of wasted Baby Boom promise. "Our current president embodied the potential of a generation. So many talents. So much charm. Such great skill. But, in the end, to what end? So much promise, to no great purpose.... This administration had its moment. They had their chance. They have not led; we will."

Then, the use of humor to point out Al Gore's timidity and lack of vision—making good use of his tenuous claim to have invented the Internet. "Our nation today needs vision. That is a fact … or as my opponent might call it, a 'risky truth scheme.' Every one of the proposals I've talked about tonight, he has called a 'risky scheme,' over and over again…. If my opponent had been there at the moon launch, it would have been a 'risky rocket scheme.' If he'd been there when Edison was testing the lightbulb, it would have been a 'risky anti-candle scheme.' If he'd been there when the Internet was invented, well…" At this point, the laughter of the convention didn't allow Governor Bush to finish.

Bush reaffirmed his promise to change the party he was chosen to lead—to ensure it is the "party of reform, not the party of repose." "Big government is not the answer," he said. "But the alternative to bureaucracy is not indifference. It is to put conservative values and conservative ideas into the thick of the fight for justice and opportunity. This is what I mean by compassionate conservatism. And on this ground we will govern our nation."

Near the end came a personal note. "I believe in tolerance," he said, "not in spite of my faith, but because of it. I believe in a God who calls us, not to judge our neighbors, but to love them. I believe in grace, because I have seen it. In peace, because I have felt it. In forgiveness, because I have needed it." Not the usual tone of a convention speech—but the deepest meaning of the faith he holds, the faith we share.

As Governor Bush spoke these words at the Philadelphia convention center, I was wandering the streets of the city in a sprinkling rain. As usual, my nerves would not allow me to attend the speech. As the rain got harder, and the neighborhoods in which I found myself got rougher, I had to ask a policeman for directions back to the hotel. Damp but safely returned to my room, I quickly got a call from the candidate, who sounded intoxicated with enthusiasm. "Well, Gerson, what did you think?" Having not seen a word, I paused a moment. Then said: "It looked great to me."

In the weeks after the conventions, a presidential campaign gains a steam-train momentum of charges and countercharges, negative ads and debate handicapping—but a policy advisor and speechwriter is mainly a spectator. Most of the serious policy has already been announced. The ambitious rhetoric of the announcement speech and the convention gives way to the shouted refrains of the stump speech, and the daily scramble for a hard-hitting sound bite. After our successful convention—perhaps stung by the charges of timidity—Vice President Gore's convention speech hit on a more effective populist theme: "I'm for the people, not the powerful." He attacked drug companies and insurance companies, and used the words "working families" nine times. With a long, onstage marital kiss, he attempted to humanize himself with voters. The advantage swung back and forth, with both candidates looking alternately inevitable and incredible. And Governor Bush's late, three- to five-point lead was erased by a dirty trick—the well-timed release, five days before the election, of an old DUI arrest record, an incident that had happened when Bush was twenty-four years old. Karen Hughes did her best to explain it away, but it successfully undermined some of the candidate's advantage on values and character.

Election night came in Austin along with a cold and steady rain. I paced in the campaign headquarters, then walked up Congress Street to the large, outdoor platform that had been constructed for the victory celebration. I expected a narrow win. But I had, folded in my pocket, the only copy of a concession speech, which had not been shown to Karen, Karl, or the candidate, out of superstition and awkwardness. It began: "My friends and fellow Americans, thank you. I've just spoken to my opponent, who is not my opponent anymore, but the president-elect of the United States. I promised him my full support as he prepares to lead our country. In a political campaign, you always look for your opponent's weaknesses. But you learn something about his strengths, too—and President-elect Gore has many. Our country has given its greatest trust to a skilled and able man. I congratulate him, and I wish him well."

The uncertainty of the night lasted so long I went home. Finally, the networks announced Bush the winner, and I went to sleep, exhausted and satisfied. I was awakened by a call from Gloria Borger: "It isn't over."

The election crisis, which sent nearly every Republican lawyer in America to Florida, left me completely unoccupied. Occasionally, we would revise the victory speech, in anticipation of some legal decision. But mainly I slept in, watched cable news, took long lunches, and went to movies. Governor Bush spent much of his time at his ranch near Waco. One afternoon, just back from the ranch, he showed me his arms, which were marked in several places by long, deep gashes—the result of cutting cedar trees. The vegetation of his ranch was clearly suffering from his frustration. Eventually, I packed up and went back to Washington, knowing I'd be going home either way, win or lose. Each day I reported to a desk down the hall from Dick Cheney, at a Potemkin transition office in McLean, Virginia. The security cards and sober meetings had a comic-opera quality, because the whole operation had no legal status until the election was decided. When the Supreme Court finally made that decision, the staff was scattered, the country was divided, and the victory had been drained of much of its joy.

But it was clear to me that compassionate conservatism—though controversial within the party, and scorned by some outside it—was one of the main reasons we had won. In 1996, voters trusted Bill Clinton over Bob Dole on education by an overwhelming 31 percent margin. In the 2000 election, the gap between Gore and Bush had narrowed to a single percentage point. Gains were also made on welfare policy, health care, and even Social Security. In 1996, Clinton led Dole on the indicator "cares about people like me" by fifteen points. In 2000, Gore and Bush were nearly even.

It was a major shift, and a difficult one. The images of the two political parties are the most durable feature of American politics. Democrats are seen as compassionate, profligate, and weak on defense. Republicans are hard-hearted, fiscally responsible, and strong on defense. Changing these images requires policy innovation, vivid language, and constant repetition—and we successfully employed all three.

Where did this shift put President Bush in the Republican tradition? Contrary to the fears of some conservatives, who were always suspicious of his father's moderation, Bush is hardly a liberal, Rockefeller Republican. He is anti-elitist, socially conservative, and convinced that the moral chaos of the 1960s must be reversed in a number of ways. But he is also not a Barry Goldwater Republican. Senator Goldwater, the Republican nominee in 1964, came to stand for a Western, rugged, libertarian individualism—the belief that government was the enemy of freedom, and should not poach beyond the fences of personal privacy. Governor Bush did not use anti-government rhetoric, and did not run as an anti-government candidate.

President Bush's ideological relationship with Ronald Reagan is mixed. Like Reagan, he is both a cultural conservative and a cultural optimist. He combines his moralism with a religiously rooted belief that individuals are capable of change, and thus societies are capable of progress. Like Reagan, he is a committed tax cutter; he believes that leaving more wealth with those who earned it is both an economic necessity and a moral goal. As a candidate, Bush earned and kept the allegiance of both these essential Republican constituencies—cultural conservatives, and pro-growth conservatives.

But it is impossible to imagine Bush attacking "welfare queens," as Reagan did. Governor Bush uniformly talked about the poor, addicts, and even illegal immigrants in sympathetic ways. And the Democrats cooperated in this role reversal, by focusing almost exclusively on "working families" and the middle class, seldom mentioning the homeless, the fatherless, the poor. In the 2000 election, the Republican candidate for president talked more consistently and passionately about poverty and hopelessness than the Democratic candidate. That was certainly not true of the Reagan era.

And unlike Reagan, Bush did not say, and did not believe, that "government is not the solution, government is the problem." His phrase "the American government is not the enemy of the American people" was intended as a conscious response to that sentiment. On issues from education, to welfare, to Social Security, Governor Bush was willing to use active government as an instrument of reform—not to create towering bureaucracies, but to break up an unjust status quo, by giving individuals and non-governmental institutions more resources and choices. The objective, he felt, was not "small" government, or "big" government, but effective government. In making this case, he repudiated one narrow element of the Reagan coalition: libertarians who are anti-government the way Sherman was anti-Georgia. They thought they were being assaulted, and were correct to think it.

After eight years of the Clinton era, Republicans were prepared to accept some heterodoxy in exchange for electability. Clinton himself, as a candidate, had benefited from the same dynamic. After twelve years of the Reagan/Bush era, Democrats willingly accepted his support for the death penalty, his opposition to same-sex marriage, and his pledge to "end welfare as we know it" in order to win. Republicans embraced or tolerated compassionate conservatism with the same goal. In politics, desperation is often the father of creativity.

The crowds that came to the Capitol to see the Bush inauguration were greeted with a cold and spitting rain, leaving dignitaries in rather undignified, transparent rain ponchos. That morning, in a careful choreography of symbols, the president-elect and his wife moved from a short service at St. John's Episcopal Church on Lafayette Park (the blessings of Providence), to a coffee with the Clintons at the White House (the orderly transfer of power), to a formal greeting at the Capitol (deference to the legislative branch, which must be both appeased and led). A little after 11:30, the governor of Texas walked with confidence toward his seat on the podium at the West Front of the Capitol, a short journey, with its own dramatic symbols. Past his father, who had held the office just eight years before. Past a sitting vice president who had gotten more votes on Election Day. Past members of the Supreme Court, who had determined the election's outcome. A short walk, but an historic one.

We had gone over the inaugural speech for weeks, mainly at Blair House, across Pennsylvania Avenue from the White House, where the president-elect stays by tradition. We read through the speech by the blazing fireplace in his upstairs bedroom, and practiced it with a tele-prompter in the back parlor. As Inaugural Day approached, I was con-scious of a change in atmosphere. The president-elect's casual manner—the teasing and banter—did not change. But as he drew closer to this objective, he drew away from the rest of us. He did not take himself seriously, but he clearly took the office he was about to assume seriously. And the nature of his duties set him slightly apart. He grew more accustomed to authority, more demanding in small things. I grew more deferential of the man I would soon call "Mr. President." But it encouraged me that he had not lost his belief that absurdity stood at the heart of all formality. At the most solemn moments, he was still apt to break out in a wink or a grin, as if to say, "Who'd a thought?"

As he took the rostrum, in a heavy black overcoat, the overcast skies cleared, and the sun cast weak shadows. The speech began with an indi-rect reference to Providence, calling American history a story, which implied an Author. "It is the story of a new world that became a friend and liberator of the old, a story of a slave-holding society that became a servant of freedom, the story of a power that went into the world to protect but not possess, to defend but not to conquer."

The speech's main theme was unity—appropriate after a divisive election. Yet the sources of our division ran deep. "While many of our citizens prosper, others doubt the promise, even the justice, of our own country. The ambitions of some Americans are limited by failing schools and hidden prejudice and the circumstances of their birth. And sometimes our differences run so deep, it seems like we share a continent, but not a country.

"We do not accept this, and we will not allow it," he went on. "Our unity, our union, is the serious work of leaders and citizens in every generation. And this is my solemn pledge: I will work to build a single nation of justice and opportunity." That unity, in America, is not created by bloodlines or birth, but by shared ideals. And "the grandest of these ideals is an unfolding American promise that everyone belongs, that everyone deserves a chance, that no insignificant person was ever born." That aspiration, in turn, creates responsibilities. "Where there is suffering, there is duty. Americans in need are not strangers, they are citizens, not problems, but priorities. And all of us are diminished when any are hopeless."

Toward the end, President Bush turned briefly away from the themes of unity and compassion, and directly addressed potential adversaries. "The enemies of liberty and our country should make no mistake: America remains engaged in the world by history and by choice, shaping a balance of power that favors freedom. We will defend our allies and our interests. We will show purpose without arrogance. We will meet aggression and bad faith with resolve and strength. And to all nations, we will speak for the values that gave our nation birth."

As he spoke, and the skies cleared, a different storm was gathering—a set of challenges that were ignored, or unknown, or unimagined. At about the same time, hijacker Mohamed Atta was traveling to Germany to deliver a progress report on the training of al-Qaeda pilots to Ramzi Binalshibh, who traveled to Afghanistan to deliver the information to al-Qaeda leaders. In this period the muscle hijackers were in al-Qaeda camps to get special training in disarming air marshals and handling explosives. They were also trained in butchering sheep with knives to prepare for the use of knives in their attack. In North Korea, Kim Jon-Il was secretly guiding a highly enriched uranium program, in direct violation of an agreement with the Clinton administration. At a deeply buried lab, he would begin assembling a nuclear weapon. That January, Saddam Hussein's son Uday proposed that all maps in the country be modified to include Kuwait as part of Iraq … illegal oil shipments were routinely leaving the country … and organized protests burned US flags on the tenth anniversary of the first Gulf War.

For eight years and more, America had been drifting through prosperity, leaving grave problems unconfronted, taking a pleasing and costly break from history. Now, on the west steps of the Capitol, a young, ungreyed president spoke, without knowing the violence and complex choices that were even then in motion. "After the Declaration of Independence was signed," he concluded, "Virginia statesman John Page wrote to Thomas Jefferson: 'We know the race is not to the swift, nor the battle to the strong. Do you not think an angel rides in the whirlwind and directs this storm?' Much time has passed since Jefferson arrived for his inauguration. The years and changes accumulate. But the themes of this day he would know: our nation's grand story of courage and its simple dream of dignity. We are not this story's Author, Who fills time and eternity with His purpose. Yet His purpose is achieved in our duty, and our duty is fulfilled in service to one another. Never tiring, never yielding, never finishing, we renew that purpose today, to make our country more just and generous, to affirm the dignity of our lives and every life. This work continues. This story goes on. And an angel still rides in the whirlwind and directs this storm."

And the whirlwind was coming.

Chapter 3

9/11, Good and Evil

It is a strange and sobering thing when the thin strand of your own life is wound into the strong cable of American history, when your own small story briefly intersects with an epic that began at Plymouth and Philadelphia.

My day began on September 11, 2001, working on a speech to unveil a never-announced, never-missed initiative called "Communities of Character"—much as some speechwriter might have been immersed in remarks on the Tennessee Valley Authority as planes approached Pearl Harbor. With the president away in Florida, I had the luxury of working at home in Alexandria, Virginia, a short drive from the White House. My deputy, Pete Wehner, was covering for me at the 7:30 senior staff meeting in the Roosevelt Room, across from the Oval Office. At 8:41, he sent me a brief e-mail: "Very little of note happened. The economy dominated the discussions, but little new was said. Senior staff should plan to attend at least some of tonight's congressional barbecue." Very little of note.

A little after 9 a.m., I was interrupted at my computer by a call from Pete: the World Trade Center had been hit by two planes; something very big and dangerous was going on. After watching some of the apocalyptic images on television, I got in my car and headed north on Interstate 395 toward the city. The traffic was slow, and as I neared the Pentagon, I saw a plane flying very low over the highway ahead— so low I could see the windows clearly. I thought, *That plane isn't going to make it to the airport. It is going to crash.* The impact was hidden by a bend in the highway, but I saw smoke begin to rise. I heard no sound or explosion. Traffic stopped completely, and people began getting out of their cars, telling each other, "I saw that. I saw the crash." I tried to use my cell phone to reach my wife, Dawn, who worked on Capitol Hill, or anyone at the White House, but the lines were overwhelmed. Emergency vehicles began coming up both sides of the road. Back in my car, I listened for information on the radio, and began to sketch out some thoughts on a yellow pad for the inevitable speech. We were stationary an hour or more, until the police turned us around, and directed us to drive the wrong way on the highway. I reached home quickly.

It would not be until later, after the rush of events had slowed, that I would think about those small windows, and the fear behind them.

Rumor ruled the morning, as reports came in that the State Department had been hit, that other explosions could be heard around town. I finally reached my wife by phone. After being evacuated from a House of Representatives office building, she had collected our infant son from day care, and had made her way safely to a bar on Capitol Hill. Our other son's school in northern Virginia was not evacuated. Dawn eventually got out of the city, but I was not able to enter—the highways and subway from our area were closed.

Because the White House complex was thought to be under threat, my staff was making a hurried journey across the city. At first, the antiquated alarm system didn't go off in parts of the massive Old Executive Office Building. Then, as many staffers milled around, the police began to shout "Run!" creating a mild panic. The writers who worked for me first made their way to the offices of *The Weekly Standard* magazine, then to the DC offices of Chrysler (where a staffer had contacts). There I finally talked to them. We produced a short, tough, dignified, but not very inspired statement. It included two elements: First, that the attacks were "more than acts of terror, they were acts of war." The traditional language of response to terrorism—the language of crime and punishment—was not, in my view, sufficient to this dramatic escalation of mass violence. And second, that we will "make no distinction between the terrorists who committed these acts and those who harbor them."

As the draft was sent along via e-mail to Karen Hughes, I felt a deep sense of frustration. I wanted to be at the White House working on the speech, which was now entirely out my hands.

Elsewhere, the president flew westward into a cloud of confusion. There were reports that Air Force One was a target, taken seriously by Chief of Staff Andy Card and the Secret Service. Leaving Florida, the president stopped in Louisiana for fueling, flew to a secure base in Nebraska, and was taken by armed military transport to an underground bunker. I passed along to Karen my strong conviction that the president should return to Washington, as a symbol of strength and leadership. Without needing my advice, he insisted on returning himself.

That night, the president's speech was unequal to the moment— too much sentiment, not enough resolve, too much forced word play: "These acts shattered steel, but they cannot dent the steel of American resolve." The president looked stiff and small. He had used the line about making no distinction between the terrorists and their sponsors, but rejected the mention of "war." Both he and Karen felt that America needed to be comforted before it could be rallied. But by 11 the next morning, in remarks made in the cabinet room, the president was referring to "acts of war." The first day of the crisis had not been a good day for the president. He was being accused, unfairly, of running from danger and, fairly, of lacking rhetorical inspiration. But behind the scenes, he was calm and determined, as I would see in the next few days.

Before sunrise on September 12, I drove across the Fourteenth Street Bridge into Washington with my windows open, smelling the Pentagon burning in the dark. It evoked feelings of anger and protest that must have been similar to what the citizens of the Roman Empire felt while smelling the Forum in flames: How could the chaos of distant places—anarchy at the fringes of the world—reach the center of the world? The transformation of Washington was total. The security perimeter of the White House was extended several blocks. The streets were empty of traffic. Other than the sound of circling helicopters, the silence was eerie and complete. Later in the day, the president made a solemn visit to the Pentagon, where a large flag was draped over the scorched side of the building. A powerful symbol, but not an assertion of presidential leadership. That evening, I went to Karl Rove's office on the second floor of the West Wing and told him: "If we think our response has been a success so far, we're wrong."

But the next day began a remarkable recovery—an example of how the words and gestures and character of an American president can change the tone and posture of a whole nation. On Thursday, the president had reporters into his office as he talked to the mayor and governor of New York. When the conversation ended, a reporter asked the president to describe his prayers, what he was feeling in his heart. He turned away a moment, then turned back, his eyes filled with tears as he jabbed toward the desk. "Well, I don't think of myself right now. I think about the families, the children." Fighting his emotions, he continued: "I'm a loving guy. And I am also someone, however, who's got a job to do and I intend to do it. And this is a terrible moment. But this country will not relent until we have saved ourselves, and others, from the terrible tragedy that came upon America." So much emotion and determination in a single moment.

Not long after the event ended, I was in the Oval Office, and told the president it had been an important moment for the country. He seemed surprised, slightly embarrassed by his tears, but encouraged by my comments. Later that day, in a meeting in the cabinet room, Secretary of State Colin Powell handed Bush a note, warning that a president shouldn't show too much emotion in public. Clearly amused, Bush read the note to the whole group, and added, "Don't worry. I'm not losing it."

I had been in the Oval Office to discuss a speech planned for the following day. The president had insisted on a service of prayer and remembrance, now set for the Washington National Cathedral, and he wanted a draft quickly. We talked about the themes of the speech—then he paused, and said: "We are at war." He had made that statement before, even in public, but now he was saying it to me, and he still seemed astounded by the words—repeating them, like they were still sinking in. I went off and worked with Matt and John on the Cathedral remarks, which we got to him by the end of the day.

The next morning, September 14, I was back in the Oval Office, in the chair next to the Resolute Desk, going over the speech. The first draft, produced in hours, was very close to his intentions—the result of over two years of close interaction. At around 11:30, I boarded the motorcade in the pouring rain, sitting in the van with Karl Rove, Counsel to the President Al Gonzalez, and some others. It was a quiet trip, past embassies with their flags at half-mast, past crowds at the side of road clutching American flags. In the cathedral, I sat several rows behind the president. Amid the stained glass and soaring limestone, he took the lectern: "We are here in the middle hour of our grief." The purposes of the speech were simple. To express sorrow at a tragedy that was actually many tragedies: "We have seen the images of fire and ashes and bent steel. Now come the names.... We will linger over them, and learn their stories, and many Americans will weep." To begin to show the intensity and direction of American resolve: "Just three days removed from these events, Americans do not yet have the distance of history.

But our responsibility to history is already clear: to answer these attacks and rid the world of evil." (The draft of the speech had read, "this evil"—the president had misspoken.) And to express confidence in a source of justice beyond the evidence of our eyes: "This world He created is of moral design. Grief, and tragedy, and hatred are only for a time. Goodness, remembrance, and love have no end. And the Lord of Life holds all who die, and all who mourn."

After the speech, three former presidents, and all of official Washington stood in the great cathedral and sang "The Battle Hymn of the Republic": "As He died to make men holy, let us die to make men free. While God is marching on." We were truly a nation at war, and I cried for the first time in the crisis, for all the suffering that had come, and might be coming.

On the way back from the service, Karl tried to talk to me, but I was too emotional to respond. I finally felt like I had done something to serve the country, something like those workers still digging in the rubble. At only a few moments in any decade do the words spoken by a president really matter to the nation—matter like sending a fleet or winning a battle. On that day, the written words mattered like a battle.

But the same day was to demonstrate another element of presidential leadership. From the cathedral, we drove to the National Mall near the Washington Monument, where helicopters waited to take the president to Andrews Air Force Base, on his way to New York and Ground Zero. The Secret Service had opposed the visit, in part because their office in New York had been destroyed in Building 7 of the World Trade Center. But the president was intent on making the trip. At the site, he mounted the wreckage of a fire truck, with his arm around a sixty-nine-year-old retired firefighter, and started speaking into a bullhorn. The crowd shouted, "We can't hear you!" Bush replied, "I can hear you. I can hear you. And the rest of the world hears you. And the people who knocked these buildings down will hear all of us soon."

It was the modern equivalent of Henry V before Agincourt: "We few, we happy few." Or Elizabeth I facing the approaching Armada: "Let tyrants fear." The Cathedral speech had used carefully crafted words to comfort the grieving and set a historical context. The Ground Zero speech—spontaneous and simple—had revealed the president's character. Both were necessary. Only one I could help to provide.

The first eight months of the Bush administration had been a time of success and innocence. Governor Bush had slipped easily into the role of president, cheerfully unawed by its burdens. Chief of Staff Andy Card presided with a light touch over a collegial senior staff. I had quickly put together an exceptional staff of my own, which efficiently produced remarks for between one and three presidential events a day. Ambitious tax reductions passed the Congress with broad support. The domestic promises of the campaign began to be checked off, one by one.

But, in retrospect, those successes had a quality of randomness, disconnected from larger purposes. At the White House, I appreciated the trappings of history—a West Wing office, meetings in the Executive Mansion, trips on Air Force One—but had little sense of being part of history. This changed decisively on 9/11. A series of days and experiences became a narrative, with heroes who ran toward burning buildings and villains who sent children to a fiery death. What had seemed a job had become a story—but a story with a brooding sense of threat, and a happy ending by no means assured.

The day after 9/11, I asked John Gibson, one of my writers at the National Security Council, to work on remarks in the event of another terrorist attack, an event we expected, and almost assumed. False alarms led to the periodic evacuations of the White House complex; I learned to work through them without disruption. Environmental samples were regularly taken to check for chemical or biological agents. This atmosphere of uncertainty and physical risk was difficult for many at the

White House—some I knew would jump at sudden noises and cry without reason; the White House brought in counselors to help deal with the pressure; some staffers quickly and quietly resigned. My reaction was surprising, especially to me. During a quiet life, I had gained little reason to be confident in my physical courage. But my predominant reaction to 9/11 was fatalism and exhilaration. If an attack came on the White House, there was little I could do; worry seemed pointless and unproductive. And during the fourteen-hour days of the initial crisis, with every presidential speech carried live to the nation, adrenaline flowed freely—a powerful antidote to fear.

The president himself was a model of upbeat steadiness. During periods of crisis, I always had the impression that Bush was keenly aware of being watched, and convinced that any sign of uncertainty would be communicated to the staff and the nation. His good spirits—the continued banter and enthusiasm—were a natural inclination, and another element of "team building." And this manner had theological roots. President Bush combined a disciplined style of work with a deep conviction that the results were not entirely in his hands. He was intent on controlling what he could control, planning what he could plan—but he was also aware of the large, unpredictable role played by God and fate. For Lincoln, this Providence was harsh and just, requiring blood spilled in war for blood spilled in slavery—a conception of God that led to resignation before His inscrutable purposes. For President Bush, this Providence is ultimately loving and personal and concerned to vindicate the right—a conception of God that leads to trust and confidence. During the crisis, he indicated that he was sleeping well at night. He regarded this as a victory of discipline and faith over chaos and emotional disorder.

Following the Cathedral remarks, I began to get hints that a big speech would be necessary to explain the nature of the enemy, and the new kind of war we were about to undertake. I was sitting on the couch near the fireplace in the Oval Office when I heard the president describe "al-Qaeda," a group about which I knew little. He explained it was a decentralized but coordinated network of terrorist cells, based in Afghanistan, with a particularly vicious anti-American ideology. After that meeting, I asked John Gibson of the NSC to prepare some material over the weekend on the nature of this threat. Karl was pushing for the president to speak to a joint session of Congress, which I opposed. I feared that we didn't have enough action to announce to justify that dramatic setting—the same setting where Franklin Roosevelt had called for "absolute victory" against the Japanese empire. Karl thought a joint session would be a symbol of unity, and a good setting for the president. He was right.

On Monday, I got a call from Karen Hughes about 10 or 10:30 a.m.: the president had requested the draft of a joint-session speech by 7 p.m. that night. After reading the speech, he would make a decision on whether it should be given. I told her the task would be difficult in that time frame—I was really thinking it would be impossible. She agreed, but said the president insisted. I sat down in my office for about a half an hour, collected my thoughts, and wrote down an outline. I called Matt and John, and we started to work, making use of the information John Gibson had provided. There was no time to look at historical precedents, or to talk with experts—at such a moment you can only depend on historical and literary capital that has already been accumulated. The president had his draft around 7 p.m.—a heroic effort, if striking computer keys in a quiet room can ever be called heroic. An hour or so later, Karen called to say that the president was happy enough to move along with the project, without a final decision. Walking to my car on West Executive Avenue, I called Karl on my cell phone and told him that in a couple of days we might have an historic speech on our hands.

The next morning in the Oval Office, I said I was still concerned the speech did not have enough action to announce. At this point, the National Security Advisor Condi Rice passed me a State Department draft of an ultimatum to the Taliban—the brutal government of

Afghanistan—demanding that the regime hand over al-Qaeda leaders, close terrorist camps, and give America full access to verify those actions. This clearly met my hope for news. That evening, as I entered my driveway, the president called me on my cell phone with an extensive series of edits to the speech. He was now clearly assuming the speech would be delivered.

The next morning, after working in an extensive round of strengthening changes from Karen, the president read the speech aloud and said, "Great job. Let's tell the Congress." There was a teleprompter practice that night, then two the following day, in which the president continued to make word changes. The announcement of Governor Tom Ridge of Pennsylvania as the new Homeland Security Advisor was added during one session. A reference to al-Qaeda "fatwas" was removed, because the word would sound so strange to American ears. The domestic-policy staff at the White House made a determined attempt to insert a passage on education reform and healthcare. This would have been a gasp-provoking intrusion—a tin ear of historic proportions. It made me wonder if some White House staffer had proposed in Roosevelt's declaration of war: "This date which will live in infamy found us making progress on many other issues, including agriculture...."

On the afternoon of September 20, the president took a nap, a typical, disciplined effort to collect his strength for the evening. Before he left for the Hill, he said, "Mike, I see you are on the manifest. Are you coming tonight?" I told him I had missed too many nights with my boys and was going home.

The Joint Session speech begins with comparisons to Pearl Harbor, another surprise attack that launched America into a new role in the world—but points out that the intentional targeting of civilians at the center of our cities is unprecedented, and marks a change of eras. "All this was brought upon us in a single day—and night fell on a different world." The speech largely focuses on one question, directly posed in

the text: "Who attacked our country?" Addressing this issue was unnecessary for Roosevelt in 1941—the empire of Japan was known and
feared. But al-Qaeda was known mainly to terrorism experts and
required explanation. The speech describes a transnational movement,
with roots and safe havens in nations like Afghanistan—a modern political ideology that distorts Islam instead of an authentic expression of
that ancient faith. "The terrorists are traitors to their own faith, trying,
in effect, to hijack Islam itself." The triumph of their political vision is
found in Taliban Afghanistan, where women are oppressed and brutal-
ized, and "a man can be jailed … if his beard is not long enough." Their
intention is to use dramatic acts of murder to demoralize us. "With
every atrocity, they hope that America grows fearful, retreating from the
world and forsaking our friends."

Then the president, nine days after 9/11, set out the elements of a
new foreign-policy approach. The "instant retaliation and isolated
strikes" of the past had failed. America intended to take the offensive
against terrorism, "to stop it, eliminate it, and destroy it where it grows."
Nations that sponsor and harbor terrorists dramatically increase their
destructive reach, so, "from this day forward, any nation that continues
to harbor or support terrorism will be regarded by the United States
as a hostile regime." Afghanistan, in particular, must "hand over the
terrorists" or "share in their fate." Yet this is more than a military struggle, it is an ideological one, a war between "freedom and fear." "This
country will define our times, not be defined by them…. This will not
be an age of terror; this will be an age of liberty." The proper response
to an attack on our beliefs, the president argued, was confidence in the
truth and power of our beliefs—a line of argument that would have
been familiar to Franklin Roosevelt.

However distinctive the current threat, it is World War II and the
Cold War that provide the context for the Joint Session speech. "We
have seen their kind before. They are the heirs of all the murderous

ideologies of the twentieth century. By sacrificing human life to serve their radical visions—by abandoning every value except the will to power—they follow in the path of fascism, and Nazism, and totalitarianism. And they will follow that path all the way, to where it ends: in history's unmarked grave of discarded lies."

After these broad historical brushstrokes, and the expression of large national commitments, the speech comes down to a single man at the podium, selected by events for a lonely role. Americans, the president says, will go back to their lives and routines, and return almost to normal. "Even grief," he says, "recedes with time and grace." And yet "our resolve must not pass." Every American should remember "what happened that day, and to whom it happened." "Some will remember an image of fire, or a story of rescue. Some will carry memories of a face and a voice gone forever. And I will carry this." The president holds up the police shield of George Howard, who died at the World Trade Center saving others. "This is my reminder of lives that ended, and a task that does not end. I will not forget this wound to our country or those who afflicted it. I will not yield; I will not rest; I will not relent in waging this struggle for freedom and security for the American people."

The speech was a nearly universal American experience; bars and restaurants turned up the sound, sporting events were interrupted to play it on the large screen. Afterward, the *Washington Post* columnist Michael Kelly, who later died reporting from Iraq, wrote a note to one of my colleagues: "Well, that was extraordinary. Thinking about it, stunned by its greatness, afterwards, it occurred to me that that speech was the only one I have ever witnessed—probably will ever witness—that was the true, historical McCoy—the once-in-a-hundred-years, history-changing, nation-defining, generationally-epic Real Thing. The other big speeches of my lifetime—various inaugural and convention addresses, 'Mr. Gorbachev, tear down this wall!' all seem now what they were, perfectly fine but in a different, vastly lesser category than this.

That was the first time in my life I have viscerally understood what it meant, in a time of fear and crisis, to have mere words change everything so immensely for the better—what it must have felt like for the British in their darkest hour to hear Churchill's 'We will fight on the beaches …' or for Americans in the Depression to hear FDR's dressing down of fear itself."

I watched the speech on television at home. I saw a president who was engaged, passionate, confident, and as strong as the country itself. And I would never view him the same way again. Whatever faults I had seen, whatever failures might come, George Bush had completely filled that historical moment. Josh Bolten called me almost immediately afterward to report on the strongly positive reaction in the chamber. Then a few minutes later, the president was on the phone. He told me quietly, "I have never felt more comfortable in my life." I took that to mean he was comfortable with his place at center stage … comfortable with his role in history. I told him, "Mr. President, this is why God wants you here." He replied, "No, this is why God wants us here."

Some have had tried to interpret this as messianic arrogance. They misunderstand the Christian idea of calling. Every Christian believes there is a golden thread of purpose in our lives, which, usually, is difficult to find. But especially when our talents are useful in the service of others, that purpose seems more definite and discernible. This isn't a reason for pride. God has a tendency to use the weak and unworthy to serve His purposes; in Paul's words, to "use the foolish things of this world to confound the wise." And if Al Gore had been elected president, it would have been equally his calling to face these challenges. But it is not a Christian belief that events unfold randomly, in a meaningless tumble. We have a part to play, all of us, in an unfolding drama, which has an Author. Lincoln, Washington, and others traced the hand of Providence in their own lives—and that Providence was not absent or asleep on 9/11.

• • •

In the weeks and months after 9/11, the habits of mind I'd seen fore-shadowed in Austin and the early months of the presidency hardened into a style of war leadership. Its defining public characteristic is directness. Some presidents, like Jefferson, operated through the "feints of front men." It was said of Martin van Buren that he "rowed to his object with muffled oars." President Bush steamed toward his objects with flags flying and horns blowing, more in the tradition of Teddy Roosevelt or Harry Truman. In this period, he used speeches to set out a series of ultimatums, arguments, and doctrines that left no one, friend or enemy, with doubts where he stood.

In the West Wing, however, the tone was different. President Bush's defining private characteristic is discipline. His management approach puts an emphasis on orderly process. For the speechwriters, that meant a careful process of editing and practice, and a discomfort with hurried, last-minute changes, which he often attributed to "hand-wringers." Bush would be in the Oval Office early, usually providing speech edits to me around 6:45, before the rigors of his daily schedule began. And the White House day normally ended before 7 p.m., as he walked down the colonnade to the residence, allowing his staff some semblance of a family life. His editing instincts are as disciplined as his schedule. He insists on straightforward, active language, and obvious, orderly out-lines—the result, he says, of a formative rhetoric class at Yale, but also the result of a careful and logical mind. He can be intolerant of sloppy work, especially after repeated warnings. One young speechwriter on my staff was called directly to the Oval Office by the president, an experience that can cause fear and trembling. Bush's gentle assistant, Ashley, called me hurriedly on the phone, and asked me to come over: "He won't yell if you are around." Reading aloud in the Oval Office, wearing reading glasses and chewing on a cigar (I never saw it smoked in the West Wing), he invariably knew when some awkward insertion had been made by others in the editing process, what he called a "cram in." And he could often identify who had done the cramming, without being told.

The same belief in order and process characterized his style of decision making. In contrast to his public image of acting according to his "gut," the president regarded hasty and impulsive decisions as a sign of indiscipline and weakness. He wanted choices to be carefully debated and considered on the staff level before they were brought to him for discussion. Instead of being headstrong and intrusive, he was a delegator on principle, investing his key staff with confidence that was difficult to revoke. His approach was to trust people, and let them run. And this applied with special force to the military. Former generals like Eisenhower respected the military, but had a realistic view of its internal politics and dense bureaucracy. Without that background, President Bush showed the military a strong deference, often contrasting himself with Lyndon Johnson, whom he felt had improperly micromanaged the Vietnam War. Bush's management challenges and failures, when they came, did not result from stubborn insistence on his views and vision, but from the lack of it.

Yet this tactical caution was matched with a strategic boldness. The main outlines of what came to be called the "Bush Doctrine" came from President Bush's own reading of recent history, and reaction to the events of 9/11. Unlike some other participants in the drama—such as Secretary of State Colin Powell, or Vice President Cheney—the president did not filter his views of 9/11 through a set of previously adopted ideological commitments and foreign-policy views. His judgments were more intuitive and organic than academic, which left him open to major departures in analysis and policy. And unlike many conservatives, the president is a "root cause" thinker, consistently asking the question: What, in the long term, would solve this problem, not just mitigate it? This willingness to think anew, combined with a desire to address root causes, led to an ambitious foreign policy—what Professor John Lewis Gaddis of Yale called "the most important reformulation of US grand strategy in over half a century."

First, it was clear that the enemy had been at war with us for decades without a response serious enough to change or complicate their intentions—a one-sided war that we had never chosen to fight. Shia extremists had begun the offensive with the Iranian revolution in the late '70s; the taking of American hostages for 444 days; and the killing of US Marines in Lebanon in 1983. Then came the first attack on the World Trade Center in 1993, and the killing of eighteen American soldiers in Mogadishu. Osama bin Laden, not a Shia but a Sunni of the extremist Wahhabi persuasion, issued his first fatwa against America in 1996, and his second in 1998, in which he called on "every Muslim who believes in God and hopes for reward to obey God's command to kill the Americans." Then the destruction of two US embassies in Africa in 1998, and the attack on the USS *Cole* in 2000.

America's response to these escalating attacks could not be called decisive—a few cruise missiles fired at a terrorist training camp in Afghanistan and a pharmaceutical plant in Sudan with ties to al-Qaeda. When the World Trade Center was bombed the first time, or a navy ship was attacked at harbor in the Persian Gulf, it was generally viewed as part of the price of living in the modern world. Governments like Pakistan and Saudi Arabia quietly appeased and supported terrorist groups in the hope they could avoid becoming targets themselves. The terrorists used these events to create a mythology: a mythology of American weakness and decadence, which they employed as a recruiting tool. Osama bin Laden believed that Muslims would be attracted to the "strong horse" of radicalism, because America and the West had proven to be a "weak horse." He said in 1998: "We have seen in the last decade the decline of the American government and the weaknesses of the American soldier who was ready to wage cold wars and unprepared to fight long wars. This was proven in Beirut when the Marines fled after two explosions in 1983. It also proves they can run in less than twenty-four hours, and this was also repeated in Somalia.... Our youth were surprised at the low morale of American soldiers.... After a few blows, they ran in defeat.... They forget about being the world leader and the leader of the new world order. They left dragging their corpses and their shameful defeat."

President Bush set out radically to change this course of events and smash this myth. His statement, "You are either with us, or you are with the terrorists" was directed at nations such as Pakistan and Saudi Arabia, which could no longer be allowed to play both sides in the global struggle with terrorism—and the message eventually had some effect. But Bush also realized that it was not likely that diplomacy or deterrence alone could have prevented the 9/11 attacks. It would have required the destruction of terrorist safe havens in Afghanistan, and of the regime that actively protected them. The next stages of the War on Terror, he concluded, would have to be conducted "on the offensive," requiring the elimination of threats "before they arrive." The attacks of 9/11 dramatically reduced the threshold of acceptable risk. The president was willing to be accused of overreaction rather than being left to comfort the grief-stricken after more funerals.

This policy tool, called preemption, was not new in international law or in American history. Much of America's frontier was secured through preemptive action in the nineteenth century. President Franklin D. Roosevelt made this argument for early involvement in World War II: "When you see a rattlesnake poised to strike, you do not wait until he has struck before you crush him." President Bush fully intended to crush the snake before it could strike again.

Second, the president quickly asserted that, in the long term, the response of force was not sufficient; political and ideological change would need to come to the greater Middle East. The enemies that revealed themselves on September 11 were part of what Condoleezza Rice called a "pan movement"—a transnational, subversive network with clear political goals: to advocate a violent version of "jihad," to impose an oppressive version of Sharia law wherever it gained power, to overthrow "apostate" Arab states, to rid the Middle East of Zionism and of American influence, and to demoralize the United States and the West through dramatic acts of murder. This movement, over the previous decade, had developed active jihads in places from Israel to Somalia to Algeria, to Chechnya to Kashmir to the Philippines. It found safe havens along the mountainous Pakistan border, and was expanding havens in Africa's Sahel and even the triborder area of Latin America. But the roots and ambitions of the movement were found in its hallowed ground of the Middle East. Success there would increase the terrorists' reach and strength, and add to their myth of inevitability. Failure in the Middle East would shatter their confidence and morale. And without this sense of inevitability, "pan movements" have historically withered and died.

This was (and remains) a bold strategic insight. The twentieth century had been dominated by the problem of Europe; that continent's internal ideological struggles and conflicts had resulted in gulags and genocide on a previously unimagined scale, and spilled out in violence across the world. Those conflicts were only eventually resolved by the ideological victory of democracy and free markets, which turned some of history's most bitter rivals (the Germans versus the French, the Germans versus the Poles) into partners in an unprecedented project of European unity. The twenty-first century confronts the problem of the Middle East—a region of aimless young men, in economically and socially stagnant societies, increasingly listening to voices of resentment and radicalism. For decades, aging autocrats have deflected attention from their own failures by encouraging anti-American and anti-Semitic scapegoating. Heavy-handed oppression has weakened democratic reform, while driving nearly all opposition into the mosque—frequently, the extremist mosque. Tyranny and terrorism have reinforced each other in a cycle, producing ideologies and individuals that murder American citizens with increasing skill and ambition. Just as the political sicknesses of Germany and Russia led to a series of world crises, the political sicknesses of the Middle East have become acute and uncontainable. Bernard Lewis, the scholar of Islam, puts the situation bluntly: "They will change, or they will kill us."

There is no effective way to oppose the diseased dreams of radicalism without some hopeful alternative. As Condoleezza Rice often said: "You can't beat something with nothing." The difficult task is to stimulate reform and progress in places like Saudi Arabia and Egypt without triggering the collapse of those governments, a collapse that radicals could use to their advantage. This is a challenge that demands the diplomatic skills of Bismarck, combined with the idealism of Jefferson. But the vision of democracy, open societies, and free markets has some tremendous natural advantages. It is more economically efficient and productive than the ideological alternatives; it has proved adaptable to diverse cultural circumstances, from Catholic Latin America, to Orthodox Eastern Europe, to Confucian East Asia; and it fills deep human needs for creativity and autonomy. Encouraging the political and social progress of the Middle East is one of history's most difficult goals, but the appeal of human liberty is one of America's great non-military advantages—what scholars call a type of "soft power." Without exercising that soft power, our long-term safety is unachievable.

The pursuit of a democratic Middle East is, by definition, destabilizing. If American security depends not merely on the external behavior of nations in the region, but on their internal character, our attempts to change that character are bound to be seen as intrusive by those who benefit from the status quo. But this effort is not motivated by a woolly-headed idealism. The "stability" of the Middle East has proved to be as stable as the mind of a terrorist, or the explosive he straps to his body. The choice, it seems apparent, is between some instability today, and massive instability down the road. The overfed and unproductive tyrannies of the Middle East have no future. The vacuum of their massive failure will be filled either by radicalism, or by something better. And America has a direct and vital interest in encouraging something better.

The third realization that dawned after 9/11 is this: it could have been worse. There was no question that if Osama bin Laden had had access to a nuclear weapon, he would have used it on that day. No barrier of conscience or humanity would have prevented it. Such an attack would have exponentially magnified the economic and psychological effect of the attack, perhaps crippling America in some unrecoverable way. Some experts have predicted that a nuclear attack in a major American city could result in five million deaths. And there was no question that al-Qaeda was seeking weapons of mass destruction, by their own admission. When asked by *Time* magazine about chemical and nuclear weapons, Osama bin Laden replied, "Acquiring weapons for the defense of Muslims is a religious duty." Terrorists view these weapons as the great historical equalizer, allowing the wrongs of history, and the military and political weakness of Islam, to be reversed in one blinding flash of retribution.

This danger led to some obvious conclusions. Though weapons of mass destruction are getting easier to produce, they are still not easy to produce. So, for the foreseeable future, terrorist networks are likely to depend on outlaw regimes as their source of nuclear, chemical, or biological weapons. The number of regimes that seek weapons of mass destruction and maintain ties to terrorism is actually quite small. But the options for dealing with them are limited. It is important to interdict these weapons and technologies as they are transported by sea or air—but that is hit or miss. It may be possible to apply diplomatic and economic pressure to force regimes to give up on proliferation—but a determined despot may care little about international isolation or the economic cost to his people. It may be necessary to prevent proliferation with military strikes or forced regime change—but military options are often limited and intelligence (as we found) can be fragmentary.

These considerations reinforced the president's commitment to political and social transformation in the Middle East—the kind of gradual regime change that would produce more responsible governments. Proliferation is far less urgent and problematic when destructive weapons are possessed by free governments. For all our disagreements, no one suspects a nuclear France will provide weapons of mass destruction to terrorists. Though a nuclear Iran would create regional tensions under any circumstances, it would not be nearly as threatening if Iran were a democracy that had cut its ties to terror. And some representative governments, such as South Africa, have actually given up nuclear weapons in the past. In a variety of contexts, President Bush made the point that "tyrants won't give up weapons." "The alternative," he said, "is to change the nature of regimes by promoting democracy."

The war in Afghanistan marked the first application of the president's new foreign-policy approach—and confirmed the realization that my life had utterly changed. On a Saturday morning in early October, I received a call on my cell phone from the president, asking me to come to Camp David as soon as possible. A car was sent, and my wife and I arrived, for the first time, at the president's retreat in the Catoctin Mountains of western Maryland. The entrance is heavily fortified, but once inside, the president and his staff have a freedom of movement unthinkable at the White House—no passes or checkpoints, no ever-present White House photographer, a casual atmosphere like a national park lodge. Guests stay at cabins separated by thick woods, and get around the complex on golf carts. One large cabin holds the main dining room, and the president's office. Sitting at his desk, I worked on the draft of a speech to announce the beginning of air strikes in Afghanistan, while the president and others watched a University of Texas football game in another building. He returned to his office around 6:30, sat on the couch while I continued at the keyboard, and began making calls about the impending attack to military leaders and members of Congress.

At about 7 p.m., we all went to dinner. Around the table were my wife, Mrs. Bush, Karen and her husband, Andy Card and his wife, Condi Rice, the president's brother Marvin, and two old Bush friends from Texas. President Bush obviously felt the pressure of the moment—many commentators were predicting the Afghan operation would be an indecisive quagmire—but he managed to be upbeat and humorous. He made fun of my discomfort with dogs, saying it was a Camp David tradition that I had to sleep with one of his pets. After dinner, we went over the draft for about an hour—then Dawn and I retired to the cabin, and went home the next morning. The president made his announcement from the family quarters that afternoon, in a firm, determined tone. "On my orders, the United States military has begun strikes against al-Qaeda terrorist training camps and military installations of the Taliban regime in Afghanistan...."

I had no doubts about the justice of this military operation. But the oddness of the experience deeply impressed me. Historical events look smaller from the inside than they do from a distance. Another speech, written with a group of people I had worked with for years ... a few hours of hurried writing ... a dinner of chicken fried steak, and green beans, and banana pudding ... and soon B–2 bombers were in the air and buildings and bunkers were exploding. It was like other jobs—and then suddenly not like them at all.

The project in Afghanistan was ambitious—not merely to end a regime, but to aid the rise of a working, representative government. It might have been possible to destroy the terrorist camps, remove the Taliban from power, and leave some type of military dictatorship in its place. But this would not have solved, or even addressed, the problem of a failed and divided society—a society that had trained human weapons that found targets three thousand miles away. The attacks of 9/11 originated in the chaos of a failed state, not in the armies of a great power. And unless those conditions of chaos changed, there was every reason to think the threat might reemerge—and require further military action in the future. The development of a legitimate, effective, representative government was a necessity, not merely an option.

This was a change for the president. A candidate who had campaigned on a platform skeptical of nation building was now a president in the full-time business of building nations. And this shift provoked a debate within the Republican Party, in which the president was accused of being "Wilsonian" in his ambition to "make the world safe for democracy." For many conservatives, "Wilsonian" is the nastiest foreign-policy epithet—President Woodrow Wilson is identified with the worst kind of arrogant, inflexible, costly idealism. Many conservatives in the past opposed not only Wilson's entry into World War I, but Roosevelt's entry into World War II, convinced that America should not be searching the world for monsters to destroy. Even in August 1940, Charles Lindbergh argued: "The problems of Europe cannot be solved by the interference of America."

In some respects, President Bush shares Wilson's instincts. "America," argued Wilson, "has a spiritual energy in her which no other nation can contribute to the liberation of mankind." Bush would agree—but so would Franklin Roosevelt, Harry Truman, John F. Kennedy, and Ronald Reagan. A belief in the power and appeal of democracy, and in a unique American call to spread it, is the mainstream of American internationalism, not the definition of Wilsonianism. President Wilson is justly criticized, not for the goal he set—who would want a world unsafe for democracy?—but for the method he chose to achieve it: an unrealistic belief that nations and their rivalries could be replaced by a League of Nations. Like Wilson, Bush believes that history has a moral direction, a current in favor of democratic ideals. Unlike Wilson, Bush does not believe this vision is fulfilled in the decline or replacement of the nation-state by international institutions. It is fulfilled by the growth in strength and number of democratic societies, who turn their competition and rivalry away from war and toward trade and cultural achievement.

The Bush approach is not Wilsonian, but it is an assault on certain expressions of foreign-policy "realism." Realism is a diverse system of thought. Many foreign-policy theorists don't consider themselves either idealists or realists; they lean one way or the other, viewing these categories more as tendencies than teams. But in its purest form, realism offers no millennial goal to pursue in foreign policy—neither international order, nor democratic peace. History does not offer the possibility of moral progress, only an endless cycle of interest and conflict—dog eat dog, forever. The highest goal of government is to limit this chaos by balancing power against power, even if that means cultivating friendly tyrants. In this view, stability is the only achievable goal. Any regime that contributes to stability is a friend, no matter how it treats its people.

For generations, every president—even those who regarded themselves as idealists—applied variations of realism in the greater Middle East. The need for oil, and the working out of Cold War rivalries, made this region the great exception to American idealism. President Nixon and his successors quietly allowed Syrian agents and informers to dominate Lebanon in the interest of stability. President Jimmy Carter cultivated Syria's brutal dictator Hafez al-Assad. President Clinton hosted Yassir Arafat at the White House more than any other world leader, even though Arafat was personally corrupt, politically repressive, and one of the fathers, if not *the* father, of modern terrorism. Presidents since the 1970s have given Egypt's pharaonic government billions in aid, with little expectation of political or economic reform. Realism in the Middle East has been fully and consistently applied for decades.

The result, in President Bush's view, was not "stability." It was a cauldron of resentment, backwardness, conspiracy theories, and violence for export. Foreign-policy realism was fresh from recent failure in Cold War Europe. Many realists postulated a permanent rivalry with Soviet communism that could only be managed through concession and negotiation. They could not comprehend or foresee the power of idealism and moral conviction—from Reagan to Solidarity to John Paul II—to alter fundamentally the balance of power. And foreign-policy realism, the president believed, was also failing in the Middle East. The West, he said, has "been willing to make a bargain, to tolerate oppression for the sake of stability. Long-standing ties often led us to overlook the faults of local elites. Yet this bargain did not bring stability or make us safe. It merely bought time, while problems festered and ideologies of violence took hold."

Suddenly, after the shock of 9/11, the Republican Party—the party of realism and caution—had become the party of idealism, action, and risk. The first risk, taken in the mountain vastness of Afghanistan, had largely succeeded. Other risks were coming.

Even at this early date, a number of criticisms of the president had begun to emerge. The first concerned the use of moral language in foreign affairs, especially the word *evil*. European opinion found it "simplistic," "absolutist," and "provocative." Academics like Stanley Fish of the University of Illinois argued: "We have not seen the face of evil; we have seen the face of an enemy who comes at us with a full roster of grievances, goals, and strategies."

This objection carried little weight with the president, or with me. The use of the word *evil* had the virtue of being plainly accurate. The terrorists' worship of death, exhilaration at innocent suffering, and ambitions of genocide left them in a different category from "political activist"; more in the realm of "serial killer." At some point, the insipid language of relativism—"understandable grievances," "inappropriate," "ill-advised"—becomes a moral indictment of those who use it. A refusal to see evil in Stalin's purges, or Hitler's *Holocaust,* or Pol Pot's killing fields indicates a dangerous, moral blindness ... the lack of a moral gag reflex ... a denial of the sheer reality of violent oppression. A refusal to see evil in terrorist celebration at the incineration of children—they were some of the passengers on the plane I saw heading toward the Pentagon—falls into the same category. The use of *evil* makes clear that some actions must be isolated and ostracized, that barbarism is not simply an unfortunate cultural option.

There are also very practical arguments for the use of accurate moral language in international affairs. It was necessary to communicate to Americans that this enemy was not a normal foreign power, motivated by rational self-interest. The calculated pursuit of interest might be tamed through concessions; the evil of 9/11 would not be. And moral uncertainty and euphemism are not the tools of leadership in war. It is difficult to imagine any wartime president rallying America with the message that good and evil are arbitrary social constructs, or that the viewpoint of the enemy, while unfortunate, is not unreasonable. Winston Churchill called the Nazis "a monstrous tyranny never surpassed in the dark lamentable catalogue of human crime." Ronald Reagan talked of an "evil empire" headed for the "ash-heap of history." Both were criticized as simplistic and provocative. But it is a strange and self-destructive belief that to diagnose evil is somehow to create it—as though silence and ignorance were the best tools for fighting evil in the world. The diagnosis of evil exposes it to scrutiny, and rallies others to oppose it.

This is more than a disagreement about language. On September 20, 2001, the president posed a serious question to Congress: Why was our country attacked? For some, the answer is simple: we were attacked because of American policies and actions. If only we pushed for an end to Israel's occupation of the West Bank, or withdrew our troops from "Muslim lands," this hatred might be appeased. But this underestimates the ambitions of Islamic radicals. Their goal is not merely to take half of Palestine, but to take Kashmir, and East Timor, and Spain. The list of concessions they seek is nearly infinite—not just the establishment of a Palestinian state, but the end of Israel; not just the end of Israel, but the humiliation and retreat of America; not just the humiliation of America, but the reestablishment of an Islamic empire from Southern Europe to India. Once a policy of concession is begun, it would be a matter of keeping pace with the Islamists' endless demands. For the American left, it should be harder than it evidently is to consider those demands calmly, given the fact that they include the subjugation of women, the end of all civil liberties, and the killing of homosexuals.

Others, on the right, contend that we are hated in the Islamic world because of our degraded popular culture—that conservative societies deeply and properly resent MTV and pornography and other forms of sexual liberationism. While it is true that Hollywood is not America's best ambassador in traditional parts of the world, this view also underestimates the ambitions of Islamic radicals. Their objective is not a more family-oriented culture; it is the strict imposition of a brutal interpretation of Islamic law. Their goal is not to oppose the excesses of modernity, but to enforce a joyless, totalitarian conformity—as in Taliban Afghanistan, where even the flying of kites was forbidden. They do not view American social conservatives as allies in a common moral project, but as infidels worthy of death. And most of the victims they take are not "decadent" Westerners at all, but fellow Muslims who disagree with their heretical view of that faith. How can that be a protest against Hollywood?

Still others contend that the problem we face is Islam itself, that the religion is inherently aggressive and violent. To some of our own religious leaders, Muhammad is a "terrorist" or a "wild-eyed fanatic" and Islam itself is "evil." But this is both unfair and counterproductive. There are vast differences between homicidal revolutionaries like bin Laden and traditional Muslim believers. Islamic terrorism is based on a heresy called Takfirism, which teaches that Muslims who do not share the most radical views—which means most Muslims in the world—are in a state of corrupt unbelief. For the Islamic community to return to vanished glory, in this view, unbelievers must be denounced and even physically eliminated. To argue that this narrow belief is representative of the Islamic tradition is the equivalent of saying that the Ku Klux Klan—another political heresy—is representative of the Christian tradition. In the mainstream Muslim tradition, anyone who accepts the five pillars of Islam must be accepted as a Muslim. The intentional murder of the innocent is at odds with most interpretations of Islamic law. And Islamic history offers many examples of religious tolerance. Takfirism is not an expression of Islam; it is a perversion of Islam. And though it has gained in influence, the movement remains a small if powerfully lethal minority—a minority that must be isolated within the Muslim world, not elevated as an authentic expression of that tradition.

Still others believe the challenge we face is deeper than Islam; it is really religion itself, ours no less than theirs. Violence, in this view, results from monotheism with its intolerant moral convictions and exclusive claim to truth. According to the late historian Arthur Schlesinger Jr.: "President Bush is fighting a holy war predicated on his religious convictions, much as Osama bin Laden fights for his fanatical interpretation of the creed of Muhammad." Social tolerance, in this view, requires a belief that others may be right—and religious faith shuts off the possibility. Religious certainty is what leads to Crusades, witch burning, and 9/11. Not just Muhammad, but Moses and Jesus have much to answer for.

Yet, it turns out, Moses and Jesus are not without answers—and they are not the ones the critics of religion expect.

Chapter 4

Faith and Politics

There are few events more difficult to place on the president's schedule, or more difficult to keep there, than a meeting with dissidents. And it is even more complicated when those dissidents are Chinese. For months in early 2006, along with allies at the National Security Council, I had pushed for a presidential meeting with Chinese house church leaders, independent writers, and human-rights advocates—the main targets of repression by the Chinese government. The goal was to send a signal that the American-Chinese relationship consisted of more than trade; that America was aware of recent crackdowns on religious groups and legal activists.

The president had no intention of heading toward Cold War-style rivalry with China; he and Condi Rice viewed the development of warm relationships with the "great powers" of China, Russia, and India as a central requirement of the War on Terror. I had been with President Bush in Shanghai just five weeks after 9/11, on a visit designed to reinforce cooperation against terrorism. Chinese President Jaing Zemin had greeted us at a large guest house with a soft, fleshy handshake. He moved like an old man, conscious of his dignity, and wore large, black glasses that were either terribly old-fashioned, or trendy with style-conscious older people. At the state luncheon that followed the meetings—a multi-course affair, featuring shark fin soup and steak with barbeque sauce—President Bush did his loud and hearty best to charm Jaing. But it was heavy going with the stilted Chinese leader. It was even more awkward at my table. Because the American delegation was so small, I turned out to be one of the more senior officials on the trip. So I was placed next to the Chinese equivalent of a four-star general. After the interpreter seated behind us explained who I was, the general lapsed into a silence that lasted most of the lunch, clearly confused as to why I had been invited at all.

Yet this cultivation of China in the fight against terror did not mean the president was silent on Chinese human rights. He did not accept the argument that raising human-rights issues with the Chinese or Russians would destroy our relations. Both of these great powers tended to act in their national interests when we criticized their abuses—and when we didn't criticize their abuses. And those criticisms, the president felt, might offer some encouragement to reformers and prisoners, and even influence a rising generation of leaders. So in one of his early speeches as president, while dedicating the aircraft carrier USS *Ronald Reagan*, he said, "Our nation cherishes freedom, but we do not own it. While it is the birthright of every American, it is also the equal promise of the religious believer in Southern Sudan, or an Iraqi farmer in the Tigress Valley, or of a child born in China today." Speaking to students at Tsinghua University during a visit to China in 2002, he explained: "Tens of millions of Chinese today are relearning Buddhist, Taoist, and local religious traditions, or practicing Christianity, Islam, and other faiths. Regardless of where or how these believers worship, they're no threat to public order; in fact, they make good citizens.... My prayer is that all persecution will end, so that all in China are free to gather and worship as they wish." And during this first visit with President Hu Jintao after he replaced Jaing Zemin, President Bush bluntly told him that millions of Chinese Christians would turn out to be "the best of citizens" and should not be feared or oppressed.

I was convinced the president would welcome and enjoy a meeting with Chinese religious dissidents at the White House. But it remained highly controversial with regional experts at the State Department. The traditional role of the diplomat is the management of relationships and the maintenance of ties, not the transformation of other societies or the pursuit of justice. And diplomats from the ambassador in Beijing to the regional bureau in Foggy Bottom fought the meeting with religious dissidents at every stage. At first it was delayed because "the timing was not right." As time made this objection less compelling, the meeting was frankly opposed as provocative and disruptive to our relations. The National Security Advisor, Steve Hadley, finally intervened in favor of a meeting, and it was set for late May.

Early in the morning, on the day the meeting was supposed to take place, we received an urgent communication from Beijing. A high-ranking Chinese official had made specific threats against the three men the president was going to host. They were not religious people, the accusation went, but political activists and "enemies of the state"—a phrase that threatened the severest consequences, including imprisonment and execution. If the president met with them, these dissidents would be at grave risk.

This development raised ethical questions. Should we cancel the meeting and prevent these dissidents from risking their lives? I considered some analogies. In a previous time, would I have advised Solzhenitsyn or Sakharov to lower their risky profile? Of course not. On a battlefield, would I prevent a soldier from taking on a heroic but risky mission to save others? Not if the soldier knew the odds of failure. A deep reverence for human life does not require us to oppose life-risking heroism. Life has a high value, but it is not an absolute value. Spending one's life in a noble cause—in the defense of freedom or one's country—is itself noble. That decision is legitimate, if it is fully informed. Yet it is still sobering to facilitate a decision that may cost a life, or result in terrible punishment. Matters of life and death are part of the burden of government—and, in a different way, of being a surgeon or a soldier.

So, working through the NSC, we informed the dissidents about the specific threat the Chinese government had made against them. If they wanted to cancel, it was their decision. But they needed to have the information. The three activists knew better than most the risks involved. One had spent several years in prison. Another had been previously arrested, and was under constant surveillance. All strongly restated their desire to meet with the president—and the meeting went ahead.

It took place in the Yellow Oval—a cheerful oval living room in the family quarters of the president's private residence. The president, the vice president, the national security advisor, some NSC staff, and I attended. The dissidents seemed nervous—scripted, elaborately polite, deferential to authority—hardly the manner of political revolutionaries. The president broke the ice by saying: "I'm told that you love freedom and that you love Jesus Christ. Sounds like we have a lot in common." In the course of the meeting, the dissidents described their families, their past sacrifices, and thanked America for being concerned. "European governments," one explained, "have betrayed us. They only emphasize business interests and trade. America is the only voice to influence the Chinese human-rights record."

Near the end of the meeting, the president was told the dissidents wanted to pray with him. Everyone stood, and the president asked people to join hands—the vice president looking momentarily stricken with awkwardness. (Clearly, where Vice President Cheney comes from, prayerful hand holding isn't so common.) After a short prayer for mercy, blessing, and protection, the president asked the dissidents to join him in a picture. As they were leaving, the president told them: "Now I've seen your faces and know your names. From now on, whenever I talk about human rights in China, I'll be thinking about you."

As of this writing, Chinese threats against the dissidents have not been fulfilled. Sino-American relations were not destroyed. And three brave men saw what religion means to President Bush: a deep concern for their rights and freedom.

The late historian Arthur Schlesinger Jr. called President Bush "the most aggressively religious president in American history"—a claim that was intended to be offensive. For secularists, the serious practice of Christianity is as foreign as the traditions of Borneo tribesman, and is treated with far less multicultural sympathy. In reality, Bush's mild and conventional evangelical spirituality would be familiar to tens of millions of Americans. He begins his day with a "quiet time" of Bible study and prayer, reads daily devotionals by Oswald Chambers and Billy Graham, prays before evening meals, and is honored when others pray for him. None of this intrudes on daily life at the White House, or gives any hint of off-putting zealotry.

The direct political influence of the president's religious beliefs is considerable—but not in the ways the critics often imagine. I have often been asked if the president's Middle East policies were driven by a Christian eschatology—some theory about Israel and the end times. I never once heard President Bush mention these matters. But he has been profoundly influenced by a Christian anthropology—a certain view of human beings and their natural rights. People are equal because they share equally in their Creator's image, and that image, in the long run, makes them resist servitude. Men and women eventually hate their chains because their nature is fulfilled in the exercise of freedom. The main political expression of the president's religious views is a deep belief in the power and appeal of liberty. This conviction encourages strong emotional ties to dissidents like the Chinese human-rights leaders we met in the Yellow Oval. And it creates a strong sense of optimism about the ultimate direction of history.

A Canadian newspaper once cited as evidence of resurgent American religious extremism that President Bush claimed that "God wants people to be free." That is, of course, also the extremism of the Declaration of Independence, which claims that human rights are God-given and universal. It is the extremism of Abraham Lincoln, who said, "Nothing stamped with the Divine image and likeness was sent into the world to be trodden on, or degraded, and imbruted by its fellows." It is the extremism of Franklin Roosevelt, who said that "man born in the image of God will not forever suffer the oppressor's sword." This is, in fact, a radical claim, held by few civilizations in history. Most cultures have taught that human worth is an achievement rather than an endowment, based on caste, or class, or tribe, or kinship, or race. The principle of universal human rights and dignity was born in a revolution, and remains revolutionary. It is found in religion, but also in the philosophic system of natural law or natural rights—the belief, common at our Founding and throughout American history, that moral rules could be found in nature, because they were placed there by nature's God. President Bush's moral beliefs about human rights are found at the confluence of Christian faith and the philosophy of the American Founding. "Not since Lincoln," argues one scholar, "has the putative head of the Republican party so actively sought to ground the party in a politics of natural right."

It is often assumed that these convictions make President Bush sectarian, intolerant, and triumphalistic about American purposes in the world. That assumption is false. Those who make claims of Bush's religious intolerance must ignore what the president has actually said about religion, which has been careful, pluralistic, and well within the mainstream of American history. This rhetoric on religion, over the years, has fallen into several categories:

The **first** is *comfort in grief and mourning*. Through terrorist mass murder and war and natural disaster, we had many occasions for the president to play the role of mourner-in-chief. We would have preferred to have less.

Sometimes those moments arrived suddenly, as on the morning of February 1, 2003, when the Space Shuttle Columbia disintegrated in the atmosphere following a routine mission. After an emergency weekend call, and an hour's work with Matt and John, the president delivered brief remarks from the Cabinet Room near the Oval Office. The president began in a clinical tone, with the blunt delivery of bad news. "At 9:00 a.m. this morning," he said, "Mission Control in Houston lost contact with our Space Shuttle Columbia. A short time later, debris was seen falling from the skies above Texas. The Columbia is lost; there are no survivors."

After praising the courage and pioneering spirit of the astronauts, and promising the space program would one day be resumed, the president closed on a note of hope and assurance, using a Bible verse Karen Hughes had called me to suggest. "In the skies today we saw destruction and tragedy. Yet farther than we can see there is comfort and hope. In the words of the prophet Isaiah, 'Lift your eyes and look to the heavens. Who created all these? He who brings out the starry hosts one by one and calls them each by name. Because of His great power and mighty strength, not one of them is missing.'

"The same Creator who names the stars," he concluded, "also knows the names of the seven souls we mourn today. The crew of the shuttle Columbia did not return safely to Earth; yet we can pray that all are safely home."

In circumstances like these—circumstances in which suffering is sudden and deeply unfair—a president can hardly stand before the nation and say that death is final; that separation is endless; that the universe is an empty, echoing void. This kind of secularized public rhetoric would be an act of cruelty, not an act of leadership. In times of tragedy, a president offers a story that makes sense of current suffering, a narrative of hope—the hope of reunions, and a love stronger than death, and a justice beyond our understanding.

Having lived through events like these, I know those words meant something to people. The criticisms of this kind of religious rhetoric eventually came—but only long after the fact. Skepticism about religious comfort and hope is much easier once the funerals have ended.

A **second** category of religious language points out the *historic influence of faith on our country*. President Bush has argued that people of faith have been voices of conscience in the American story.

In July of 2003, I traveled with the president to Senegal, crossing by ferry to cheerful, tropical Goree Island, bright with Caribbean colors, but oppressed by a terrible history. Goree Island was one of the main points of embarkation in the trans-Atlantic slave trade for four hundred years. On a solemn tour, the president saw the slave pens and the door of no return, a little stone opening where captive Africans left their home for the last time. In a small square near the water, under an oppressive sun, the president said: "For 250 years the captives endured an assault on their dignity. The spirit of Africans in America did not break. Yet the spirit of their captors was corrupted. Small men took on the powers and airs of tyrants and masters. Years of unpunished brutality and bullying and rape produced a dullness and hardness of conscience. Christian men and women became blind to the clearest commands of their faith and added hypocrisy to injustice. A republic founded on equality for all became a prison for millions. And yet in the words of the African proverb, 'No fist is big enough to hide the sky.' All the generations of oppression under the laws of man could not crush the hope of freedom and defeat the purposes of God."

"In America," the president continued, "enslaved Africans learned the story of the Exodus from Egypt and set their own hearts on a promised land of freedom. Enslaved Africans discovered a suffering Savior and found He was more like themselves than their masters.

Enslaved Africans heard the ringing promises of the Declaration of Independence and asked the self-evident question, then why not me?"

For years, I had wanted to help write a speech on the amazing story of Africans in America—one of the most extraordinary moral stories outside the Bible. A captive people, by their courage and persistent demands, eventually redeemed the democratic soul of the nation that enslaved them. An oppressed people embraced Christianity, and called Christians in America to live up to their own creed of love. Those who deny this contribution of religion to America, and others like it, are blind to our history.

A **third** category of religious rhetoric is the argument for *the role of faith in fighting poverty*. The case here is simple: government, in welfare reform, should encourage the provision of social services without providing those services itself. And some of the most effective providers, especially in fighting addiction and providing mentoring, are faith-based charities. In making this argument, the president has consistently called attention to the good works of people motivated by their religious beliefs.

At his first National Prayer Breakfast in February 2001, he said: "There are many experiences of faith in this room, but most will share a belief that we are loved and called to love; that our choices matter, now and forever; that there are purposes deeper than ambition and hopes greater than success. These beliefs shape our lives and help sustain the life of our nation. Men and women can be good without faith, but faith is a force for goodness. Men and women can be compassionate without faith, but faith often inspires compassion. Human beings can love without faith, but faith is a great teacher of love.

"Our country, from its beginning, has recognized the contribution of faith," the president continued. "We do not impose any religion; we welcome all religions. We do not prescribe any prayer; we welcome all prayers. This is the tradition of our nation, and it will be the standard of my administration. We will respect every creed; we will honor the diversity of our country, and the deepest convictions of our people."

President Bush's faith-based initiative has been controversial, but it hasn't been sectarian. It has welcomed and encouraged social service providers of every faith, and no faith. And the approach really isn't new. For decades, public funds have gone to Catholic Charities and Lutheran Social Services and many other large, established religious groups. The president's innovation has been to go beyond those traditional institutions and to provide resources to smaller, grassroots organizations—often African American organizations. It is hardly a threat to the Constitution to give African American faith-based charities the same benefits that establishment charities have enjoyed for generations.

A **fourth** category of religious language is *literary allusions to hymns and scripture*. In President Bush's first inaugural, he pledged: "When we see that wounded traveler on the road to Jericho, we will not pass to the other side"—a reference to the New Testament parable of the Good Samaritan. In the 2003 State of the Union, he said that "there is power, wonder-working power in the goodness and idealism and faith of the American people"—echoing the refrain of an old and popular Christian hymn.

While in the White House, I sometimes had reporters call me after a major speech to ask, "Which ones are the code words?" They assumed these references were a private language, a political ploy, the rhetorical equivalent of a secret Christian handshake. I would explain that these are not code words, they are literary references understood by millions of Americans. They are not code words; they are our culture. It was not a code when the president made reference to a line of poetry by T. S. Eliot in his Whitehall speech in London: "those who live near a police station find it hard to believe in the triumph of violence." And just because some did not understand that reference did not mean it was a plot.

An incident from the 2000 election is instructive. In the course of one interview, Governor Bush used the phrase that "people should take the log out of their own eye before taking the speck out of their neigh-bor's eye." The next day, on the front page of the *New York Times*, this phrase was mocked as "an odd version of the pot calling the kettle black." Neither the reporter nor his editors knew that Governor Bush was quoting one of the most famous sermons in history—actually, one of the most famous human utterances in history—the Sermon on the Mount. And the fact that reporters didn't know the reference was not Governor Bush's fault.

These allusions were not politically driven. They came from the president's background and my own reading of American rhetoric. The image of a "city on a hill" did not come from the Pilgrim Fathers; they were quoting the teachings of Jesus. Lincoln's "a house divided against itself cannot stand" falls into the same category. The rhetoric of civil rights is filled with references to the Exodus and a "promised land" of freedom. In political discourse, these images are given a lesser meaning, but they have an added literary resonance precisely because they have a deeper meaning. And American public discourse would be impover-ished without them.

A **fifth** category of religious rhetoric is *references to Providence*. In his speech to the joint session of Congress on September 20, 2001, Presi-dent Bush declared: "Freedom and fear, justice and cruelty have always been at war, and God is not neutral between them." In his 2003 State of the Union, he said: "We Americans have faith in ourselves, but not in ourselves alone. We do not know, we do not claim to know, all the ways of Providence, yet we can trust in them, placing our confidence in the loving God behind all of life and all of history."

It would be arrogant and theologically presumptuous to claim that God is on the side of America—that His Providence is defined by our policies. But that is not what these statements assert. Instead of arguing that God is on the side of America, the president has claimed that God is on the side of justice. And this is not an exceptional belief in Ameri-can history. It is the theme of Lincoln's second inaugural. It is a central argument made by Martin Luther King Jr.: "The arc of the moral universe is long, but it bends toward justice"; "We do not know what the future holds, but we know Who holds the future."

In all these categories of rhetoric, President Bush has applied a principled pluralism—a welcoming attitude to all religions, instead of favoring any religion in a sectarian way. He is the first president to make a reference to mosques and the Koran in an inaugural address. He began a tradition of celebrating the Muslim holiday of Eid al-Fitr at the White House, and got in trouble with some religious conservatives for asserting that Muslims and Christians pray to the same God. He is careful to include agnostics and atheists, talking of "good people of every faith, and no faith at all."

Bush's approach to God and faith is, if anything, more temperate than other presidents. Critics who talk of Bush's unprecedented religiosity should consider the religious language of President Franklin Roosevelt. On D-Day, in 1944, Roosevelt made his announcement to the nation entirely in the form of a prayer. He began: "In this poignant hour, I ask you to join with me in prayer." And he asked God for military victory, saying, "With Thy blessing we shall prevail over the unholy forces of our enemy. Help us to conquer the apostles of greed and racial arrogance." A month after Pearl Harbor, FDR said this in his State of the Union: "They know that victory for us means victory for religion, and they could not tolerate that. The world is too small to provide adequate living room for both Hitler and God. In proof of this, the Nazis have now announced their plan for enforcing their new, German pagan religion all over the world, a plan by which the Holy Bible and the cross of mercy would be displaced by *Mein Kampf* and the swastika and the naked sword.... We are inspired by a faith that goes back through all the years to the first chapter of Genesis: God created man in his own image. We on our side are striving to be true to that divine heritage. That is the conflict that day and night now pervades our lives. No compromise can end that conflict. There never has been, there never will be successful compromise between good and evil."

Suffice it to say, this religious rhetoric crosses several theological lines that President Bush has never crossed.

The backlash against President Bush's approach to religion has come in several forms. Some of the criticism is merely a vague and prejudiced distaste for religious things. At the funeral of Ronald Reagan in 2004, President Bush delivered one of the eulogies. After praising a life of conviction and kindness, the president concluded: "Americans saw death approach Ronald Reagan twice, in a moment of violence, and then in the years of departing light. He met both with courage and grace. In these trials, he showed how a man so enchanted by life can be at peace with life's end. And where does that strength come from? Where is that courage learned? It is the faith of a boy who read the Bible with his mom. It is the faith of a man lying in an operating room, who prayed for the one who shot him before he prayed for himself. It is the faith of a man with a fearful illness, who waited on the Lord to call him home. Now death has done all that death can do. And as Ronald Wilson Reagan goes his way, we are left with the joyful hope he shared. In his last years, he saw through a glass darkly. Now he sees his Savior face to face."

In preparing those remarks, the words of the apostle Paul, "now we see through a glass darkly," seemed an apt reference to Alzheimer's disease—an illness of shadows and fading light. But the media critic of the *Washington Post*, Tom Shales, found this inappropriately religious. "George W. Bush chose to proselytize," he said, "theorizing that Reagan is now in heaven having chats or perhaps playing cards with Jesus." This was, of course, the funeral of a Christian man at a Christian cathedral. And though I would not have used the "playing cards" analogy, this is, in fact, the Christian hope—the hope of resurrection—often mentioned at funerals. Shales assumes that this concept, and words like *savior*, are unsuitable for polite company—that religion is a private eccentricity or secret vice that shouldn't be inflicted on the rest of us. This kind of bigotry doesn't even rise to the level of argument. But it is a good summary of the sterile vision of secularism: funerals without hope; churches where mention of the resurrection is forbidden; a repressive "inclusion" that really means religious people should shut up.

Another example of this prejudice came at Thanksgiving a few months after 9/11. The Ad Council, a major sponsor of public-service announcements, asked President Bush to contribute a Thanksgiving message that would run in newspapers. The speechwriting office produced a text, and it was approved by the president. At the last minute, the Ad Council objected to a line in the message that referred to God as sustaining the nation in times of success and hardship. At first, the Ad Council left the impression this religious language violated its bylaws. On further questioning, they admitted their bylaws did not forbid religious references. Then we were told the line "won't pass the test with the media." It is hardly controversial for a Thanksgiving message to include thanks to God—which is, after all, the purpose of this federally mandated, national holiday. But for groups with an anti-religious bias, even the most innocuous religious references are treated as four-letter words.

But the critique goes deeper. For some, religious ideas and arguments are not just impolite, but a threat to liberal democracy. Former Labor Secretary Robert Reich asserts that "terrorism itself is not the greatest danger we face." The "true battle" is with "those who believe that truth is revealed through Scripture and religious dogma." Scientist Richard Dawkins puts this case bluntly: "To fill a world with religion, or religions of the Abrahamic kind, is like littering the streets with loaded guns. Don't be surprised if they are used." In this view, it is a belief in religious truth itself that encourages intolerance and violence. Exclusive truth-claims rooted in faith are the enemy of democracy.

This viewpoint, in some ways, claims too much. Do its advocates really intend to lump violent jihadists with, say, the Amish? Or African Pentecostals? Or Benedictine monks? All these are monotheists of the "Abrahamic kind," though their differences seem to outweigh this similarity. Are these critics really intending to say that Osama bin Laden, who seeks to impose a comprehensive tyranny, is the same as John Paul II, who fought a comprehensive tyranny? That John Wesley and Billy Graham and Mother Teresa are really Grand Inquisitors in disguise, because they are believers in "truth revealed through Scripture"? But this actually does seem to be the accusation: anyone who believes in revealed truth is already intolerant in their mind, and cannot be trusted in society.

And this assumption leads to certain conclusions. If religious beliefs are the source of social intolerance, then they cannot be the basis for laws and public policy, because this would be to impose narrow beliefs on dissenters. The separation of church and state, in this view, requires us to rigidly separate religion from government. Political philosopher John Rawls argues that religious people, when they enter the public square, must leave behind religious language and make secular arguments. A leading constitutional expert, Stephan Gey, contends: "The establishment clause should be viewed as a reflection of the secular, relativistic political values of the Enlightenment, which are incompatible with the fundamental nature of religious faith. As an embodiment of these Enlightenment values, the establishment clause requires that the political influence of religion be substantially diminished." Religious belief is protected by the Constitution—but, in the cause of pluralism and tolerance, it must be confined to the private sphere.

This turns out to be a thin kind of pluralism, and a partial kind of tolerance. In this view, it is permissible to advocate for human rights because the Constitution says so, but not because of a theological belief that the image of God is found in every human being. If your views on the value of life are informed by John Stuart Mill or B. F. Skinner, they are allowed to triumph in politics. If your views on the value of life are informed by Moses and Jesus, they can never prevail, because they are religious and therefore private. If you support gambling in your town because it will make you a fortune, that is permissible; if you oppose gambling because of your reading of Scripture, that is not. This is hardly an evenhanded "neutrality." It is a definition of pluralism that silences millions of people, by marginalizing their deepest beliefs. G. K. Chesterton called this a "taboo of tact or convention whereby a man is free to say this or that because of his nationality or his profession, or his place of residence, or his hobby, but not because of his creed about the very cosmos in which he lives."

This is the extreme expression of views that have been around since the Enlightenment, as scholars such as Michael W. McConnell have argued. After the religious wars of the sixteenth and seventeenth centuries, political philosophy reacted strongly against the role of religious beliefs in politics. Christians, particularly Roman Catholics, were suspected of dual loyalties, of divided allegiances. Under Christianity, said Rousseau, "men have never known whether they ought to obey the civil ruler or the priest." And this was seen as a source of conflict and instability. The French Enlightenment, following Rousseau, argued the religion should be actively repressed as a rival of the state. The British Enlightenment, following Locke, argued that religion should be privatized—kept in a purely personal sphere. Both traditions taught that in any conflict between religious opinion and the state, the state should always win.

America, however, took a different path. The Founders carefully separated the institutions of church and state, fearing what George Washington called the "horrors of spiritual tyranny." But they also generally believed that the virtues necessary for democracy—self-sacrifice, honesty, public spirit—were formed by religious beliefs and institutions. Washington warned against the "supposition that morality can be maintained without religion." So religious influence was both accommodated and encouraged by the new government. And the "dual loyalties" of religious people were not viewed as a threat, but as a source of conscience. "Before any man can be considered as a member of Civil Society," said James Madison, "he must be considered as a subject of the Governor of the Universe." The Founders recognized a duty to follow God in the world, not just a right to privately admire Him. And Americans have followed that duty into a series of restless reforms, from the fight against slavery to the fight against segregation.

The central problem with a rigid secularism is this: it would remove the main source of reform—the main source of passion for justice and change—in American history.

Religious communities have generally been the springs or fountains where reform movements trace their source. Abolitionism had roots in Quakerism. Nineteenth-century evangelicalism laid the foundation for the temperance movement, women's suffrage, and anti-slavery activism. American Catholicism fed into the labor movement and the pro-life movement. African American churches in the South were essential to the civil-rights struggle. In all these cases, religious ideals and institutions provided a vision of justice and a supportive community—a place where individuals gained the courage and resilience to challenge a repressive political order. The "divided loyalties" of these reformers—their pursuit of a moral and religious ideal that stood in judgment of the political status quo—was the whole reason they were willing to spend and sacrifice their lives for others.

For early abolitionists such as the journalist William Lloyd Garrison, slavery was "a national sin that all Christians in America had a duty to oppose." In the most important statement on race between the Declaration of Independence and the Gettysburg Address, Garrison spoke from the pulpit of Park Street Church in Boston on the Fourth of July, 1829. He began by attacking the holiday itself for its "glaring contradiction of our creed and our practice." Slavery, Garrison argued, was "a gangrene preying upon our vitals, an earthquake rumbling under our feet, a mine accumulating materials for a national catastrophe." And the problem, he argued, was not only slavery itself, but the racist assumptions that sustained it. Near the end of his speech, he thundered, "Thus saith the Lord God of the Africans, 'Let this people go, that they may serve Me.'"

Garrison—with his mild face and spectacles—did not look the part of the radical. He would sometimes begin his lectures by saying, "Ladies and gentlemen, I am the peace-disturber Garrison—the fanatic Garrison—the madman Garrison." And the audience would laugh at the contrast. But he convinced many Americans that even the unlikely and the ordinary could take part in the moral, heroic drama of abolition, and a mass political movement was created in the process. "The abolitionism which I advocate," Garrison said, "is as absolute as the law of God, and as unyielding as His throne. It admits no compromise. Every slave is a stolen man; every slaveholder is a man stealer.... The law that makes him a chattel is to be trampled underfoot; the compact that is formed at his expense, and cemented with his blood, is null and void." Garrison trusted absolutely in the truth of his religious principles, in the need for a free press to express those beliefs, and in the sizzling urgency of his cause. "I do not wish to think, or speak, or write with moderation," he exclaimed. "No! No! Tell a man whose house is on fire to give a moderate alarm; tell him to moderately rescue his wife from the hands of the ravisher; tell the mother to gradually extricate her babe from the fire into which it has fallen—but urge me not to use moderation in a cause like the present." Few other leaders of his time, and no major political figures, had the courage to call for immediate abolition and complete social equality for African Americans—and that courage was a result of his faith.

For progressives such as William Jennings Bryan, the only real Christianity was "applied Christianity." And he applied his faith to support legalized strikes, limits on corporate power, a minimum wage, progressive taxation, woman's suffrage, opposition to capital punishment, and public financing of elections. As a three-time nominee for president, Bryan transformed the Democratic Party into the party of the common man. "God," he told audiences across the country, "made all men and He did not make some to crawl on hands and knees, the others to ride on their backs." After his "Cross of Gold" speech, one journalist wrote that the 1896 election was "the first time in my life and in the life of a generation in which any man large enough to lead a national party has boldly and unashamedly made his cause that of the poor and the oppressed." When many of Bryan's ideas were eventually integrated by Franklin Roosevelt, Herbert Hoover dismissively (but correctly) called the New Deal "Bryanism under new words and methods."

The Great Commoner was also the most prominent evangelical in America, conducting camp meetings in Florida, corresponding on religious topics with people around the country. But it was hardly the evangelicalism of modern stereotype. His personal hero was Leo Tolstoy, for his radical identification with the poor—and he visited Tolstoy in Russia. He spoke in synagogues and was deeply tolerant of Jews and Catholics. And even his eventual opposition to evolution was based on a (justified) fear that Social Darwinism would encourage eugenics, targeted at the poor and weak. In his last convention speech in 1924, Bryan said, "If my party has given me the basis of my political beliefs, my Bible has given me the foundations of a faith that has enabled me to stand for the right as I saw it."

For civil-rights leaders such as Martin Luther King Jr., human equality was a requirement of divine law. "A just law," he wrote in his Letter from the Birmingham Jail, "is a man-made code that squares with the moral law or the law of God. An unjust law is a code that is out of harmony with the moral law." And King firmly rejected the privatization of religious belief. "It's all right to talk about heaven," he said. "I talk about it because I believe firmly in immortality. But you've got to talk about earth.... It's even all right to talk about the New Jerusalem. But one day we must begin to talk about the new Chicago, the new Atlanta, the new New York, the new America."

One of King's lieutenants, Andrew Young, recalls of the civil-rights era: "Even then, see, people didn't want to think of Martin Luther King as a minister. Most of our white supporters kind of tolerated our religion, but they really didn't take it seriously, and most of the press, too." But King took his religion seriously, and had reason to. After the Montgomery bus boycott in 1955, King was receiving dozens of phone calls daily threatening his life, and the lives of his family. One evening around midnight, a call came promising to blow up his home. King, who could see no human source of help, began to despair. In his account, he prayed aloud: "Lord, I'm down here trying to do what's right.... But, Lord, I must confess that I'm weak now; I'm faltering; I'm losing my courage." Yet his prayer was not one-sided. King goes on to say: "It seemed at that moment that I could hear an inner voice saying to me, 'Martin Luther, stand up for righteousness, stand up for justice, stand up for truth. And lo I will be with you, even until the end of the world.' And I'll tell you, I've seen the lightning flash. I've heard the thunder roll. I felt sin-breakers dashing, trying to conquer my soul. But I heard the voice of Jesus saying still to fight on. He promised never to leave me, never to leave me alone. No, never alone. No, never alone. He promised never to leave me, never to leave me alone."

What are the critics of religion in politics to make of this: the voice of God, urging persistence in a movement of political and social reform? What could be more dangerous to a secular democracy? But, of course, that moment was essential to our democracy, and commonplace in our history. Dissent often requires courage; courage is often rooted in faith. Religious dissenters have served their conception of God's purposes in movements to end child labor, improve the conditions of mental hospitals and prisons, oppose wars, and defend immigrants.

It is easy to talk about the threat of "religions of the Abrahamic kind" in the abstract. But strict secularism would mean, not only no more Pat Robertsons, but also no more Martin Luther Kings. Are we really so enlightened and advanced that religious conscience is no longer needed to call attention to the weak and oppressed? Are we really so close to the ideal of justice that a higher conception of divine justice can be banished from public debate? Every society needs a standard of values that stands above the political order, or the political order becomes absolute, and progress toward justice becomes impossible.

It is easy to lump all religious idealists into the category of bin Laden, as fanatics who take their commands from God. But surely the content of religion makes some difference. There is a difference between the Takfiri command to kill your neighbor and the Christian command to love your neighbor. There is a difference between religious extremists who crash planes into buildings and religious extremists who shelter slaves along the Underground Railroad. There is a difference between religious believers who blow up markets and mosques in Iraq, and religious believers in the American military who sacrifice for the security of strangers. And confusing these groups is a lazy and foolish slander.

Religious idealists—from Lyman Beecher and Harriet Beecher Stowe to Mother Jones and Dorothy Day—tend to be inconvenient people. Many have found their impatient purity exhausting. "When we see an eager assailant on one of these wrongs," wrote Ralph Waldo Emerson, "we feel like asking them, What right have you, sir, to your one virtue?" And realists like Reinhold Niebuhr warn us that there is a distance between the morally imperative and the historically achievable. But it is often difficult to determine what is historically achievable until some idealist demands it. And even the failures of a Bryan or a King appear nobler over time, until their incredible visions seem inevitable. Without their influence—without the demands of conscience rooted in faith—America would be a different and crueler country.

•   •   •

In American politics today, Williams Jennings Bryan would not recognize the party he led for so long—its elevation of autonomy and choice above the interests of the weak and vulnerable, its disdain for the religious beliefs of average Americans. Sometimes this condescension is not even conscious. After writing a profile for *The New Yorker* magazine that mentioned my evangelical faith, journalist Jeffrey Goldberg was talking to a leading Democratic political consultant. This advisor had read the article, and had one question for Goldberg: "But does he *really* believe that someone was raised from the dead?" Jeff Goldberg replied: "Yes, a lot of people do. They are called Christians."

Prior to the late 1960s, most Democrats would not have viewed religious communities as a strange and foreign land. Both political parties shared a rough consensus on sexual morality and the family. Both parties drew support from conservative religious voters. But that began to change with the rise of countercultural influence in the Democratic Party, and the nomination of George McGovern. The alienation of conservative Christians accelerated as the Democratic Party embraced Roe v. Wade, abortion-on-demand, and government funding for abortion. "Somehow," says Clinton aide Paul Begala, "we moved from Carter, who was really pro-choice but very much sensitive to the tragedy, to now, where we're dancing in the aisles about it." And a series of presidential candidates from Mondale, to Dukakis, to Gore made the Religious Right a consistent rhetorical target.

Today secularists have become a reliable voting block within the Democratic coalition, about as large as support from labor. Normally three out of four secularists support Democratic candidates for president. (About two out of three religious conservatives have voted for Bush.) And these Democratic secularists dislike conservative Christians with great intensity. Strongly Democratic voters are 5 percent less favorably disposed toward Catholics ... 10 percent less favorable about Protestants … and 23 percent less favorable toward Christian fundamentalists. A study of these patterns by two professors at Baruch College concludes: "One has to reach back to pre-New Deal America when political divisions between Catholics and Protestants encapsulated local ethno-cultural cleavages over prohibition, immigration, public education and blue laws, to find a period when voting behavior was influenced by this degree of antipathy toward a religious group."

Through active Democratic alienation of conservative Christians, and active Republican courting, America has moved toward the development of one secular political party, and one religious political party. And this is a true danger to democracy, because it turns nearly every political disagreement into a culture-war battle. When the sides view each other as infidels or ayatollahs, it adds jet fuel to the normal combustion of American politics.

It would be good for American democracy if both parties were to appeal to religious voters. This is not impossible for modern Democrats, but it is more than a matter of using less-awkward religious language. This appeal would require a genuine openness to religious ideals and motivations in politics. Stopping the overbroad condemnations of religious influence. Talking about helping the poor, at home and abroad, as a matter of social justice and religious responsibility. And reopening the Democratic Party to people with pro-life convictions—people who view the protection of growing life as an important measure of social justice. Most evangelicals are not libertarians. Many are troubled by materialism and the social philosophy of "winner takes all." Majorities of both liberal and conservative Christians favor increased humanitarian foreign aid, universal health care, and greater aid to poor Americans. An agenda that is "pro-life and pro-poor" would have a powerful appeal for many evangelicals. But no appeal will be effective if the deepest beliefs of religious people are viewed as suspect, and their strongest principles are declared a threat to liberty.

The Religious Right has also contributed to dangerous social divisions in our country. In the early 1980s, this movement counted genuine accomplishments. It brought many conservative Christians back into politics after a long exile that began during the Fundamentalist-Modernist controversy of the 1920s. And it discovered common cause on pro-life issues between Roman Catholics and evangelicals after generations of mutual bitterness. Early pro-life events featured busloads from Liberty University marching beside Knights of Columbus carrying statues of the Virgin Mary, in the best democratic tradition of taming durable differences.

But the focus of the Religious Right was always too narrow, too selective. It emphasized issues of sexual morality while ignoring equally urgent matters of economic and racial justice. Considering the words of the New Testament—"I was hungry and you gave me food, I was thirsty and you give me something to drink, I was a stranger and you welcomed me, I was naked and you gave me clothing, I was sick and you took care of me"—it is impossible to imagine how a "Christian voter guide" could be written without a major emphasis on poverty or disease. But these were never near the top of the agenda. The tone of the Religious Right was sometimes bitter. When I served on Capitol Hill, staffers dreaded the organized call-in campaigns of religious groups, because the comments were often the most vicious and hurtful. Religious Right leaders developed habits of certainty, which became indistinguishable from arrogance. And, in the end, the movement became too closely identified with a single political ideology—becoming a tool in the power games of others, instead of an independent witness. It simply baptized a Republican political agenda, from tax policy to missile defense, instead of challenging, humanizing, and transforming that agenda. And this is the same temptation of the religious left, which shows a mirror-image tendency to adopt the priorities of liberalism. In fact, Christian social teaching is not identical to either political ideology; it stands in judgment of both. It indicts consumerism and indifference to the poor; it indicts the destruction of the weak and the elderly; it indicts tyranny, and the soul-destroying excesses that sometimes come from freedom. When religious people identify faith with a single political party or movement, they miniaturize their beliefs and end up being reduced to one interest group among many.

And Christian political involvement also needs to be distinctive for its tone. The goal is not only to stand for Christian moral teaching, but to emulate the manner of its Founder, who showed that kindness is not weakness, and had more tenderness for moral outcasts than for moral hypocrites. The passion for truth at the heart of Christian faith will always disturb the most passionate and proselytizing skeptics. But, as Chesterton wrote, the authentically Christian approach is to be sure about the truth, and doubtful about ourselves.

Politics, like sex, is both a human necessity, and an occasion for sin. Principled people set out to change the world, and become a pale reflection of its priorities. In C. S. Lewis's *The Screwtape Letters,* a senior devil offers this advice to his apprentice: "Once you have made this world an end and faith a means, you have almost won your man, and it makes very little difference what kind of worldly end he is pursuing. Provided that meetings, pamphlets, policies, movements, causes and crusades matter more to him than prayers and sacraments and charity, he is ours."

The model of social engagement of the Religious Right is quickly passing. Its main institutions—from the Moral Majority to the Christian Coalition—are dead or dying. Only in the nightmares of *New York Times* editorial writers does Pat Robertson continue to exercise broad influence. A head-snapping generational change is favoring new leaders such as Rick Warren, focused on fighting poverty and AIDS in Africa, and Gary Haugen, confronting rape and sexual slavery in the developing world. During my time at the White House, the most intense and urgent evangelical activism I saw did not come on the expected values issues—though abortion and the traditional family were not ignored—but on genocide, global AIDS, and human trafficking. The most common request I received was: we need to meet with the president on Sudan—not on gay marriage. Since leaving government, I've asked young evangelicals on campuses from Wheaton to Harvard whom they view as their model of Christian activism. Their answer is nearly unanimous: Bono. Evangelicalism's journey from Jerry Falwell toward Bono is still partial and uncertain—but that is the direction.

President Bush talked with Bono several times over the years, including at the G–8 Summit at Gleneagles, Scotland, in 2005. The American delegation arrived by helicopter, landing on a golf driving range in a light rain. Our first meeting—the president, the First Lady, Andy Card, Steve Hadley, and myself—was with Bono and anti-poverty activist Bob Geldoff. Both were campaigning at the summit for greater financial commitments to help Africa. Geldoff was wry, very Irish, and had clearly not gotten much sleep. The president shook his hand and commented: "You look kind of strung out." Geldoff responded, "Give me a break. I put on a suit for this."

Bono, in trademark glasses and black suit, praised the president for his initiatives on debt forgiveness, AIDS, malaria, and girls' education, and then pressed hard for even bolder action. It was a typical performance—charming, grateful, but never satisfied. Sitting on a couch across from the president, he related a conversation with a Christian pastor, who had deeply impressed him. The minister had given him this advice: "Don't ask God to bless what you are doing, join in what God is doing; and it is already blessed." Bono then talked about the task of bringing life and hope to African children, and concluded, "In so many cases, it is hard to know God's will—but this is truly God's work."

It was a point of agreement between two men who disagree on much. And that is also a contribution of faith.

Chapter 5

War, Conscience, and Iraq

It is difficult to think about Iraq without deep and conflicted emotions. Hardly a week goes by without some personal reminder of a war that seems to consume sacrifice without yielding victory. A high-school friend—a man I only remember as a child—is laid to rest at Arlington National Cemetery. A White House colleague, now deployed in Iraq, must collect his dead comrades from a downed helicopter, while his wife knows that helicopter could have been his. An acquaintance struggling with a gentle sadness, I find, lost her husband in Iraq. And sometimes I have sought out those reminders myself, visiting the new graves at Arlington before Memorial Day in 2005; feeling the contrast between the peace and dignity of that place and the distant chaos and sudden violence that adds new rows of white markers.

Given the events and emotions of the past few years, it is tempting to read current doubts back into history, as many commentators and politicians have done. It is easy to claim credit for early wisdom that was entirely hidden and unexpressed. Surely all the difficulties and complications were obvious from the beginning. But they were not, at least to me.

As we headed toward our first State of the Union address following 9/11, a scrambling disorder had given way to a sense of steady progress.

The president's response after the attacks had touched and rallied Americans in a way that only a handful of presidents have achieved. An American flag flew over our embassy in Kabul, and the terrorist training camps of Afghanistan were emptied or destroyed. The American military, after innovative operations in a landlocked nation seven thousand miles away, was at a peak of respect unequaled since the end of World War II. Chairman Hamid Karzai—whose dashing robes and impressive bearing made him an Asian leader out of central casting—was scheduled to be in the gallery at the State of the Union as the grateful representative of a liberated people. The CIA was running a global War on Terror out of a conference room at their headquarters, and making a series of high-value captures. The initial reaction to 9/11 had been successful beyond expectation, and perhaps beyond precedent.

Yet the president's consistent concern was to ensure that the War on Terror was more than a series of successful reactions, on a pace and in a manner dictated by the enemy. All of his instincts tended toward a single ambition: a desire to reshape the security environment we found in the world, rather than endlessly responding to escalating dangers and attacks.

This ambition gave those around the president the sense of being part of an important historical enterprise. Like Harry Truman, he would define new security doctrines that would guide a global conflict of uncertain duration, a conflict with highest stakes. Like John F. Kennedy, who talked of a "world beyond the Cold War," President Bush would set out a vision of justice and freedom that could bring the War on Terror to a conclusion—not with the annihilation of our enemies, but with the transformation of the societies that produced them.

During this period, I worked cooperatively with National Security Advisor Condoleezza Rice, as well as her deputy, Steve Hadley. Both combined a careful professionalism—a tactical caution—with an openness to bold strategic thinking. Condi's quiet self-assurance, rooted in a life of academic, athletic, and artistic accomplishment, was impressive at any time. Her best qualities were on display in a time of crisis. She was calm and unhurried, and her steadiness managed to steady others.

The 2002 State of the Union was the first opportunity to communicate directly to Americans, in a more systematic fashion, how the War on Terror might unfold. The boldest element of this speech was to assert, after generations of tyranny and stagnation, that the Middle East might have a better future—that the advance of human rights might lower the heat on that region's boiling resentments. Even with a war waging, the president talked of "a great opportunity ... to lead the world toward the values that will bring lasting peace." And these values, he asserted, are universal, because they are rooted in human nature itself. "All fathers and mothers, in all societies, want their children to be educated, and live free from poverty and violence. No people on Earth yearn to be oppressed, or aspire to servitude, or eagerly await the midnight knock of the secret police. If anyone doubts this, let them look to Afghanistan, where the Islamic 'street' greeted the fall of tyranny with song and celebration. Let the skeptics look to Islam's own rich history, with its centuries of learning, and tolerance and progress. America will lead by defending liberty and justice because they are right and true and unchanging for all people everywhere."

This was as firm a rejection of moral and cultural relativism as an American president has ever given. And it was more than a philosophic statement; it was intended as a guide to policy. "No nation owns these aspirations, and no nation is exempt from them," he continued. "We have no intention of imposing our culture. But America will always stand firm for the nonnegotiable demands of human dignity: the rule of law; limits on the power of the state; respect for women; private property; free speech; equal justice; and religious tolerance. America will take the side of brave men and women who advocate these values around the world, including the Islamic world, because we have a greater objective than eliminating threats and containing resentment. We seek a just and peaceful world beyond the War on Terror."

Those who accuse the president of using the promotion of democracy and human rights as an *ex post facto* justification for invading Iraq were not listening that night, a year before operations in Iraq began. And those who accuse the president of an approach that simplistically equates democracy with elections were not very attentive that evening either: the president set out a reform agenda that included all the institutional prerequisites for the exercise of political freedom. His argument represented a clean break with the Middle East policies of the president's father, and nearly every other president.

But coverage of the speech was dominated by a second point. From the day of the September 11 attacks, a new strategic reality had been clear: terrorist groups were intent on using the tools of the modern world to overthrow the modern world. They employed the technologies of the twenty-first century—technologies they could never have created—to pursue a vengeance and vision rooted in the seventh century. In the September 11 plots they had made use of airplanes, the Internet, and international banking institutions. They expressed a firm intention to use other technologies—biological, chemical, and nuclear weapons—to cause death on a massive scale. And this mad ambition fit the methods of al-Qaeda in particular—a group with a preference for massive, dramatic acts of terror, intended to shock and demoralize whole societies into fear and retreat. In the cold calculus of terrorism, the use of weapons of mass destruction makes perfect sense. Serious studies show that a nuclear attack on a major US seaport could result in immediate property damage of 50 to 500 billion dollars. America's health care and financial systems would risk collapse. And the psychological effect would be difficult to predict—no acts of inspiring heroism to celebrate, just the uncounted and unburied dead, and many more dying who would envy them.

This is the single greatest danger to the American people of the next twenty years—many security experts believe that some kind of unconventional attack in that period is nearly certain. But though weapons of mass destruction are getting easier to produce, they are still not easy to produce in some mountain hideout on the Pakistan border. So the question naturally arises: where could terrorists get these weapons? In the short and medium term, those weapons would come from regimes that seek them, hate America, and maintain ties to terrorist groups. This kind of regime—every single one of them—is potentially a mortal threat to the American people.

Iraq was clearly such a regime, as were Iran and North Korea. The final language of the speech read: "States like these, and their terrorist allies, constitute an axis of evil, arming to threaten the peace of the world. By seeking weapons of mass destruction, these regimes pose a grave and growing danger. They could provide these arms to terrorists, giving them the means to match their hatred. They could attack our allies or attempt to blackmail the United States. In any of these cases, the price of indifference would be catastrophic."

Trying to overturn an instant consensus is nearly impossible, even when it is obviously wrong. But the general view that by "axis of evil" we intended to signify an allied group of hostile states is wrong, and obviously so. In the plain language of the speech, the axis is between "states like these"—meaning outlaw regimes in general—and "their terrorist allies." No alliance was asserted among Iran, Iraq, and North Korea, because none existed. The danger came, and comes, from the axis, or relationship, between rogue states and terrorist groups—hardly a controversial assertion. All three states were included on the State Department's "State Sponsors of Terror" list. All three had a history of seeking weapons of mass destruction—and, in the case of Iraq, of using them. All three were part of a small and self-selected group of the most irresponsible nations in the world.

Moving from analysis to policy, the president made clear that military action to confront this threat, while possible, was one tool among many. "We will work closely with our coalition," he continued, "to deny terrorists and their state sponsors the materials, technology, and expertise to make and deliver weapons of mass destruction. We will develop and deploy effective missile defenses to protect America and our allies from sudden attack. And all nations should know: America will do what is necessary to ensure our nation's security."

At this point, these arguments were purely theoretical—the purpose was to communicate to Americans the threats of a new world, and the broad outlines of a new approach to confronting them. But a message was being sent: dangers we had tolerated in the past would no longer be tolerated. And the message was received. In Pyongyang, the official news service said, "The remarks were merely US shenanigans aimed at continuing its policy of aggression against us." In Tehran, Ayatollah Ali Khamenei responded, "The Islamic Republic of Iran is proud to be the target of the rage and hatred of the world's greatest Satan." In Baghdad, an Iraqi official said, "I believe the US administration and Zionist entity are sources of evil in the entire world and not only in the Arab world."

To critics at home, the president's words were "shooting from the hip" that would "strengthen the hand" of anti-American enemies. As I observed in Chapter 3, there is an odd tendency in some circles to believe that the diagnosis of an international danger somehow creates that danger—like blaming a doctor for the existence of a tumor revealed by his tests. When Winston Churchill called vivid attention to the rising threat of Nazi Germany in the 1930s, he was attacked as "alarmist," "hysterical," and part of a "violent, foolish campaign to drive this country into war." When Ronald Reagan talked frankly about the limitless ambitions of Soviet communism, he was dismissed as a dangerous lunatic. Likewise, the diagnosis of the threats from North Korea, Iran, and Iraq did not create those threats; it revealed them to the American people, who are, after all, the ones being threatened, and have a right to know it. The point seems simple enough: When a light reveals a rat in a dark corner, it is not the light that is to blame. And removing that light does not eliminate the rat. In fact, this early speech of the Bush administration was a precise and accurate description of the emerging threats that would dominate American foreign policy for the next several years.

But the question remains: From among these threats, why did Iraq come to the fore? Why was it confronted first?

The answer lies in the history and actions of Iraq itself, which had been waving a red flag of defiance at the international community for more than a decade. By the time of the 2002 State of the Union address, America was in the middle of its confrontation with Iraq, not at the beginning. A cease-fire, not a peace treaty, ended the first Gulf War on March 3, 1991. And one of the conditions of that cease-fire was the "unconditional" relinquishment of weapons of mass destruction, which Iraq had built and used in the past. Within six months, Saddam Hussein began playing cat-and-mouse games with inspectors. At that point, a resumption of full-scale military hostilities by the coalition would have been legally justified. Instead, America engaged in a low-grade military confrontation with Iraq. Iraqi forces fired regularly on American planes. American aircraft flew thousands of sorties to enforce a no-fly zone. And America pushed for tight enforcement of an economic embargo, which imposed a terrible cost on Iraqi civilians. Throughout the 1990s, America was not at peace with Iraq's government.

In the middle of that decade, Saddam's son-in-law defected, providing conclusive evidence about hidden stockpiles of weapons of mass destruction, and elaborate efforts to conceal them. As international pressure increased, Saddam's resistance to inspections hardened, and he eventually halted access to "presidential palaces"—really, large government facilities. By 1997, the UN could no longer verify that Iraq was not producing weapons of mass destruction. Saddam had effectively created a fog of uncertainty around his programs. And President Clinton's Secretary of Defense, William Cohen, told a press briefing that if Saddam had "as much VX [nerve gas] in storage as the UN suspects," he would be able to "kill every human being on the face of the planet."

Late in 1998, the Congress passed, and President Clinton signed, the Iraq Liberation Act, making "regime change"—the overthrow of Saddam Hussein—the official policy of the American government, not only because of his unconventional weapons, but because his regime was genocidal, deceptive, aggressive, and destabilizing. At the end of the year, in a speech from the Oval Office, President Clinton announced a four-day bombing and missile campaign, known as Operation Desert Fox, directed at weapons of mass destruction sites within Iraq. He told the nation: "Other countries possess weapons of mass destruction and ballistic missiles. With Saddam, there's one big difference: he has used them, not once, but repeatedly—unleashing chemical weapons against Iranian troops during a decade-long war, not only against soldiers but against civilians; firing Scud missiles at the citizens of Israel, Saudi Arabia, Bahrain, and Iran—not only against a foreign enemy, but even against his own people, gassing Kurdish civilians in Northern Iraq. The international community had little doubt then, and I have no doubt today, that left unchecked, Saddam Hussein will use those terrible weapons again." With that bombing, Saddam ended all inspections, but there was no reason to think his ambitions had ended with them.

Then came 9/11. Contrary to some accusations, the president never believed or asserted that Saddam Hussein was implicated in the attacks. In fact, he directly stated in public: "We've had no evidence that Saddam Hussein was involved with September 11." But that national shock had a decisive influence on the psychology of the administration, and the course of events. The 9/11 Commission eventually faulted the intelligence community and the White House for an inability to "connect the dots"—a "failure of imagination" that prevented officials from pulling together the scattered, individually inconclusive pieces of the intelligence puzzle that might have exposed the outlines of the plot. Across the administration, there was a strong determination to prevent this from happening again. Uncertainties America had lived with for years were reexamined in a new light. And Saddam Hussein—consciously, deliberately, systematically—had created the greatest uncertainties of all.

By April, President Bush told British journalists: "I've made up my mind that Saddam needs to go. That's about all I'm willing to share with you." It was the same policy of regime change that the Clinton administration and the Congress had already formally adopted. But the president was determined to put this commitment in a wider context.

So in early June I headed with the president to West Point, for a commencement address that would be more serious and memorable than usual. I seldom traveled to this kind of event, or listened to speeches in person, but this one had the feel of history. Our army helicopters approached along the river, to the campus set dramatically on a bluff. The stadium was filled with dress uniforms and proud relatives. It was a hot day and a long speech, but we could assume (unlike other college settings) an attentive audience at a military academy. And it was appropriate to announce a new doctrine to a new generation of military leaders.

The president set out three points. First, the traditional, reactive stance of America was not sufficient in the War on Terror. In the past, America often did not act in the world until it was provoked—a direct attack (such as Pearl Harbor) or the invasion of a weak country (such as Kuwait). But in the case of weapons of mass destruction, the actual arrival of an attack would be catastrophic, and action, at that point, would come too late. America, in a new world of danger, was forced to confront threats as they arose.

"For much of the last century," the president said, "America's defense relied on the Cold War doctrines of deterrence and containment. In some cases, those strategies still apply. But new threats also require new thinking. Deterrence—the promise of massive retaliation against nations—means nothing against shadowy terrorist networks with no nation or citizens to defend. Containment is not possible when unbalanced dictators with weapons of mass destruction can deliver those weapons on missiles or secretly provide them to terrorist allies." As a result, "the War on Terror will not be won on the defensive. We must take the battle to the enemy, disrupt his plans, and confront the worst threats before they emerge."

At West Point, the president talked of this kind of "preemption" as an evolution beyond the Cold War. But, in fact, it was anticipated during the Cold War. In his October 1962 Cuban Missile Crisis speech, President John F. Kennedy argued, "Neither the United States of America nor the world community of nations can tolerate deliberate deception and offensive threats on the part of any nation, large or small. We no longer live in a world where only the actual firing of weapons represents a sufficient challenge to a nation's security to constitute maximum peril. Nuclear weapons are so destructive, and ballistic missiles are so swift, that any substantially increased possibility of their use or any sudden change in their deployment may well be regarded as a definite threat to peace."

Kennedy called the "change in deployment" in Cuba an "explicit threat to the peace and security of all Americans." And he would not allow offensive missile sites to remain. In his book about the crisis, Robert Kennedy wrote: "If the Russians continued to be adamant and continued to build up their missile strength, military force would be the only alternative." But the Russian leader, Nikita Khrushchev, after intense diplomatic maneuvering, backed down. Saddam Hussein, after intense diplomatic maneuvering, did not.

Preemption does not mean that military force is the first or preferred option to deal with emerging threats. As the president said at West Point, "We will send diplomats where they are needed, and we will send you, our soldiers, where you're needed." The tools to oppose proliferation should be as varied and flexible as the challenges we face—from carrots like improved economic relations, to sticks like diplomatic isolation, economic embargoes, targeted air strikes, and broader military action. But the central insight of preemption is undeniable: a world of irresponsible regimes with weapons of mass destruction and links to terrorist groups would be a nightmare of risk and confrontation. It is easy for those without executive responsibility to dismiss that risk when it is prospective. After a catastrophic attack on America, those critics would likely be silent, hoping that no one recalled their reckless complacency.

The president's second point at West Point was that opposing totalitarian ideologies is a moral calling. "America confronted imperial communism in many different ways—diplomatic, economic, and military. Yet moral clarity was essential to victory in the Cold War. When leaders like John F. Kennedy and Ronald Reagan refused to gloss over the brutality of tyrants, they gave hope to prisoners and dissidents and exiles, and rallied free nations to a great cause. Some worry that it is somehow undiplomatic to speak the language of right and wrong," he continued. "I disagree. Different circumstances require different methods, but not different moralities. Moral truth is the same in every culture, in every time, and in every place. Targeting innocent civilians for murder is always and everywhere wrong. Brutality against women is always and everywhere wrong. There can be no neutrality between justice and cruelty, between the innocent and the guilty. We are in a conflict between good and evil, and America will call evil by its name."

It is sometimes argued that using the word *evil* alienates foreign countries. But that needs to be qualified with a question: whom in those countries does it offend? Certainly, oppressive rulers, who understandably prefer the normal language of diplomacy—the civilities and euphemisms exchanged around polished tables. But there are other audiences as well. Men and women starving in slave labor camps. Women beaten by clerical thugs, or threatened with beheading for adultery. The prisoners of conscience and victims of systematic rape. Are they offended when their oppressors are called "evil"? When a president speaks, he can identify with these victims, or ignore them. As a speechwriter, I tended to value the opinion of this audience more highly than the opinion of their jailors and persecutors. Sometimes, foreign policy must consist of more than what G. K. Chesterton called "easy speeches to comfort cruel men." Foreign policy must have the realism to see evil from the perspective of its victims.

Third and finally, the president at West Point talked of extending "a just peace, by replacing poverty, repression, and resentment around the world with the hope of a better day." "The twentieth century," he argued, "ended with a single surviving model of human progress.... A truly strong nation will permit legal avenues of dissent for all groups that pursue their aspirations without violence. An advancing nation will pursue economic reforms, to unleash the great entrepreneurial energy of its people. A thriving nation will respect the rights of women, because no society can prosper while denying opportunity to half its citizens. Mothers and fathers and children across the Islamic world, and all the world, share the same fears and aspirations. In poverty, they struggle. In tyranny, they suffer. And as we saw in Afghanistan, in liberation they celebrate."

The encouragement of freedom and economic progress, in this argument, was not merely an altruistic add-on to a military strategy—it was a central part of our national security strategy. Human dignity, rights, and progress were the long-term answers to terrorism. "America cannot impose this vision—yet we can support and reward governments that make the right choices for their people. In our development aid, in our diplomatic efforts, in our international broadcasting, and in our educational assistance, the United States will promote moderation and tolerance and human rights."

The speech at West Point was meant to combine a hard-nosed realism about emerging threats with an idealistic national purpose that could sustain Americans through a long, ideological struggle. And what was argued in a stadium at West Point would be quickly applied by some of the graduates themselves.

It would be of little use for me to rehearse the details of pre-war intelligence on Iraq. I worked closely with the president and the national security advisor to set out broad strategy in the War on Terror, but I was not a part of the war council. I was not given raw intelligence, or the National Intelligence Estimate, the authoritative summary of intelligence judgments. Chief of Staff Andy Card often talked of the large distinction between "need to know" and "want to know" when it came to intelligence—and he enforced that distinction vigorously.

But the outlines of the case were clear enough, and the puzzle pieces, in this case, were neither scattered nor inconclusive. Saddam Hussein was the only leader in the world who had personally ordered the use of weapons of mass destruction—a mixture of mustard and nerve gases—against civilians, killing thousands of Kurds in dozens of villages. In the mid–1990s, he was forced to admit possessing tens of thousands of liters of biological agent, enough to kill millions of people. He had failed to account for tons of biological weapon growth media, and chemical weapons precursors—the materials used to produce biological and chemical weapons. He employed a special department of the Iraqi government to coordinate elaborate deception plans designed to fool weapons inspectors. He had fired medium-range missiles against Israel, Saudi Arabia, and other nations—missiles that might be used to deliver weapons of mass destruction. And his intelligence services had a series of contacts over the years with terrorist groups, including al-Qaeda. (Just because Iraq was not involved in the 9/11 plot did not mean there had been no contact with al-Qaeda. That contact had been informal but serious, both while al-Qaeda was based in Sudan and in Afghanistan.)

Both the Clinton and Bush administrations concluded that Saddam was continuing his weapons of mass destruction programs (which President Clinton tried to destroy by bombing in 1998). That judgment was shared by the intelligence services of many nations, including Great Britain, Russia, Israel, Germany, and France. Even most of the critics of military action assumed that Iraq had weapons of mass destruction, sometimes using the fact that Saddam might unleash them as an argument against intervention.

These were the facts as we knew them. But the case against Iraq was given added momentum by several psychological factors. Many senior officials involved in the second confrontation with Iraq had also been involved in the first, including the vice president and the secretary of state. And one of the most bitter lessons from the Gulf War had been that Saddam's progress on weapons of mass destruction had been *under*-estimated in the pre-war intelligence. In 1991, following the first war, Saddam was found to be much closer to a nuclear weapon than American intelligence had suspected—perhaps a year away. There was a suspicion that the reality of Iraq's weapons might be worse than our estimates, because this is exactly what had happened the last time.

Another psychological factor concerned the burden of proof. We were not operating in a court of law. Saddam was *not* considered innocent until proven guilty. He had been guilty in the past, so he was under an obligation—according to the cease-fire and United Nations resolutions—to prove his own innocence through unconditional cooperation. Not only did he refuse that kind of cooperation, but he acted in the guiltiest possible manner. When inspections eventually resumed, satellites showed suspected chemical weapons sites cleaned out just ahead of inspection teams. Close to thirty chemical and biological sites got this kind of housecleaning. Communications were intercepted between Iraqi officers who talked of removing "nerve agents." Instead of trying to demonstrate his innocence, Saddam acted like a sweating suspect in a police lineup.

The momentum toward confrontation was also increased by the decay of sanctions against Iraq. Those sanctions, over the years, hurt many Iraqi civilians, who paid the price of international efforts to isolate Saddam. As a humanitarian response, the United Nations created the Oil for Food program, allowing Iraqi oil sales to fund the purchase of food and medicine for the poorest of the poor. It was the largest humanitarian program that the UN had ever undertaken—and perhaps the largest corruption scandal in the history of the world. Not only did Saddam smuggle massive amounts of oil outside the program, but, with the help of corrupt officials in Russia, France, and at the UN itself, he used the program to enrich his regime. Money intended for the poor and disabled in Iraq was diverted to military spending and the construction of presidential palaces. At the same time, France and Russia, along with UN officials, pushed to lift the sanctions entirely. By 2002, the choice was *not* between stronger action and the continued containment of Iraq. Containment was crumbling. The choice (increasingly) was between stronger action and Saddam unbound.

Finally, the momentum toward conflict was built by the character of Saddam Hussein himself. Saddam was not merely a dictator. He was arguably the most vicious, homicidal butcher since Pol Pot, the author of the Cambodian genocide. Saddam was twice guilty of genocide himself, against the Kurds and the Marsh Arabs. His torture chambers employed electric shock, burning with hot irons, dripping acid on the skin, mutilation with electric drills, systematic rape, and the cutting out of tongues. And Saddam, refusing to leave the enjoyment to others, would sometimes take a personal hand in his murders. For me, these were not just elements of a public argument. I felt a deep moral revulsion toward a ruler who ordered the torture of children in front of their parents. Bringing such a man to justice fit the president's foreign-policy idealism, and his conception of America's purposes in the world. And this helps explain the president's own intensity of purpose in the run-up to the war.

Would this moral reason have been sufficient to justify a war to depose and punish Saddam Hussein? The answer to that question cannot be separated from a thousand practical considerations. No theory of international affairs allows national sovereignty to shield acts of genocide—and America has formally endorsed the "responsibility to protect" innocent civilians in other lands when their own government conducts war against them. A war to punish genocide and prevent mass murder might be a moral duty if the costs to America were low, and the chances of success were high. This is the argument for intervention in Rwanda in the 1990s, where the authors of genocide were armed mainly with machetes. A war to punish and prevent mass murder would be morally problematic if the costs to America were prohibitive and the chances of success were remote. Intervening to stop the Cambodian genocide in the 1970s, in the immediate aftermath of Vietnam, might have been strategically and politically impossible. Iraq fit somewhere along that continuum—though it is very hard to predict just where before a war is undertaken.

The case for humanitarian intervention in Iraq was at least arguable. And even if this was not a sufficient reason, it was a contributing reason. In the run-up to the war, I believed that the punishment of genocide was an act of justice. I believed that the prevention of further violence by one of the world's cruelest despots was a noble goal. I believed that the liberation of millions of people from oppression was a moral good. And I believe those things still.

America's "rush to war" looked much slower from the inside, and *was* in fact much slower than critics allege. Since 1991, the UN Security Council had passed sixteen resolutions demanding that Saddam Hussein demonstrate his disarmament and respect human rights. All had been defied or ignored. Vice President Cheney was convinced that no further provocation or authorization was necessary for America to act. Secretary of State Powell believed we should go back to the United Nations at least one more time to make clear that every peaceful avenue had been exhausted. A real rush to war would presumably have avoided this lengthy and difficult series of steps. But it was Secretary

Powell (strongly supported by Prime Minister Blair) who won the argument.

In early September of 2002, I had prepared and sent along an outline for the president's upcoming speech to the United Nations that focused almost entirely on democracy and reform in the Arab world. The president and Condi Rice set an entirely different direction. He had made the decision to go back to the Security Council to make a final demand for full Iraqi compliance with inspections. And he wanted to challenge the UN to live up to its responsibilities. Condi contributed that we should urge the United Nations to avoid the lot of the League of Nations before World War II—the fate of being judged by history as feckless, ineffective, and irrelevant.

When the speech was given, the audience applauded at only one spot—when the president announced that America would resume its membership in UNESCO. But the remarks—a lawyerly recounting of Saddam's aggression, brutality, and deception—gathered to a crescendo of solemn intensity. And the president was at his grim and determined best. "The conduct of the Iraqi regime," President Bush said, "is a threat to the authority of the United Nations, and a threat to peace. Iraq has answered a decade of UN demands with a decade of defiance. All the world now faces a test, and the United Nations a difficult and defining moment. Are Security Council resolutions to be honored and enforced, or cast aside without consequence? Will the United Nations serve the purpose of its founding, or will it be irrelevant?"

He went on to outline, in a kind of velvet-wrapped ultimatum, a series of steps that the Iraqi regime could take if it "wishes peace"—disclosing all WMD, ending support for terrorism, ending persecution of minorities, accounting for missing personnel from the Gulf War, ending all illicit trade outside the Oil for Food program. "The United States has no quarrel with the Iraqi people," the president continued. "They've suffered too long in silent captivity. Liberty for the Iraqi people is a great moral cause, and a great strategic goal. The people of

Iraq deserve it; the security of all nations requires it. Free societies do not intimidate through cruelty and conquest, and open societies do not threaten the world with mass murder. The United States supports political and economic liberty in a unified Iraq."

The president concluded with a promise and a threat. The promise was to "work with the UN Security Council to meet our common challenge." America would not act immediately or unilaterally. "But the purposes of the United States should not be doubted. The Security Council resolutions will be enforced—the just demands of peace and security will be met—or action will be unavoidable. And a regime that has lost its legitimacy will also lose its power."

A few days later, the US Congress added its support for the president's approach, authorizing the use of force against Iraq by a strong vote of 77 to 23 in the Senate, and 296 to 133 in the House—a much larger majority than had approved the first Gulf War in 1991. During the debate, Senator Hillary Clinton stated: "In the four years since the inspectors left, intelligence reports show that Saddam Hussein has worked to rebuild his chemical and biological weapons stock, his missile delivery capacity, and his nuclear program. He has also given aid, comfort, and sanctuary to terrorists, including al-Qaeda members." Senator Joe Biden argued: "The speed and stealth with which an outlaw state or terrorists could use weapons of mass destruction, and the catastrophic damage they could inflict, require us to consider new ways of acting, not reacting." Leaders of Congress, the White House, Prime Minister Tony Blair, and others were making the same arguments, because they were all operating with roughly the same information.

The first week of November 2002 set the course for the months to follow. Secretary Powell was lobbying heavily in the Security Council for a strong resolution. And the midterm elections were upon us—a test of political strength at an important moment. Karl Rove had sent the president on a nationwide scramble for votes—seventeen events in seven days, with a few days off here and there to rest and conduct presidential business. For these political events, we gave the president some material on local candidates, and a few notes. He extemporized the rest.

On Tuesday, Election Day, I sent to President Bush in Crawford the draft of a statement reacting to the UN Security Council resolution. The speech assumed a Security Council "yes" to a new inspections resolution, and pressed for unconditional Iraqi cooperation. I thought the president would be tired after his campaign swing, and did not expect a call—but it came almost immediately. I took some edits on a secure line in the Situation Room—a warren of offices and conference rooms in the basement of the West Wing where secure communications are possible.

At this point, the situation at the UN was unsettled. France was moving toward support of a resolution, but Russia might veto. This course would have put Prime Minister Blair at great risk. If he went to his Parliament for approval of military action without UN support, he would likely fall in a vote of no confidence. It was essential to get the resolution.

At the same time, the election news seemed very mixed. The exit polling was all over the map—a pattern we would see repeated in other elections. Three analysts interpreted the data with three different outcomes—varying as much as twelve to fourteen points.

On that Tuesday in November, the administration seemed poised on a precipice. A veto at the Security Council would be a political disaster. A poor midterm election result would be a sign of weakness. But by the end of the week, the world looked very different.

Late that evening, it became clear that the president had won an historic midterm election victory, gaining seats in both the House and the Senate. The next morning, when Karl Rove entered the senior staff meeting, he was given a standing ovation. And the news at the United

Nations got better each day. On Thursday night, as I left the West Wing, I saw Secretary Powell coming into the building. He patted me on the back, obviously a happy man.

On Friday, the vote in the UN Security Council was 15 to 0, and had even included Syria. Resolution 1441 found Iraq in "material breach" of its obligation to disarm, and promised "serious conse-quences" if it did not comply. Within thirty days, Iraq was to provide "a currently accurate, full and complete declaration of all aspects of its programs to develop chemical, biological, and nuclear weapons, ballistic missiles, and other delivery systems such as unmanned aerial vehicles and dispersal systems designed for use on aircraft."

The president wanted to do his reaction statement in the Rose Garden immediately, so I headed to the Oval Office, where I found Condi, Steve, Dan, and Andy. The president, his face bright with suc-cess, shook my hand. Then Secretary Powell entered. He reported that the previous night the Iraqi ambassador was wandering around the UN looking for someone to talk with—and found that no one would. The president asked Powell to stand next to him at the podium as he deliv-ered his statement. We all filed out the door of the Oval Office to the Rose Garden, and Condi and I stood to the side, silently reading the statement as the president soberly delivered it. "The resolution approved today presents the Iraqi regime with a test—a final test. Iraq must now, without delay or negotiations, fully disarm; welcome full inspections; and fundamentally change the approach it has taken for more than a decade.... If Iraq fails to fully comply, the United States and other nations will disarm Saddam Hussein."

This was not merely the resumption of inspections, but a new theory of inspections. Past UN approaches had emphasized long-term, accounting-oriented, methodical monitoring—inspections at a slow pace, with a low level of intrusiveness, so inspectors would not be thrown out. The new inspections would take a "zero-tolerance" approach to further deception. The administration was pushing for early tests to show whether the regime had made a strategic shift toward complete cooperation.

Quickly it was apparent that Saddam Hussein had done nothing of the kind. He continued to deceive and obstruct inspectors and sanitize WMD sites. By January, conflict seemed inevitable.

Was the invasion of Iraq justified? I can only say that the evidence on weapons of mass destruction seemed very strong—far more conclusive than any of the fragmentary warnings before 9/11. I had no evidence that my colleagues had lied to me, or to one another. And it would have made little sense to lie about such matters, since the truth would be dramatically revealed to everyone in just a few months. The views we held about Iraq's weapons of mass destruction were not a deception; they were an assumption. And that assumption was shared not only by George Tenet and Colin Powell, but by Hillary Clinton and Nancy Pelosi, and by Tony Blair and Jacques Chirac, and by the *New York Times* and the *Washington Post*. Saddam Hussein had been guilty in the past. He acted guilty in the present. And the president was not prepared to tolerate the dangerous uncertainty he cultivated. Given what we knew, and thought we knew, ignoring that uncertainty would have been a betrayal of the president's most basic constitutional responsibility to protect the American people.

The pre-war debate did not generally focus on the existence of Iraq's weapons of mass destruction, but on the most prudent method to deal with them. And here the president took a middle-ground approach. He rejected the vice president's counsel of a military operation without returning to the United Nations. But he also was not willing to return to the Clinton strategy of dire warnings, limited strikes—and then further Iraqi violations that began the cycle all over again. So he took the approach urged by Secretary Powell and Prime Minister Blair: a new UN resolution, and a final chance for Saddam Hussein to comply. This left the final decision for war in the hands of Saddam himself. Saddam did not make a responsible, or even a rational, decision. But it is unlikely that a few more months of diplomacy and pressure would have made any difference to the final outcome. Saddam Hussein would have needed to change his behavior fundamentally. And after all the years of brutality, and megalomania, and boot-licking subservience of those around him, Saddam was not about to make that change.

Once the president declared that Iraq's traditional methods of deception would no longer be tolerated—that continued defiance would lead to war—there were only two possible outcomes. Either Saddam would back down, or America would back down. We hoped for the first. But when that transformation didn't come, to have accepted the second option would have entailed unbearable costs. Saddam himself, as the sanctions against him collapsed, would likely have been released from all constraints—free to pursue, once again, his agenda of mayhem in the Middle East. American resolve in the War on Terror would have been revealed as shallow, sending a message of weakness to the terrorists, and a message of permission to other outlaw regimes. This kind of retreat was not a possibility for the president I had come to know.

This consideration—that is, protecting our national interest—was our primary task, the one we all had sworn ourselves to in an oath. But a Christian has an additional burden. Was this war not only justified, but just? For the Christian pacifist, every war is morally unacceptable, because the followers of Jesus do not use violence. And there is something to this position. It is true that Jesus never took up the sword, declaring the arrival of a Kingdom "not of this world." The use of force to establish this Kingdom was impossible. God's rule expands through voluntary acceptance—heart by heart, not conquest by conquest. And the Sermon on the Mount teaches the believer to reject all violence and vengeance—even violence in self-defense—in his or her daily life.

I have a deep respect for a principled Christian pacifism, but I am not a pacifist. When John Courtney Murray was asked how foreign policy could be reconciled with the Sermon on the Mount, he replied: "What makes you think that morality is identical with the Sermon on the Mount?" There is more to Christian ethics than this one passage of Scripture. Other passages assert that government has a different role from individuals: to protect the innocent and prevent injustice. While private individuals cannot use force, a legitimate government authority may use force to keep the peace.

In the mainstream of the Christian moral tradition, as George Weigel and other scholars have pointed out, the policeman and the soldier have valid, even noble, professions. All governments are established by God to restrain the cruel and unjust; and the restrainers risk their own lives to show love for their neighbors. War breaks the peace, but peace is not always the highest moral good. We should resist what John F. Kennedy called "the peace of the grave, or the security of the slave." In these cases, war is not a "dirty business," or a "necessary evil"; it can be a moral duty, rendered honorable by necessity. "It is the other side's wrongdoing," said Saint Augustine, "that compels the wise man to wage just wars."

But the same Christian moral tradition also places a series of moral limits on war, to prevent the strong from abusing the weak. First, a just war must have a just cause and intention. This is clear in the case of self-defense, but the justified use of force is not limited to self-defense. The just-war tradition also talks of punishing organized evil and protecting the innocent from harm. This would allow humanitarian wars to prevent genocide and mass killing. And this tradition also allows for preventive wars, when the threat is clear and aggressive. I believe that an attack against Nazi Germany in 1936, when it remilitarized the Rhineland in direct violation of its treaty obligations, would have been justified, even though no self-defense was involved. Given what we knew about Iraq, a war to disarm Saddam Hussein, punish his genocide, and liberate his country seemed justified to me as well.

Second, a just war must employ just methods. It is not permissible, for example, to kill innocent people on purpose—to do evil, even in pursuit of a good outcome. This tradition recognizes that collateral damage is unavoidable in pursuing military objectives, though every effort must be taken to avoid it. But just-war theory does not permit the targeting of noncombatants, however useful it might appear.

This is not an easy or noncontroversial standard. America has sometimes conducted wars in the tradition of General Sherman— since "war is hell," we should make that hell as hot as possible, to demoralize the enemy, shorten the war, and ultimately save lives. This was the theory behind the fire bombing of civilians in Dresden during World War II, and the justification for the nuclear destruction of Hiroshima and Nagasaki.

But Christian thought has consistently rejected this purely utilitarian perspective. It does not permit the purposeful incineration of children and old people in the pursuit of military goals. It forbids acts of barbarism, even in a fight against barbarism. It warns that lawless methods, once tolerated, quickly become preferred. And it asserts that the soldier can and should be a man or woman of character—a threat only to the enemy.

This is the spirit I have seen in the American military. In the Gulf War, Afghanistan, and Iraq, men and women in uniform have taken remarkable precautions to minimize collateral damage, and new technologies have made that job easier. Bombing raids are analyzed with lawyerly precision to limit civilian casualties. The killing and abuse of civilians are investigated and punished. The American military, on the whole, has fought in the best just-war tradition. And our soldiers do not, in my experience, regard those moral rules as a frustrating limit on their deadly work. They regard those rules as evidence of their honor, and a natural reflection of the cause they volunteered to serve. And they believe that indiscriminate brutality, particularly in a counter-insurgency campaign, undermines the long-term goal of leaving behind a stable, orderly society.

This second standard of the just-war tradition—just methods—also contributes to the argument for limited and preventive wars. As World War II shows, in a total war all moral restraints are quickly abandoned. Winston Churchill and Franklin Roosevelt, at the start of the war, issued a joint statement condemning civilian bombings; by the end of the war, Britain and America had perfected the technique. Almost no one, at that point, expressed moral reservations, because a war for survival gains an unstoppable momentum. An early, limited, preventive war against Hitler would not have needed to cross those boundaries—an intervention in 1936 would have made the fire bombings of Dresden unnecessary. Or consider the case of a threatening outlaw regime seeking WMD. Attacking WMD facilities before the deployment of weapons allows for a limited, proportionate conflict. Were an outlaw regime actually to destroy an American city, America would likely pursue a policy of annihilation against that whole nation—and few of our citizens, in their justified rage, would question it. Preventive war makes the use of moral methods more likely.

There is a third element of this tradition. A just war must establish the conditions of a just peace. A nation undertaking a war must plan and act to leave the situation better than before the war started. Here some serious concerns begin for me when it comes to Iraq—which I will address in a later chapter.

By late January 2003, the president and Prime Minister Blair were convinced they had gone the extra mile to disarm Saddam without war. Resolution 1441, the inspection regime, and the movement of troops to the region were providing maximum pressure. At one point, Prime

Minister Blair estimated to the president there was a 20 percent chance that Saddam would cooperate. Both thought it was possible that his regime might collapse internally with the right outside pressure.

In the State of the Union, we made the case against Saddam once again, and spoke directly to two audiences. "Tonight," the president said, "I have a message for the brave and oppressed people of Iraq: Your enemy is not surrounding your country—your enemy is ruling your country. And the day he and his regime are removed from power will be the day of your liberation."

President Bush also addressed the American armed forces: "Many of you are assembling in or near the Middle East, and some crucial hours may lie ahead. In those hours, the success of our cause will depend on you. Your training has prepared you. Your honor will guide you. You believe in America, and America believes in you.

"Sending Americans into battle is the most profound decision a president can make. The technologies of war have changed; the risks and suffering of war have not. For the brave Americans who bear the risk, no victory is free from sorrow. This nation fights reluctantly, because we know the cost and we dread the days of mourning that always come. We seek peace. We strive for peace. And sometimes peace must be defended. A future lived at the mercy of terrible threats is no peace at all. If war is forced upon us, we will fight in a just cause and by just means—sparing, in every way we can, the innocent. And if war is forced upon us, we will fight with the full force and might of the United States military—and we will prevail."

A week later, Secretary Powell made his vivid presentation to the United Nations Security Council. All along he had been the least inclined to use force, making him the best test of the credibility of the case against Iraq. Powell and Director Tenet pored over the evidence, line by line, in preparation for the remarks. After this due diligence, Secretary Powell's presentation was compelling—the fullest explanation of what was known at the time. He talked of elaborate and recent deception, captured by satellite photos ... communications intercepts mentioning "forbidden ammo" ... death threats against scientists who provided information to inspectors ... Iraqi ties to al-Qaeda and Abu Musab al-Zarqawi ... mobile laboratories to make germ weapons ... hidden missiles in the western desert ... and Hussein's authorization to use poison gas if an invasion went forward. Secretary Powell concluded: "We know that Saddam Hussein is determined to keep his weapons of mass destruction. He's determined to make more. Given Saddam Hussein's history of aggression, given what we know of his grandiose plans, given what we know of his terrorist associations, and given his determination to exact revenge on those who oppose him, should we take the risk that he will not someday use these weapons at a time and a place and in a manner of his choosing, at a time when the world is in a much weaker position to respond? The United States will not and cannot run that risk to the American people. Leaving Saddam Hussein in possession of weapons of mass destruction for a few more months or years is not an option, not in a post–September 11 world."

At Prime Minister Blair's request, the administration was seeking a second resolution from the Security Council to give a final ultimatum to Saddam. President Bush did not believe it was necessary, but pursued it out of deference to Blair, who was on the brink of a vote of no confidence in Parliament. By Wednesday, March 12, President Bush was beginning to lose patience. The process in the Security Council was messy. Some leaders were hiding from calls and feigning illness to avoid a decision—like schoolchildren dreading a test. All the players were acting according to form. Condi's mood—calm and serious—never varied. Andy looked out for the president's needs—is he sleeping enough?—with a motherly concern. I was nervous, chewing through several plastic pens a day. I remember thinking: *It is Lent, every day closer to the cross.*

The next day, the waiting was becoming unbearable. Andy Card had proposed a summit in the Azores with Blair. The president was interested. The prime minister was wary. He didn't want to leave Britain for even eight hours, remembering that Margaret Thatcher had been deposed while out of the country. But Blair eventually agreed.

On Saturday, I was headed on Air Force One to the Azores with the president, the draft of an ultimatum in hand. Saddam and his sons would have forty-eight hours to leave, but military operations could begin before the deadline. In the Azores, the meeting took place in a conference room on an air base. During the discussion, the news came that Jacques Chirac would not support an ultimatum under any circumstances—the second resolution would need to be pulled. The leaders talked about post-Saddam Hussein Iraq: maintaining its territorial integrity, the need for humanitarian relief, the release of UN money in escrow, the need to go back to the Security Council to build international consensus on reconstruction. Blair argued for a strong push in the Middle Eastern peace process. As the leaders filed out of the meeting, I stood against the wall. President Bush loudly asked, "Gerson, are you trying to avoid attention?" Then Condi asked for the ultimatum speech I was holding, and gave it directly to Blair. It came back right before we left with a series of edits to make it more conditional: "If conflict comes…" The prime minister clearly wanted to hold out hope that war could be avoided, even at the eleventh hour. This was fully consistent with the president's beliefs. Friendly Middle Eastern leaders, at the time, were delivering public and private messages urging Saddam to leave Iraq. The speech would make the same point.

On Sunday, there was a teleprompter practice session in the cross hall of the Residence. When the president read the words, "Saddam Hussein and his sons must leave Iraq within forty-eight hours. Their refusal to do so will result in military conflict, commenced at a time of our choosing," there was a catch in his throat, and he had difficulty going on. At the end of the remarks, there was a moment of heavy silence. To diffuse it, he rolled up the draft of the speech, and hit me on the head with it.

The president called twice with minor changes on Monday morning. At the Residence that evening, with the camera set up and a tangle of cords all over the marble floor, the president saw me hovering in the back of the room. "Gerson," he said, "you are being too quiet. Are you nervous?" Then he told me a story about how he and one of his brothers were too nervous to watch his father during his first debate with Governor Michael Dukakis. So they went to a Woody Allen movie, and kept going out to the phone, at intervals, to get reports. Then came the call: "One minute." The president's face hardened as he stepped to the podium. He solemnly delivered the ultimatum to Saddam, and still offered this hope: "It is too late for Saddam Hussein to remain in power. It is not too late for the Iraqi military to act with honor and protect your country by permitting the peaceful entry of coalition forces to eliminate weapons of mass destruction. Our forces will give Iraqi military units clear instructions on actions they can take to avoid being attacked and destroyed. I urge every member of the Iraqi military and intelligence services, if war comes, do not fight for a dying regime that is not worth your own life."

The president also delivered this warning to the Iraqi military, consistent with our belief about Saddam's capabilities and intentions: "In any conflict, your fate will depend on your actions…. Do not obey any command to use weapons of mass destruction against anyone, including the Iraqi people. War crimes will be prosecuted. War criminals will be punished. And it will be no defense to say, 'I was just following orders.'"

I still needed to work with John McConnell and Matt Scully on a short speech announcing the beginning of military operations. On March 19, I got a call from Andy on my cell phone about 6 p.m.: "Is it done?" He wanted to meet me outside the Oval Office at 6:30. As I sat in the waiting area just outside the president's office, Director Tenet and his aides, intense and animated, were rushing in and out of the Oval Office, talking on the phone. I could see that Secretary Rumsfeld, General Franks, and Secretary Powell were also with the president. The president called for Karen and Dan, who entered. Andy came out of the Oval Office to get the speech, and brought it back in. The meeting broke up at 7:30. Leaving the office, Secretary Rumsfeld said, "I was just butchering your speech." Actually, his edits were light; he wanted to make sure the remarks said we were in the "early stages" of the operation.

From inside the Oval Office, I heard the president's voice: "Gerson, come in." He stood just inside the door. "We're going after him," he said. I didn't understand at first, but he told me he meant Saddam himself. "The information is good. Let's hope we're right," he said, tearing up. After making Secretary Rumsfeld's changes back in my office, Karen Hughes and I walked along the columns of the Rose Garden, to the basement of the Residence, then climbed the steps to the private quarters. The president was in his office. He started going through the remarks: "At this hour, American and coalition forces are in the early stages of military operations to disarm Iraq, to free its people, and to defend the world from grave danger." He looked ashen as he read the words aloud. Quickly the phone rang. It was Andy Card, informing the president that the forty-eight-hour ultimatum had passed.

Chapter 6

Can Government Do Good?

The act of writing a narrative can convey the impression that events at the White House unfolded in a rational and ordered pattern. In fact, they came in a rush of disorienting variety that left little time for reflection, only a sense that history and absurdity were shaken together in equal measure.

A single day in the spring of 2004 makes the point. It started, as usual, with devotions in my living room at 5:15—some time to myself in the calm darkness. I fell asleep during prayer, perhaps the lingering effects of the Ambien I took far too often to guarantee rest. A rush to the office along nearly empty highways. Then breakfast in the White House mess, a dining room run by the navy in the basement of the West Wing for senior staff.

The senior staff meeting took place every morning at 7:30 in the Roosevelt Room near the Oval Office, presided over by the chief of staff. First, from the press secretary came a short summary of news that might require a public response: a disgruntled former National Security Council staffer is pressing an attack on his book tour; Israel has killed the spiritual leader of Hamas, setting off a swell of protest in the Middle East. Then an overview of the president's schedule for the day. The president's assistant appeared at the door and called me into the Oval Office—President Bush, who seemed subdued and distracted, had some edits on a ceremonial speech to be given later that day on Capitol Hill. Walking back to take my seat in the senior staff meeting, I heard a heated discussion underway on a topic in my area: in the humorous remarks the president would give the next night, should he say the word *testicles*?

Having no pretensions of being a humor writer myself, this kind of speech was generally contracted out through the Republican National Committee to a very talented writer named Landon Parvin. The slide show Landon had prepared for the dinner included a picture of the president looking intently at his dog, Barney, who appeared angry. The president was supposed to comment: "This photo was taken down at the ranch, and as you can tell, Barney's not very happy with me. This is the day I told him he didn't have any testicles." Andy Card and White House Counsel Harriet Meyers opposed the joke as undignified and unpresidential. I thought the word in question was more clinical than crude, and spoke in favor of the joke. Then-Director of the Office of Management and Budget Josh Bolten took my side. The senior staff was deadlocked; the decision would be brought to the president.

On my way out of the Roosevelt Room, I passed the national security advisor, Steve Hadley, looking burdened. As the director of the CIA, George Tenet, passed by on his way to the Oval Office, Steve commented to him: "Though I walk through the valley of the shadow of death, I will fear no evil." Not for the first time, I was thankful not to be afflicted with the secrets they held.

My morning was spent revising a speech on housing set for the following week—a speech that announced no news, offered no interesting arguments, and acted (like so many events) as filler on the president's schedule. I was always surprised that the president's time was wasted in this way, as though his hours were as plentiful as water or sand. Over the years I consistently argued that the president should have one or two major, newsworthy speeches a week, instead of a proliferation of forgettable events. It was an argument I consistently lost, because the schedule generally reflected Karl Rove's hyperactive imagination. For lunch I headed over to the cafeteria in the Old Executive Office Building instead of the White House mess, because my wife had complained about the size of my mess bill (the food is not free). I was approached in the hall by a very young, very nervous female staffer, who called me Mr. Gerson, and who was reading the same book I said I was reading in a recent newspaper profile. The flattery of the moment clashed uncomfortably with the realities of lacking exercise, gaining weight, spiritual distraction, and assorted failures as a husband and father.

Early in the afternoon there was a cabinet meeting, in the cabinet room next to the Oval Office, with blooming tulip trees outside the window that kept attracting my view to the Rose Garden. Staff seating is assigned, and Steve Hadley was to my left. I awkwardly offered: "Tough few days." He only responded: "Going to get worse." Andy Card began with a prayer. Secretary Rumsfeld left early to testify before the commission investigating the events of 9/11. A scrum of reporters and photographers entered at the end; then the ritual questions no one expected to be answered.

Soon afterward, Andy, myself, and a few others were with the president in the family theater over in the East Wing—rows of theater seats in a small auditorium, decorated in unfortunate orange hues by the Reagans—where teleprompter practices take place. President Bush ran through the remarks twice—each time he could not deliver the "testicles" line without laughing.

An hour later, I attended the weekly scheduling meeting, where invitations and proposed events are discussed. A large calendar on the wall told the story of the next few days: a major economic speech; interviews with a number of fishing magazines; a visit by Prime Minister Blair. The testicles joke was still a matter of controversy. By the end of the day, after persistent appeals, it was removed. Another loss in the White House power game.

No day like that could be considered typical, but it was consistent with my experience of many other days. The small decisions that become large when made by the president. The large matters that become familiar through repetition. The president's good humor. And the consistent undercurrent of global danger.

National security issues have overshadowed the Bush administration, as they did the Johnson administration in the late 1960s—but in neither case did this prevent significant domestic accomplishments. President Johnson, in the aftermath of the Kennedy assassination and as Vietnam ramped up, used enormous (and temporary) assets of public support to pass the Civil Rights Act and Medicare. President Bush pushed for No Child Left Behind education reform, and a prescription-drug benefit in Medicare, against considerable ideological opposition in the leadership of his own party. Were it not for the Iraq war, these accomplishments would seem larger, because they are actually quite large.

Over 23 million seniors now receive prescription-drug coverage through Medicare, saving, on average, over a thousand dollars a year in drug costs. The program itself has been less costly than predicted, as competition between providers and the use of generic drugs has kept down prices. And low-income seniors receive the most help, paying little or no premiums, and getting 95 percent of the costs of their medicine paid. The drug benefit is a good example of the power of presidential leadership: without Bush's consistent advocacy, this issue would never have risen to the top of the Republican agenda on Capitol Hill. As a result, millions of low-income seniors have one less source of fear, and that is a contribution to the justice and fairness of American society.

No Child Left Behind has its detractors among educators, but they are often the ones who didn't want to be bothered by standards and accountability in the first place. The great achievement of this law is simple: every public school in America must now prove yearly progress in reading and math among minority students or face consequences (though the consequences of betraying poor and minority children are still not severe enough, in my view). Parents have at least some idea if their local elementary school is succeeding or failing. And this scrutiny has encouraged steady progress. The gap in achievement between African American and white nine-year-olds in reading and math is now at an all-time low. More reading progress has been made by nine-year-olds in five years than the previous twenty-eight years. A Republican president refocused the American elementary-school system on the performance of minority children. And that is both admirable and unprecedented.

President Bush's domestic-policy instincts generally fit a pattern: He is open to increased spending, if that spending was accompanied by reform. He raised federal education spending nearly 34 percent—but tied those increases to testing and accountability. He increased Medicare spending to cover prescription drugs—but insisted that coverage be provided through private companies chosen by the individual. He increased spending on overseas development through the Millennium Challenge Account—but made grants contingent on political and economic reform. In none of these cases did President Bush roll back government, but he did restructure and modernize it. At its best, this approach has been more than a cut-rate liberalism; it has been an active, reforming conservatism, aimed at empowering individuals and encouraging performance with public funds.

If these programs were merely elements of a cynical political strategy, it didn't work; little credit has come to the president on education or prescription drugs, any more than has come on the global

AIDS initiative. And I never saw such cynicism on the president's part. My experience in the White House policy structure was consistent: President Bush was the most touched by stories of personal suffering, and the most open to government activism that would relieve that suffering. Before the State of the Union in 2005, I was pushing for a proposal that would encourage more training for defense lawyers in death-penalty cases. The vice president's office—which was conventionally and narrowly conservative—opposed it. So did the Domestic Policy Council and the White House Counsel's Office. All were adamant that the president should not raise issues of fairness related to the death penalty. So the DPC called a policy meeting with the president in the Roosevelt Room to kill my ill-considered idea. The critics, one by one, made their presentations—the problem was exaggerated, implementing the proposal would be difficult. Then I was asked to defend the proposal—the only person who would. I made a simple, not particularly articulate case: if someone was at risk of being executed, he or she deserved a lawyer who knew what they were doing. The president said abruptly, "I want this in the speech" and dismissed the meeting. This pattern, repeated on a number of issues, sustained my commitment in an exhausting, frustrating job. If I could get compassionate proposals raised to the highest level of decision—a task that got harder over time—I could rely on the president's decency.

This would not be reassuring to a certain kind of Republican. In these policies, anti-government conservatives have detected a subtle conspiracy. In 1999, candidate George W. Bush proposed expanding Medicare to cover prescription drugs—then, as president, expanded Medicare to cover prescription drugs. He supported an increased federal role to raise standards in public education—then increased the federal role in public education. He attacked the "destructive mind-set" that "if government would only get out of our way, all our problems would be solved"—

then refused to get government out of our way so that all our problems could be solved.

After six years assembling the jigsaw puzzle of this consistency, conservative critics have concluded that Bush is a "Christian socialist," "a Reagan impostor," and "more compassionate than conservative." They talk of a "spending orgy" and a government "out of control." They contend that future political success will require a return to the anti-government purity of the Reagan era—the Golden Age of limited government. And their agenda provides a hint of how that purity is defined: the severe pleasures of cutting food stamps; steep reductions in foreign assistance; paying the costs of Katrina by postponing or ending the Medicare prescription-drug benefit.

At one level, this debate is simply factual. Conservative accusations on out-of-control domestic spending are a distortion, based on a caricature and a myth.

The caricature concerns the Bush budgets, which, in my experience, were not profligate, but frustratingly restrictive. From the inside, the domestic "spending orgy" was considerably less stimulating, because it never happened. Apart from signature commitments like education and prescription drugs, domestic spending was tight, and got tighter with time—pressured by war spending and a presidential pledge to halve the deficit. Most of President Bush's spending increases went to a range of unexpected security necessities, including military Imminent Danger Pay; unmanned aerial vehicles; doubled funding for special operations; biological-weapons vaccines; nuclear-detection equipment. By one calculation, security spending—on homeland security, defense, and international affairs—grew 32 percent from 2001 to 2006, when adjusted for inflation and population growth. Non-security, domestic discretionary spending—spending on things like agriculture, roads, and new social initiatives—increased about 2 percent in the same period. (Critics often try to artificially inflate this figure by including homeland-security spending as domestic spending—an accounting ploy intended to magnify the president's crimes against conservatism.) Why don't anti-government conservatives mention spending increases on defense and homeland security when they make their critique? Because a minimalist state cannot fight a global war—so it is easier for critics to ignore the global war. But after the next attack comes, no one will complain that we didn't cut government enough.

Deficits grew in the early Bush years. But much of that problem was caused by the economic effects of a recession, the 9/11 attacks, and corporate scandals that rocked the stock market in 2002. The rest of the deficits were mainly the result of tax relief (which helpfully stimulated economic growth) and security spending. In 2003, for example, just 8 percent of the deficit was caused by non-defense, non-homeland security spending. Put another way: if increases in non-security, domestic discretionary spending had been frozen that year—not a penny higher—the deficit would have been $380 billion, instead of $455 billion, hardly an earth-shaking difference in a vast, continental economy. Bush's deficit in relation to the size of the total size of the economy stands at about the historical average of the last forty years. He has reduced the growth of non-security, domestic discretionary spending every year that he has held office. And his 2005 and 2006 budgets proposed real cuts in this category of spending.

It is worth noting that conservative criticism of the president "profligacy" came during the years when the president's budgets were the most restrictive on domestic spending—reaching a crescendo just as deficits were rapidly declining. It has clearly been easier for anti-government conservatives to attack the president when his poll numbers are low—courage gets easier when your opponent seems weaker—but the tendency is not very attractive, or principled.

Congressional courage on spending cuts has been … selective. Many Republicans are eager to cut discretionary spending on food stamps or foreign aid—but all of them know that the real economic threat comes from mandatory spending, especially on Social Security and Medicare. Assuming current spending trends and a tax burden at historical levels, entitlement outlays and interest payments will consume *all* federal revenue by 2035. And the reason the problem is so massive is because entitlement benefits America's massive and long-lived middle class. Yet when President Bush proposed to rein in the costs of Social Security by making it more progressive, the overwhelming response of members of Congress was to wince and fidget. By targeting the hungry and foreigners in need, and avoiding middle-class programs, the anti-spending crusade has managed to look cruel and cowardly at the same time.

The criticisms of spending under President Bush also depend on unflattering comparisons to President Ronald Reagan. But the Golden Age of austerity under Reagan is a myth. During the Reagan years, big government got bigger, with federal spending reaching over 23 percent of the economy in 1984 (compared to just over 20 percent under President George W. Bush). Reagan expanded Social Security coverage, expanded Medicare coverage, and did not eliminate a single cabinet agency—in fact, he added one (Veterans Affairs). The federal workforce increased in size, and farm subsidies grew massively. In 1982, the libertarian CATO Institute complained: "Soaring military spending for overseas commitments and the refusal to make significant cuts in most major domestic programs have created the worst deficits in American history.... People around the country seem to understand what no one in Washington will admit: the budget is out of control."

Yet the Reagan reality is more admirable than the myth. He wisely chose what was historically necessary—large defense increases and tax reductions—over what was politically unattainable—a massive rollback of government. Then, as now, spending increased, deficits expanded, and America experienced some of the most vigorous economic growth in our history. Reagan employed a harsher anti-government rhetoric than

Bush, but their records on spending are similar. Those who criticize President Bush on this basis should also criticize President Reagan. Neither man deserves such criticism.

In reality, the objections of many conservatives to President Bush have little to do with the level of spending, and everything to do with their conception of the role of government. They are correct that Bush is not an anti-government conservative. They are wrong to call him a liberal. Surprisingly, the key to understanding the domestic policy of this evangelical president can be found in the teachings of the Church of Rome.

Anti-government conservatives are attempting to set before the Republican Party a stark choice, but a false choice. On one side, they assert, is statism, the accumulation of coercive governmental power. This coercion in the economic realm amounts to liberalism. And some argue that the use of government to reinforce moral traditions amounts to "theocracy" (a charge that covers everything from defending unborn life to preserving thousands of years of traditional practice on marriage). On the other side, they argue, is the philosophy of freedom, reduced to a single principle of unrestricted individual economic and social choice. True conservatives, they argue, will choose freedom. Anything else ... anything less ... is a betrayal of "limited government."

But this formulation completely ignores the other main intellectual tradition in American politics. There *are* two belief systems contending for the soul of the Republican Party, but one is not the straw man of liberalism (much less the imaginary monster of theocracy). The two intellectually vital movements within the Republican Party today are libertarianism and Roman Catholic social thought.

I am not a Catholic, for a variety of theological reasons. But I recognize that my own theological tradition, just emerging from decades of cultural isolation and anti-intellectualism, has not developed a compelling philosophy of public engagement. The Catholic Church, after a history of suspicion toward democracy, has become its most insightful defender in the modern world—and its most courageous defender, given the Cold War leadership of Pope John Paul II. Catholic teaching on these issues does not require assent to Catholic theological distinctives; it summarizes the best of the Christian tradition, and is addressed to all people of goodwill.

This tradition begins with a principle called "subsidiarity," the belief that human needs are best served by the institutions closest to human beings: strong families, religious congregations, charitable groups, local unions, civic associations, the whole complex web of community. These institutions are important because they are the setting in which naturally selfish individuals learn to care for and take responsibility for the young, the weak, and the poor. These institutions are also real—meaning that the family and church, for example, are not created by individual consent or by the decrees of the state; they are part of a divinely created order. Government has a duty to respect these institutions, rather than undermine them, because their health is essential to the justice of society.

This is a form of limited government. The Catholic Catechism says: "The principle of subsidiarity sets limits for state intervention." It rules out every form of totalitarianism, religious or secular. Larger communities, such as state and federal governments, must respect and promote smaller communities. But responsibility runs the other way as well. When smaller communities fall short or fail in serving the common good, larger communities have a duty to intervene. So, for example, when state governments trample individual rights with Jim Crow laws, the federal government has a responsibility to overturn those laws and enforce legal equality. Education is properly a local responsibility, but when poor children are consistently betrayed by local schools that refuse to reform, state and federal intervention is required. When communities are overwhelmed by national disaster or economic depression, government has a responsibility to help. The role of the state is both narrow and noble.

Subsidiarity is fully consistent with the philosophy of the American Founding, and clearly draws upon it. The more clear-eyed and conservative founders, such as Washington and Adams, believed that a people without internal moral restraint could not govern themselves for long. And these civic virtues were learned in a variety of institutions. Families teach manners and self-restraint. Religious congregations provide instruction in compassion and the moral virtues. Participation in the community encourages public spirit and patriotism. All these elements of civil society were seen as schools of responsible citizenship. The founders were well aware of the central paradox of democracy: the strength of liberal political institutions—institutions characterized by autonomy and free choice—depend on the health of illiberal social institutions—communities that teach moral rules and obedience.

There is, however, one more element of Roman Catholic social teaching that takes a large step beyond traditional conservatism: a principle called "solidarity." In this belief, the justice of any society is measured by the treatment and status of the weak and the oppressed. "As a disciple of Jesus," the Catechism states, "we are called to become neighbors to everyone, and to show special favor to those who are the poorest, most alone, and most in need." An impartial rule of law—equal legal treatment for everyone—is not enough to guarantee justice. Instead, we have a positive obligation to order society in a way that benefits the powerless and suffering. Hebrew law made special provision for the destitute (requiring, for example, a portion of crops to be left in the field, so they could be gathered by the poor). The Hebrew prophets raucously confronted the political and economic exploitation of the poor. And Jesus of Nazareth took this tradition even further, asserting that when we reject the homeless, weak, and hungry, we have rejected Him.

This is a startling teaching: that poverty and sickness are the guises of God. And this emphasis on the rights of the weak is the great contribution of Judaism and Christianity to the politics of the West. The Roman world had a highly developed system of legal justice for male citizens, but children, women, and slaves had little worth. Christian belief put a heavy hand on the other side of the scale. Early Christians criticized the routine Roman practice of infanticide—the main form of birth control in antiquity, in which infants were placed (the saying went) "in the mouth of a dog." Others, such as Gregory of Nyssa, offered unprecedented criticisms of slavery. All Christians were supposed to practice charity to strangers—a revolutionary idea at the time (and in every time).

These principles—subsidiarity and solidarity with the poor and weak—do not fit comfortably within any of the political traditions of our day. American liberals tend to be enthusiastic about solidarity (at least for the poor), but dismissive of subsidiarity—often turning first to federal power and bureaucratic control, and showing a distrust for the traditional family and enthusiastic religion. Traditional conservatives tend to embrace subsidiarity, but remain suspicious of solidarity, which sounds ambitious, radical, and liberal. Libertarian conservatives reject both principles in favor of unrestricted individual rights—any idea of the common good is viewed as a dangerous myth. Surely it must be possible to escape these barren alternatives and combine a conservative respect for value-creating institutions with a radical, active concern for the poor and oppressed. This has always seemed to me a proposition worth testing.

Has the Bush administration tested that proposition? In one way, the question is unfair. This religiously informed view of social justice is a prophetic vision, not a policy agenda. Jesus taught a radical concern for the poor and weak; but He didn't announce a legislative "contract with the Roman Empire." No political platform will perfectly embody a Christian vision of social justice, because religious people (and those who come to the same goals through different convictions) always will disagree on the best methods to achieve it. Are the poor best served by new social spending or tax cuts that stimulate economic growth? Probably some of both, in proportions that will be endlessly debated. A belief in social justice sets a destination; the path is determined by facts and circumstances.

But it is fair to say that the initial Bush agenda was inspired, at least in part, by Catholic social teaching. It was my primary intellectual influence (on domestic issues, many evangelicals have effectively accepted a Catholicism without rosaries). It fit the president's policy instincts. And it shaped some of the most important policy statements during my time in the White House. The clearest evidence can be found in both inaugural addresses, usually the most careful and formal presentations of a president's basic philosophy. In the first inaugural: "The grandest of these ideals is an unfolding American promise that everyone belongs, that everyone deserves a chance, that no insignificant person was ever born." That is solidarity. In the second inaugural: "Self-government relies, in the end, on the governing of the self. That edifice of character is built on families, supported by communities with standards, and sustained in our national life by the truths of Sinai, the Sermon on the Mount, the words of the Koran, and the varied faiths of our people." That is subsidiarity. These references were intentional.

Judged by the aspirations set out in these speeches, the Bush administration had some successes … some mixed results … and at least one clear failure.

Apart from education reform, prescription drugs, and global initiatives on disease and development, one of the largest successes, in my view, concerned the issue of human life. President Bush signed legislation to end partial-birth abortion—a procedure the late Senator Daniel Patrick Moynihan called "as close to infanticide as anything I have come upon." Bush signed the Born Alive Infants Protection Act, which protects the lives of children who survive an abortion procedure. And the greatest test came on the most difficult possible issue. Early in the president's term, scientists talked excitedly about the eventual use of human stem cells to treat diseases like Parkinson's, Alzheimer's, and spinal cord injuries (a promise that is real but distant, and often oversold). And one of the sources of those cells is human embryos, which must be destroyed to harvest the useful material. Scientists wanted public funds to conduct their research initially on "spare" embryos produced during in vitro fertilization. But this line or limit was unlikely to hold: the most convenient and useful source of cells is likely to be cloned embryos, produced in the laboratory in order to be destroyed. The political calculation was simple enough. At this early stage of development, human life is at its least recognizable, and gains the least emotional sympathy (there are seldom funerals for an early miscarriage). Embryos have few advocates and no votes; adults with diseases have both.

But President Bush, after a careful scientific review, rejected the obvious political course, and made two points. First, though human embryos do not look like us, they are distinct from the mother, biologically human, and have the capacity to develop into a child. This makes them different from the cells of a hangnail or a tumor. At what point does this developing human life deserve protection? When neurological activity develops? When the fetus can feel pain? When a child is born? When an infant can think and reason? All these "achievements" are, in fact, scientifically and ethically arbitrary—they don't mark the start of a new life, just the development of an existing life. Second, the president went on to draw a bright ethical line in a debate filled with mists and fogs: in a just society, he said, "We do not end some lives for the medical benefit of others."

The practical effect of the president's stem-cell policy was limited. The government would not cut off private stem-cell research, but it would only fund public research using existing stem-cell lines. It would not fund research based on the destruction of new embryos. This has given time for research to move forward on more ethically defensible sources of stem cells, taken from adult cells, umbilical cords, and placenta. The more dramatic effect of this approach has been in the realm of ideas. The president introduced a large philosophic debate into a political argument. He rejected utilitarianism—the belief that morality consists of doing the greatest good for the greatest number. This ethical system sounds appealing and democratic. Why shouldn't the interests of a few be sacrificed for the health and happiness of millions? But there is a problem with this creed: it does away with the Jewish and Christian view of human rights and dignity. In utilitarianism, no action is forbidden, no matter how cruel, if it will reduce the net amount of suffering in the world.

The most rigorous and consistent defender of this view is Peter Singer of Princeton University. "When the death of a disabled infant," he argues, "will lead to the birth of another infant with better prospects of a happy life, the total amount of happiness will be greater if the disabled infant is killed." Infants with hemophilia and Down syndrome, according to Singer, can be destroyed. Parents should be permitted to produce a child, then kill them to implant their organs in an older sibling. Singer approves of organ farming, in which children are bred for medical spare parts on a large scale. These are the logical consequences of abandoning a belief in the sacredness of human life—of making life a means to other social ends: Lethal discrimination against the handicapped. Contempt for deformity. The transformation of life into a tool, a resource, a commodity. What begins as an attempt to relieve suffering ends with the abolition of man.

Medical ethics untethered to human rights is a frightening thing—and will only grow more frightening as our genetic control increases. By rejecting a cold, utilitarian vision, President Bush affirmed the principle of solidarity—the belief that the powerless are not expendable in the interests of the strong. Human life, he argued, is an endowment, not an achievement. And this is really another way of asserting that all men are created equal. Protecting the weak—loving and caring for people who don't look like us or share our achievements—is the price of believing in equality. "Equality," says ethicist Eric Cohen, "often requires heroism— the heroic sacrifice of the caregiver and the heroic courage of the patient, who see the other as equal to themselves, even when the equality of the other is hardly obvious and the suffering of the self is very great."

Another success on the domestic agenda concerns judges, particularly Supreme Court justices. Grasping, arrogant judges who use their power to impose their personal views are a threat to constitutional government. They have abolished legal protections for unborn children, and undermined the authority of states, communities, and traditional institutions. And this arrogance leads to acrimony—because people are more likely to accept controversial decisions when they are the product of democratic self-government, instead of being imposed by courts from on high. Resentment of liberal judicial activism unites conservatives of most backgrounds. But even here, some have attempted to attack President Bush. One conservative writer complains: "Reagan's oft-repeated vision of limited constitutional government played an important role in putting Chief Justice John Roberts and Justice Samuel Alito on their path to the Supreme Court. It is far from clear that Bush will inspire the next generation of conservative jurists to take their place." Accusations like these combine dishonesty and comedy. It is, of course, President Bush who appointed Roberts and Alito. President Reagan, in contrast, was responsible for Sandra Day O'Connor and Anthony Kennedy, hardly conservative heroes. At some point, Reagan worship descends into silliness.

On another major domestic emphasis of the Bush administration—the faith-based agenda—the outcome has been mixed. I have a long-term interest in these issues. While working for Prison Fellowship Ministries, I saw how faith could turn violent criminals into responsible citizens, while government approaches to rehabilitation seldom had much effect. While working on Capitol Hill, I visited effective volunteer efforts around the country. At a public elementary school in one of the poorest areas of South Philadelphia, I talked with senior citizens who came in several times a week to befriend and mentor the children, with the government (through Senior Corps) paying for their bus fare. One of their roles was to teach games like hopscotch. No one had ever taken the time to show the children organized play, so they fought continually on the playground. Another role was to celebrate birthdays for the children, who often had no celebration at home. As a father of two boys, I could hardly imagine the message of worthlessness communicated to a child if their birthday caused no one in the world to rejoice.

On one hand, conservative criticisms of welfare programs are often correct. On complex human challenges like addiction, homelessness, and the moral choices of youth, government bureaucracies are blunt and ineffective instruments. "Take a number and wait" compassion has little to offer men, women, and children in spiritual and emotional crisis. Sometimes the most urgent human need is for love and concern, and here community and religious institutions—staffed by compassionate and idealistic volunteers—have a comparative advantage. On the other hand, these efforts, particularly in our cities, are not equal to the scale of the need. Religious charities in the inner city are often overwhelmed, and based in churches with limited funds. And the question naturally arises: can government increase the scale of these private efforts, without changing the distinctives that make them so effective?

The president's faith-based initiative involved a shift, not a revolution. Since the Great Society and before, federal social spending has gone to large, faith-based groups like Catholic Charities, Lutheran Social Services, and Jewish Federations. President Bush set out to encourage greater funding for smaller, community-based charities, often based in African American and Hispanic churches. (In one survey, two-thirds of African American churches expressed an interest in public funding for their social services, compared to about a quarter of predominantly white churches.) The legal basis for this spending is clear and relatively non-controversial: government funding can be provided to religious groups to achieve legitimate public purposes, but it can't be used for proselytization or worship services. And those who take the money need to provide services without discrimination, to people of every religious background. This strong, constitutional consensus was embodied in several bills, known as Charitable Choice, signed by President Bill Clinton—an approach later supported by Senator Hillary Clinton.

This is applied subsidiarity. As President Bush put it: "In every instance where my administration sees a responsibility to help people, we will look first to faith-based organizations, charities, and community groups."

Over the years, the faith-based office at the White House sponsored a series of well-attended conferences to teach small charities the basics of applying for public money—Grant Making 101. Some have alleged a political motive for this outreach, but most who attended—social-service providers and inner-city pastors—would not have voted for the president in a million years. The administration focused periodically on tax incentives to promote charitable giving, eventually passing provisions that encourage food-bank donations, and the rollover of IRAs for charitable purposes. Through executive orders, the president created faith-based offices in most federal departments, and leveled the playing field on contracting, so religious groups could apply for funding on the same basis as secular ones. And every State of the Union included specific initiatives focused on the most intractable social problems: mentoring the children of prisoners, fighting domestic AIDS, confronting the problem of youth gangs.

These are successes. But the ambitions of the faith-based initiative were consistently limited by two factors. First, the Republican leadership of Congress was almost completely uninterested. Some, according to the first White House faith-based director, John DiIulio, didn't want to spend any money on the effort. Others, such as Congressman Dick Armey, thought it sounded like a Democratic idea. After grudgingly accepting the new spending in No Child Left Behind, conservatives on the Hill had little appetite for more spending on the poor. The tax-writing committees of Congress, run by Congressman Bill Thomas and Senator Charles Grassley, insisted that charitable incentives have offsets and be as small as possible. Eventually, according to Jim Towey, the second faith-based director, Tom Delay and Dick Armey would not even meet with him to talk about strategy—because they had no intention of making this issue a priority. At the same time, other conservatives on the Hill wanted to pick a fight about homosexuality, proposing unnecessary legislation that would permit religious institutions to hire and fire according to their religious beliefs (a right they already have under the Civil Rights Act of 1964). This had the effect of turning a bipartisan effort to help the poor into a culture war debate—exactly what some intended.

Second, the lack of congressional enthusiasm was often reflected in the West Wing. White House Legislative Affairs—the people who pushed for our agenda on Capitol Hill—tended to report congressional indifference as an unchangeable fact, instead of challenging it. And some in the White House did not share the president's vision. In the run-up to the 2004 State of the Union, one staff-level policy discussion focused on the prisoner reentry initiative—an effort to help released prisoners find jobs and make the transition back to a productive life. A representative of the vice president's office complained: "Who cares about these prisoners when we have law-abiding people looking for jobs?" And no one, other than the faith-based director Jim Towey, would speak up for the idea. Again, the proposal was only saved by Jim's direct appeal to the president, who personally intervened to revive it.

When asked about his legacy, the president always mentions two issues: the democracy agenda, and the faith-based initiative. He is deeply committed to the idea of helping the poor through community and faith-based institutions. It is a defining part of his idealism. But on domestic policy, a president's powers are limited by the Congress—and the party of Tom Delay and Dick Armey had no intention of making compassion for the poor a major focus. Even at the White House the number of compassionate conservatives was always small, and they had little influence in the Office of Management and Budget and the National Economic Council—the institutions charged with formulating and implementing the president's vision. The faith-based initiative was not tried and found wanting. It was tried and found difficult—then tried with less and less energy.

But even this mixed record is likely to have lasting importance. The president has put a concept into wide usage that will not go away, because the irreplaceable contributions of community and religious groups are not going away. Over forty governors, Republican and Democrat, now have faith-based offices, along with hundreds of mayors. The culture of government is clearly shifting, welcoming religious charities as allies instead of resenting them as rivals. And it is worth noting that the Katrina Recovery Act included charitable choice, because faith-based institutions were the heroes of a tragedy with few heroes.

At first, on Sunday, August 28, 2005, Hurricane Katrina seemed like a glancing blow; New Orleans appeared to dodge the bullet. Then on Monday morning the levees gave way ... the water took just seventeen minutes to reach far into the city ... the electricity went out, and the panic began. Faith-based groups and the Coast Guard distinguished themselves by throwing away the normal procedures and doing what needed to be done—rescuing the stranded and providing shelter to the homeless. The government response was a failure at nearly every level. The city's plan was incoherent, herding evacuees into the Superdome. State officials were unprepared, squabbling, and incompetent; the state National Guard was two days late. The federal reaction was sluggish and uninspired. Over the next few days, it became clear that FEMA—the

Federal Emergency Management Agency—was unequal to the task. The Department of Homeland Security, created to deal with terrorists, had little skill or sensitivity dealing with confused people who had lost all their possessions. And the White House staff seemed overwhelmed by a thousand operational decisions that prevented the exercise of decisive leadership.

The president, with his background as a governor who had dealt with hurricanes, was forced to micromanage a dysfunctional process. In meetings, he asked a series of obvious questions: "Where are people going to cash the checks we give them?" "Who is going to provide case management for people who are confused?" "How are we going to take care of mortuary services?" "When people come back, where are they going to get health care?" Officials from various departments had few answers; often the answers they gave were contradicted the following day.

But the primary failure of Katrina was not in the management of details. It was a failure of urgency and imagination from the very beginning. This was not a normal hurricane, with houses blown down and rebuilt. Because of the flood, this was a massive logistics and security operation, involving food distribution, the maintenance of public order, and long-term evacuations—more like a nuclear or biological attack than a storm. FEMA is incapable of dealing with a crisis on this scale, even with the best leadership; it is actually a small organization that expands through contracting in time of need. There is only one part of the US government capable of logistics and response on the scale of Katrina: the military. The possibility of military involvement was raised early in the crisis. Andy Card supported it. But Secretary Rumsfeld resisted, raising concerns about the legal status of the troops, and arguing that the TV coverage of the crisis was overblown. There was some truth to his point—media outlets had run with rumors and complicated the rescue by frightening bus drivers away from the Superdome. Yet the fact remained that 85 percent of New Orleans was under water.

The crisis was not exaggerated; it was unprecedented. But the federal response, in the end, was conventional.

This disaster was different. The state and locals were incompetent. FEMA wasn't up to the job. We needed the military to take over immediately. But no one, to my knowledge, came to the president and said that the job was too large for them. People want to tell the president of the United States, "We are ready." But they could not have been ready for this.

In this period, I traveled with the president on Air Force One to visit Louisiana and Mississippi. Jim Towey, the faith-based director, was concerned that the president had not spent enough time with African American victims of the storm. So we were headed to a church in Baton Rouge that was sheltering hundreds of people, accompanied by the great African American preacher T. D. Jakes. The motorcade passed fallen church steeples and downed trees, and came to a church gymnasium packed with cots. The reception was interesting. Usually the president is the center of attention, and he was politely received that day. But the real celebrity in this crowd was Pastor T. D. Jakes. So many wanted to touch him, or have him talk to relatives on their cell phone. A disaster like Katrina is as much a spiritual as a physical crisis. People need to hear: "I'm sorry all your photographs were destroyed" and "God has some plan for you." I remember a little girl fighting boredom, playing with blocks on the floor. A 101-year-old woman in a wheelchair, confused by the loss of everything familiar. A man who had driven to Houston, slept at rest stops, and come back to Louisiana because he had no place else to go. He told me, "Something good will come out of all this."

It was my hope, as well. I hoped that Katrina would force the American political class to confront extreme poverty and racial injustice in the shadow of our affluence. I hoped the president's speech at Jackson Square on September 15 could begin serious national dialogue on race and poverty. Those hopes were disappointed.

In giving out benefits, the administration had discovered men and women who had never had a bank account—completely disconnected from the mainstream economy. People who had never flown in an airplane. People who couldn't evacuate because they had no means of transportation. At Jackson Square, the president told the nation: "That poverty has roots in a history of discrimination, which cut off generations from the opportunity of America. We have a duty to confront this poverty with bold action. So let us restore all we have cherished from yesterday, and let us rise above the legacy of inequality." That evening, the president proposed a Gulf Opportunity Zone to promote entrepreneurship in the region; worker recovery accounts to pay for job training; an Urban Homesteading Act, which would allow the building of homes on deserted federal property. Even these modest initiatives had been internally controversial—with the vice president's office again throwing up roadblocks of skepticism and the president again overruling those objections. But however modest, these proposals seemed a start, a down payment on larger ambitions.

Yet the Jackson Square Speech became, for me, a lesson in the limited power of words. Some of the proposals passed. Billions flowed to the region for reconstruction. But a serious effort to confront the poverty and inequality revealed by the storm died for lack of interest. After Katrina, national Democrats were focused almost entirely on the apportionment of blame. Congressional Republicans were focused almost entirely on the cost of the recovery. The Republican Study Committee used Katrina to announce "Operation Offset," which proposed cuts in foreign assistance, in subsidized student loans, in anti-drug education, and a postponing of prescription-drug coverage for the elderly. With hundreds of thousands of the poor still homeless and desperate, it was difficult for me to understand how this "operation" could be considered the most urgent. The storm had also revealed a political and moral chasm in the Republican Party. The president and I saw Katrina as an opportunity to open a debate on race and poverty. Anti-government

Republicans saw Katrina as an opportunity to cut off medicine to old people. It confirmed the worst image of Republicans as the party of shriveled hearts.

But Katrina also left its mark on the Bush administration. Along with events in Iraq, Katrina raised questions of competence, and added momentum to a serious slide in public support. And the initial failures alienated many of the African American leaders who had previously worked with the administration on the faith-based initiative. The boldness and leadership of 9/11 had not been matched on another day of disaster—and the price was high.

In 1999, with the innocence required at the start of all great enterprises, President Bush set out not just to lead the Republican Party, but to transform it. He defined a series of traditionally liberal goals: better education for minority children, help for addicts and the homeless, prescription drugs for the elderly. And he proposed to meet those liberal goals through conservative means: the empowerment of individuals and communities. This, in his view, required a strong, energetic executive to break up existing bureaucratic arrangements—the use of federal power to push power beyond government. And this willingness to use executive power put him at odds with some in the Republican Party whose governing agenda is to reject governing.

As a candidate in the 1964 election, Senator Barry Goldwater had said that he had little interest in reforming government "for I mean to reduce its size." President Bush knew that Americans did not seek or desire to undo the Great Society, much less the New Deal. So he had a large interest in reforming government. His guiding objective was not to make it bigger or smaller, but more effective. This approach achieved more than it is given credit for—and less than it intended. Education reform and prescription drugs are genuine accomplishments. The faith-based initiative raised an issue that all future presidents will need to address. And the president counts more legislative accomplishments on the pro-life agenda than any of his predecessors. I found his commitment to build a culture of life courageous, particularly when it was politically costly.

But events conspired to overshadow and undermine these domestic achievements. The agenda of any administration is determined by a shockingly small number of people at the top of the pyramid of executive authority—perhaps half a dozen decision makers. Their attention and energy are finite, and the conduct of a global war consumes both. After 9/11, President Bush defined his personal mission in terms of the War on Terror. In interviews, or the State of the Union, it was clear that his emotional intensity would rise on international issues, and fall on domestic ones. And this personal tendency was reinforced by a constitutional reality: on foreign policy, the president has a relatively free hand; on domestic policy, he is bound by 535 congressional cords. I found this same dynamic in my own writing. Speeches on Social Security or the economy were generally factual, complicated, and dull. Speeches on Iraq and the War on Terror were opportunities for Churchillian resolve and moral purpose.

Other factors slowed the domestic momentum of the Bush administration. By late 2005, much of the innovative agenda Bush had passionately advocated in 1999 was either passed (education and Medicare reform); defeated (Social Security); or smothered by congressional indifference (faith-based initiatives). The domestic-policy shop at the White House did little to replenish that agenda with issues that engaged the moral passions of the president. And the budgetary situation made that job difficult. Iraq and Katrina required enormous resources, eventually leaving budgets strained, and those who wrote them deeply skeptical of domestic spending. In the policy process leading up to the 2006 State of the Union, I advocated two compassion initiatives. One was a domestic AIDS proposal, which set the goal of ending new infections in America in five years through education, broader testing, and the work of faith-based groups. The other was an initiative to help vulnerable children, particularly runaways who often end up in the sex trade. It was a very limited agenda, requiring perhaps 300 or 400 million dollars a year (not much in a 2.8 trillion dollar budget). But the Office of Management and Budget objected to both proposals. A smaller version of the domestic AIDS initiative was eventually included in the State of the Union, but I felt increasingly frustrated by budgetary constraints that made creativity on the domestic agenda nearly impossible.

It was the war in Iraq, however, that most directly undermined the president's attempt to redefine the ideology of the Republican Party. If Iraq had gone well, the president could have been a colossus in American politics, and dissent within his party would certainly have been muted by his success (as it was in the months after 9/11). Under these circumstances, no one would have questioned that President Bush was a transformative figure, a Republican Roosevelt. But as Iraq became more messy and complicated, the worst elements of the Republican Party felt liberated by the president's political weakness. The advocates of isolationism, nativism, and a libertarian indifference to the poor were emboldened. And some Republicans in Congress eventually blamed the president's "reckless spending" for the midterm defeats of 2006—conveniently forgetting that more than fifteen Republican members of Congress had been implicated in sexual and financial scandals. Americans generally change control of Congress when its leadership appears corrupt and arrogant—and by that standard it is difficult to argue with the judgment of the American people in 2006.

Many conservatives argue it is necessary to move "beyond" Bush's domestic policy when they are really recommending a return to the conservatism of the 1990s—the era in which leaders like Newt Gingrich, Tom Delay, Dick Armey, and Senator Phil Gramm controlled the message of the movement. Their stewardship was not a pretty sight. Dick Armey declared Medicare—a life-and-death matter for many of the poor—"a program I would have no part of in a free world." Phil Gramm proposed to eliminate all federal education programs. And when Republicans forced a shutdown of the federal government in 1995, Gramm appeared on television saying, "Have you missed the government? Doesn't it strike you as funny that … large sections of the government are shut down?" It did not, in fact, strike most Americans as funny that parks were closed, Medicare claims were not processed, and federal workers were not paid. A justified critique of government excess became an unbalanced hostility to government itself. And anti-government conspiracy theories—from Ruby Ridge to the suicide of Vince Foster—flourished in this toxic atmosphere. Republican anti-government extremism allowed President Clinton—even when politically wounded and bleeding—to outmaneuver Republican leaders at every turn.

It turns out that most Americans, and most conservatives, do not hate their government. They tend to agree with Ben Franklin that the strength of the nation depends "on the general opinion of the goodness of government." And this was one of the main reasons that Republicans turned to George W. Bush with such hope and enthusiasm in the late 1990s—because he was a direct contrast to shut-government-down Republicanism. Bush was a successful governor who had reformed government, not disdained it. Unlike members of Congress from gerrymandered districts in which nearly everyone looks and thinks like them, Governor Bush had appealed to Hispanics and other minorities with policies that took their lives and interests into account. He combined a moral conservatism with a social conscience, and this appealed to millions of Americans who care for the unborn for the same moral reasons they care for the poor. In 2000, Bush saved the Republican Party from itself—and his message brought political success for Republicans in 2002 and 2004. The political complications flowing from Iraq do not change a basic political reality: no presidential candidate can win without a message of solidarity, a vision of justice, and hope that includes the whole country.

That hope is not a false one. In the 1980s it was fashionable for conservatives to claim that all social policy was doomed by the "law of unintended consequences." Idealism and government activism, in this view, are counterproductive, because they usually leave the situation worse than they found it. And this skepticism became an excuse for paralysis. When welfare reform was proposed in the mid-1990s, a number of conservatives actually opposed it, arguing that the poor are incapable of work because they lack the habits and self-discipline necessary to hold a job. This is a traditional conservative temptation: cultural determinism, combined with disdain for the poor. Likewise, many conservatives argued that crime in America would only grow worse, as values and families disintegrated in an inalterable cultural decline.

But an odd thing happened on the way to American cultural collapse. Welfare reform that required work had a dramatic effect. In less than a decade, welfare rolls were reduced by 60 percent … women went to work and earned more money than they had on welfare … and rates of child poverty went down, hitting all-time lows for African American children. Most of the poor were fully capable of making responsible decisions when the welfare system no longer sent mixed messages on the need for work and self-sufficiency. The same story can be told on the issue of crime. Government policies that restored basic order to communities and imprisoned dangerous and repeat offenders for longer terms had a swift and powerful influence. In the course of a decade, violent crime in America reached the lowest levels in the history of the federal survey … similar reductions were recorded in property crime … and schools became as safe as they had been four decades before. Progress also has been made in the last decade on providing health insurance to poor children and teaching reading to minority students.

Republicans should draw some lessons from this revival of social policy: Progress can come faster than many conservatives think possible, and unintended consequences can sometimes be better than we expect.

Effective, well-designed public policies can serve the common good, and make our country stronger and more just. Human beings, even in the most difficult social circumstances, can rise to expectations. American society and culture are more resilient than some imagined. And all these lessons confirm a greater lesson: pessimism is an easy pose; hope is a moral virtue.

A retreat from hope and idealism would be a political disaster for Republicans, and leave a flawed Democratic ideology uncontested in addressing the social challenges of our time. Republicans need a positive, active agenda on health care, and racial healing, and the economic empowerment of the poor, and the fight against global disease, and the struggles of disadvantaged youth, and energy independence, and a humane bioethics. Without this agenda, the Republicans Party will fade into irrelevance, and deserve its decline.

Carrying this message in the Republican Party, or any party, is not easy, and no one promised it would be. Indifference and ideological hostility are large obstacles. And even the best intentions of a president can be frustrated by events, and undercut by political allies. But retreat and disillusionment are signs of political adolescence, not options for adults. Societies are naturally ruled by narrow and personal interests. Those interests—from slavery, to segregation, to the economic exploitation of the poor, to biomedical horrors—are never overcome by skepticism, weariness, and disillusionment. They are only overcome through passion, idealism, and persistence. And these are the virtues for which conservatism can be known.

Chapter 7

Has Iraq Killed Idealism?

On April 30, 2003—twenty-one days after the toppling of the Stalin-like statue of Saddam Hussein and the end of his Stalin-like rule—I approached the USS *Abraham Lincoln* by transport plane, facing backward, strapped in tightly and anxious about my first landing on an aircraft carrier. Along with National Security Advisor Condi Rice, Press Secretary Ari Fleisher, Karl Rove, and other members of the senior staff, I was to arrive on the *Lincoln*—then sailing about sixty miles off the coast of San Diego—before the president landed in a S–3B Viking jet. The men and women of the crew were nearly home after a ten-month deployment in the Afghan and Iraq campaigns, during which they had launched and landed aircraft 12,700 times without a mishap, and dropped 1.6 million tons of ordnance on the enemy. The president was coming to the ship to thank the troops in a victory speech, and the setting was too dramatic for me to miss. As we touched the deck, the jolt of the tail-hook landing came like an injection—a sharp prick, quickly over.

In the days since the fall of Baghdad, my overwhelming emotion had been one of relief. None of the predicted horrors had come to pass—no bloody siege of Baghdad; no dams destroyed and no massive flooding; no burning oil fields; no refugee crisis; no use of chemical weapons against our troops (a serious possibility, General Franks had warned). It was like being a patient told that the tests are negative, or that the lump is benign. We had, it seemed, been spared the worst, and I felt not giddy, but grateful.

We watched the president's jet land on the deck—as a former National Guard pilot, he had flown about a third of the way himself—then President Bush emerging from the cockpit in his flight suit. Given later complications in Iraq, the *Lincoln* visit has been dismissed as an unseemly stunt. But to the military, this event was significant. I saw the reaction of the sailors, who view their commander in chief as a cross between pope and rock star. Their pride at his presence was moving. "It's like when you thought everybody forgot about you," one said. "He came out here and made everything better because he didn't forget."

After being settled in our cabins, the staff was given a briefing on the *Lincoln*'s recent combat operations. We were shown grainy video footage of jets landing in a dust storm so thick that the deck was invisible until the wheels were just feet off the surface—a breathtaking act of skill and faith. We talked to the pilots—including professional and idealistic women who melted my skepticism about women serving in this combat role. Then we climbed down ladder after ladder into the depths of the massive ship, put on protective gear, passed thick containment doors, and entered the nuclear power generator. Through a periscope, we could see the rods in the reactor itself. Peering into the core, Condi commented to the rest of us: "Those are what the North Koreans have."

After the official tour, a young officer asked me if I wanted to take the real tour later on. During four or five hours after dinner—taking much of the night—we walked the 4.5 acre flight deck in a blue glow of stars, and climbed and crawled through most of the ship. In the mess, I was told that for months the only meat the crew had been served was chicken. "When I get home," the officer said, "I'm never eating chicken again, unless it's homemade or Hooters." I asked young sailors about the sexual tension on a coed ship, and was told, "Everyone knows where to go if you want privacy." I talked to the doctors on duty in the medical center, who cheerfully related horror stories of sailors (on other ships) cut in half by flying cables on the flight deck; most military people take macabre pride in the danger of their work. The *Lincoln* seemed to me a microcosm of the military: officers of great skill and surprising gentleness, enlisted men performing repetitive and risky duties, hormone-driven teenagers anxious for the comforts of home— all volunteers, bound together by an oath, intense training, and a sense of honor, and forged into the most lethal fighting force in human history.

Contrary to claims in the press, no draft of the president's *Lincoln* remarks, from first to last, contained the phrase "mission accomplished." That was found only on a banner, raised by the White House advance team in consultation with the crew. The sailors of the *Lincoln* had, indeed, accomplished their own mission. But the banner, though plainly at odds with the speech itself, was easily misinterpreted. The draft went on to say: "We have difficult work to do in Iraq. We're bringing order to parts of that country that remain dangerous. We're pursuing and finding leaders of the old regime, who will be held to account for their crimes. We've begun the search for hidden chemical and biological weapons and already know of hundreds of sites that will be investigated." In short, the *Lincoln* speech set out a series of missions that had yet to be accomplished—pacifying the country, finding Saddam, discovering WMD stockpiles. All would prove to be more difficult than I imagined.

The setting *was* extraordinary. The president walked through silent rows of sailors to a podium on the flight deck under a clear sky, surrounded to every horizon by the Pacific Ocean—a massive stage of limitless blue. But it is not the setting I remember most; it is the oddly prophetic quality of the speech itself. "In the images of falling statues," the president said, "we have witnessed the arrival of a new era. In defeating Nazi Germany and Imperial Japan, Allied forces destroyed entire cities, while enemy leaders who started the conflict were safe until the final days. Military power was used to end a regime by breaking a nation. Today, we have the greater power to free a nation by breaking a dangerous and aggressive regime. With new tactics and precision weapons, we can achieve military objectives without directing violence against civilians. No device of man can remove the tragedy from war; yet it is a great moral advance when the guilty have far more to fear from war than the innocent."

The conduct of the Iraq War—the extraordinary care taken to minimize civilian casualties—was indeed a moral advance. But precisely because the center of the regime collapsed so quickly, many hardened Baathists in Saddam's military and intelligence forces were not destroyed in battle. They removed their uniforms and melted away, only to reemerge in time. The region of Saddam's birthplace and his stronghold, known as the Sunni or Baathist Triangle, never tasted the total defeat that Japan and Germany experienced—the kind of defeat that deflates resistance.

The president went on to say: "Other nations in history have fought in foreign lands and remained to occupy and exploit. Americans, following a battle, want nothing more than to return home." This also was predictive. From the beginning, the plan was to liberate Iraq and to leave as soon as possible. America did not want the duties of an occupier. But some of those duties—particularly the establishment of security and order—turn out to be necessary in order for a liberator to return home.

Less than one year later, on Thursday, April 8, 2004, a few days before Easter, the full crisis of Iraq was breaking over us. American casualties had spiked in urban combat with Sunni insurgents in Fallujah, west of Baghdad. Shiite militias loyal to Muqtada al Sadr had taken control of two regional capitals.

After the senior staff meeting that morning, Andy Card pulled Dan Bartlett and me into his office. A major Shiite holiday called Arba'een, he said, was about to begin, and hundreds of thousands of people were gathering at Iraq's major Shia shrines. At least three groups had an interest in promoting chaos and violence—Muqtada al Sadr's Shia thugs, the Sunni insurgency, and Abu Musab al-Zarqawi's al-Qaeda terrorists. "A bomb that kills 5,000 will look like 50,000 on TV," Andy predicted. America had agreed with the Iraqi Governing Council—an appointed group of Iraqi officials—to allow the Iraqi police and military to provide security for the pilgrimage. But these local forces had little effective leadership. Ultimately, Iraqis expected the US to provide security—and we would be blamed if the worst happened.

Dan pushed for a press conference for early the next week, with a long opening statement that would begin answering some questions: Who is the enemy? Who is supporting them? Why the increase in US casualties? How will we win?

On that day, according to Steve Hadley, we were "on the knife's edge." The Iraqis are a fiercely independent people who wanted freedom and sovereignty, but were not fully confident they would get it. So they were tempted to throw in with demagogues like al Sadr. At this point, al Sadr did not enjoy widespread support among the Shia—only 2 percent identified him as their "most trusted leader." Most of the residents of Najaf—the holy city where al Sadr was based—were impatient with his Mahdi Army. Grand Ayatollah Sistani, the leading Shia cleric in Iraq, strongly opposed al Sadr's influence. As long as the mainstream Shia viewed clashes as a confrontation between al Sadr and the Coalition, they would watch passively. But if they thought the Coalition was attacking the Shia as a whole, the result could be a broader uprising. So it was not possible to intervene with a massive show of force in Najaf— this would offend religious sensitivities. The strategy was to defeat al Sadr's forces everywhere surrounding Najaf—first to isolate the rebel cleric, then to listen if he put out feelers for a political settlement.

All this was complicated by the pilgrimage. If Sunni extremists and terrorists killed Shia pilgrims in large numbers, the Shia might blame the Coalition or seek destabilizing revenge. And this would add to the momentum of existing discontent. The Iraqi population was growing disappointed with what the Coalition had delivered, unhappy with the appointed governing council, disillusioned with the political progress so far, and uncertain about the future. The next few weeks before the scheduled transfer of sovereignty to Iraqis on June 30 would be decisive. Many Iraqis were on the fence—still committed to a political process that crossed ethnic and religious lines but tempted, if that process failed, to throw in with violent groups of their own sectarian background.

The next morning, as I talked with Andy in the Roosevelt Room, the fog of war was thick. Some reports said that Baghdad was quiet. Others said that firefights had continued all night. During a crisis, I found, information at the White House is often no better than the latest cable-news reports. It was clear that fewer Shia pilgrims than predicted had gathered for Arba'een observances—good news. Our troops were massed around Fallujah for decisive action against Sunni insurgents, but a twenty-four-hour cease-fire had been declared to bring in humanitarian aid. Some were concerned that ongoing military operations in Fallujah and Ramadi were stoking anti-Coalition sentiments in Sunni areas, and undermining political moderates in the Sunni community. I began working on the president's opening statement for next week—a grim task on Good Friday.

Coming in to work on the Monday after Easter, however, I found the situation dramatically different. The military operations in Fallujah had not gone forward; it seemed that Sunnis on the governing council had threatened to resign if the assault took place. Instead, Sunni council members were now negotiating with the locals for a return of central authority to the city. A similar shift had taken place in the south. Shia members of the council were talking to al Sadr about a solution short of conflict. The administration had decided to let the governing council do the cease-fires, in order to give them greater legitimacy.

At his press conference the next day, the president performed in typical style. Four or five questioners pressed him to apologize for 9/11, the invasion of Iraq, and nearly every other action he had taken as president. The reporters were hungry for a public expression of self-doubt in the tradition of Jimmy Carter. But Bush was the anti-Carter—firm, passionate, morally clear. "The person responsible for 9/11 was bin Laden," he insisted. To skeptical questions about democracy in Iraq, he replied: "Some people don't think Muslims and people with brown skin can govern themselves." The press was so enraged by his self-confidence that they largely missed the story. Because the president said, several times, "stay the course," they didn't realize that the course had been shifted. On every front, in two short days, the strategy had gone from military confrontation to negotiations, designed to encourage the strength of Iraqi political institutions. Iraqis were put in the lead, in the hope that political progress could calm resentments and lead to better security.

In this situation I also saw how the demands of communication can conflict with the demands of governing. Over that Easter weekend, I had been besieged with e-mails from nervous conservatives, arguing that we were failing to communicate at a key time; that we weren't speaking to "Joe six-pack," who resented the ungrateful Iraqis; that the president was "losing the communications war." One blogger called the president "silent and inarticulate"—though it is hard to be both, at least at the same time. Seen from the president's side, things were not so clear. The Shia pilgrimage could have become a bloody tragedy, then a riot, then an uprising. If the president had spoken at length at that point, his information would have been flawed, and the policies he announced would have dramatically reversed in the next three days. The president actually has a job—and that job is not to be a pundit on cable television, responding to every criticism in an ever-shorter news cycle. His job is to get good information and make informed decisions—and *then* communicate them. And sometimes the problem is not communications at all.

Sometimes the problem is events—like cities in revolt and dying soldiers and images of chaos on TV.

Speeches must attempt to explain why the cost is worth the effort. But sometimes, eroding public support is the result of objective circumstances that must be addressed through policy and action. In the spring of 2004, the objective circumstances were serious and deteriorating, and no speech or press conference could change that fact. The immediate crisis passed—the pilgrimage was orderly—but the problems that caused the crisis had not passed.

What had happened between the *Lincoln* speech and that Easter on the knife's edge? The initial military operations in Iraq rank among the best-executed plans in the history of warfare. American forces charged across 350 miles of hostile ground, grabbed key bridges before they could be destroyed, and took Baghdad before its defenses could be fully prepared. A massive military force, amazingly, achieved tactical surprise. A siege of Baghdad was avoided. The campaign was a swift and humane success, which rightly added to the reputation of the military and its leaders.

But the challenges began to accumulate almost immediately. I saw those events in Iraq from a distance, but I had trusted colleagues and friends who saw them firsthand, serving in the Coalition Provisional Authority, the military, embassy staff, and the Iraq Survey Group. And they describe a series of misfortunes, errors, and failed theories that turned a dramatic success into a long, hard slog.

Some of the problems might be traced to bad luck. A poorly handled vote in the Turkish parliament prevented the Fourth Infantry Division's planned invasion of Iraq from the north. Such a full-scale invasion of the Sunni heartland would likely have killed some of the most determined and dangerous Baathists; but it never took place. The Sunni Triangle—where most insurgent attacks eventually originated—never felt fully conquered by the Coalition, and a portion of Saddam's army and security apparatus quickly reconstituted itself with local support.

Some of the problems could be traced to Saddam Hussein himself. Over the years, he had turned his country into a vast ammunition dump, with countless arms caches in cities and towns all over Iraq. And as the invasion began, Saddam, in a final disservice to his country, opened all of Iraq's prisons. So the Coalition was eventually greeted by a highly weaponized society, and tens of thousands of felons on the loose.

These difficulties were compounded by errors. Coalition forces did little to stop the looting and destruction of Baghdad following the fall of the regime. A friend later told me, "Every night for weeks I stood on the roof of the palace and watched the city burn." Soldiers in Humvees stood by as government buildings were sacked. Buildings were looted down to the tiles on the floor. America did not have enough troops on the ground to halt the chaos, and the troops that were there had no orders to intervene. Many Iraqi families in Baghdad hardly left their homes for months, imprisoned by the fear of violence. This culture of chaos brought out the worst elements of Iraqi society, while responsible citizens learned to lie low. Confronting the looters would not have been easy. Refusing to confront them helped nurture habits of lawlessness and distrust that remain to this day.

In those early days, the Coalition also did not confront al Sadr and the Shia militias (al Sadr's forces only numbered two or three hundred at the time). Soon after the liberation, al Sadr had been involved in the assassination of a moderate Shia cleric, Majid al-Khoei, whom America had brought back from exile in London. An Iraqi judge had indicted al Sadr for the crime, and the British thought the case was strong and tightly constructed. But the military was nervous about the backlash that might result from going after al Sadr, and action wasn't taken. A key moment—a chance to arrest street-level extremism before it gained momentum—was lost.

The disbanding of the Iraqi army has also been cited as an early failure. This judgment may be true, but it is not obvious. An official told me, "There was no Iraqi army to keep together. We didn't disband it because it didn't exist." The only option would have been to go on TV and radio and offer money to lower-level soldiers who would return to duty. Another American involved with the occupation told me: "It would have been a ragtag bunch, but it might have helped a bit to stop the looting."

In fairness, all of these options would have been controversial. How would the American media have reacted to the shooting of hundreds of looters? Would the arrest of al Sadr have made him into a Shia folk hero? How would the Shia and Kurds have reacted to the quick reconstitution of Saddam's hated army? Decisions made in battle and its aftermath are difficult. Historical "what ifs" are an easy parlor game.

But it is valid to ask whether adequate planning was done, and adequate preparations were made, to deal with the challenges the Coalition eventually faced. *Military* operations had been planned in exhaustive detail, gamed out in "rock drills" that covered every contingency. Serious planning had also been done in the event of a humanitarian nightmare—dealing with burning oil fields and hungry refugees on the move. But planning for an effective occupation—the quick return of order, security, and basic services—was hurried and incomplete. "Victory in Iraq," one former CPA official told me after I left government, "was defined as decapitating the regime. No one defined victory as creating a sustainable country six months down the road."

This lack of adequate planning resulted from an assumption and an attitude. It was assumed that we could take off the top of the pyramid of Iraqi society—Saddam and his Baathist henchmen—and the rest of the pyramid would remain in place. Iraqi generals would hand over intact units. Iraqi citizens would return to work the day after the liberation. Iraqi institutions would function under new leadership. But the rest of the pyramid did not stay in place. The Iraqi military disintegrated … workplaces were burned … and Iraqi institutions proved to be weak and fragmented as a result of Saddam's brutal rule. America was confronted with a huge nation-building enterprise. Yet the United States government had not developed the capacity for nation building on this scale.

And this reflected an attitude—what might be called the first theory of the Iraq War: the theory of liberate and leave. The initial assault had worked with a small, nimble invasion force. In post-war Iraq, the theory went, America could also have a light footprint and hand over responsibilities quickly to Iraqis and international forces. The military thought it would be down to thirty thousand troops in Iraq by the end of 2003. America had no intention of being an occupier, and every intention of leaving as quickly as conditions improved.

What happened instead was the growth of a classic insurgency. In early May, the week of the *Lincoln* speech, there had been about thirty insurgent attacks in Iraq, from small arms, rockets, roadside bombs, and ambushes. By the first full week in June, there were about seventy. The first week in July, there were about ninety. By the final week of that month, there were nearly 150. In the first week of October, there were nearly 250 attacks. The insurgents were targeting not only our troops, but also Iraqi security personnel, judges, and economic infrastructure—all the pillars of reconstruction. Lists went up in mosques, with the names of "collaborators" crossed off when killed. Some of the insurgents were bitter and disenfranchised Saddam loyalists. Others were Sunni religious extremists seeking to maintain their political and religious dominance. Still others were international *mujahidin*, the roving veterans of other jihads. And others were al-Qaeda terrorists associated with al-Zarqawi. All shared the goals of creating chaos, weakening American political will, and forcing our retreat from the country.

The army and Marines were not losing whole units in battle; the level of casualties was low compared to other conflicts in our history. But the losses were steady and growing. The conflict looked less and less like Afghanistan—a difficult but hopeful campaign against Taliban holdouts—and more like the West Bank—a bloody, drawn-out counter-insurgency campaign.

While the Iraqi insurgency festered, the attempts to find stockpiles of chemical and biological weapons became less and less productive. I found myself, at first, stubbornly insistent that the weapons would eventually be found. Then convinced that the survey effort must be weak and incompetent. Then angry: *How could this have happened?* But I found little opportunity to vent these feelings and concerns because, at the White House, the issue was covered in a blanket of silence. The lead-up to the war had been an unending series of meetings and discussions. But after the liberation, there was no general meeting to explain to confused White House staff what had happened to the weapons stockpiles we had expected to find. The national security staff was inhibited by growing recriminations in the press between the White House, the CIA, and the Department of Defense—and perhaps inhibited by its own uncertainty.

There was, however, an explanation. After 1991 it seemed Saddam Hussein had destroyed much of his stockpile of WMD. He may have destroyed more in the mid- to late-1990s. The inspectors had kept him from openly pursuing his programs, so these were embedded within other dual-use facilities. Saddam believed he would escape the sanctions at some point, and would be quickly able to resume WMD production. But much of the information about these programs was destroyed in the looting.

This general version of events was confirmed by a number of in-depth investigations. David Kay, the head of the Iraq Survey Group, would report that the regime had concealed labs and safe houses containing equipment for chemical-weapons research. He noted the existence of a prison-lab complex for human testing of biological weapons; biological reference strains hidden in a scientist's home; new research on biological agents; nuclear documents and equipment hidden in scientists' homes; advanced design work on prohibited missiles. In October 2003, Kay had told Congress that the regime "maintained programs and activities, and they certainly had the intentions at a point to resume those programs. So there was a lot they wanted to hide because it showed what they were doing was illegal." Charles Duelfer, who led the Iraq Survey Group at a later point, would concur: "Saddam pursued a strategy to maintain a capability to return to WMD production after sanctions were lifted by preserving assets and expertise. In addition to preserving capability, we have clear evidence of his intent to resume WMD production as soon as sanctions were lifted." Duelfer concluded that Saddam Hussein retained the capability to resume anthrax production within one week of making the decision to do so, and could have resumed production of mustard gas within days or weeks.

Saddam, it turns out, was hiding something in all his efforts at deception, but it wasn't actual weapons of mass destruction; it was his ongoing programs. In the mid-1990s, he concluded it would be safer to maintain a smaller, covert program than to keep large, easily discoverable stockpiles—waiting until the international pressure was off to produce the chemical and biological weapons themselves. At the same time, in order to deter Iran and others, Saddam wanted to maintain the appearance that he had such weapons—a deception that much of his own government (and the rest of the world) believed. In sum, Saddam never gave up his aspirations to produce WMD, and he maintained the programs that would allow him to resume production quickly; but he didn't keep the weapons themselves on hand. This was far from "no threat"—but it was a different threat from the one we had diagnosed.

Why did American intelligence have a different explanation? My own limited contacts with the CIA, in policy meetings on issues like Sudan, had been positive. Its people were professional, careful, and public spirited. Their response to 9/11 had been impressive—by September 17, operational officers had hooked up with the Northern Alliance in

Afghanistan and begun preparations to remove the Taliban. The counter-terrorism center run out of the CIA headquarter *was* the War on Terror in the months after 9/11, making daily progress in capturing high-value targets.

Yet the CIA at the beginning of the War on Terror was also a decimated institution. During the 1990s, in the name of the "peace dividend" accruing to us with the ending of the Cold War, the CIA and NSA (National Security Agency) had suffered massive budget cuts. Attrition was high, and the agency was forced to retreat from covering many parts of the world. Three years after 9/11—even after a series of large budget increases—the CIA had still not returned to the intelligence collection levels it had in 1993. New sources of human intelligence—scientists, engineers, military officers—are cultivated over time, not created overnight. Yet the agency would be asked quickly to establish a large operation in Iraq at the same time that its people were running flat out in the broader War on Terror.

But the largest challenge was Saddam Hussein's own bizarre behavior, which made the reality in Iraq hard for anyone to predict. Concerning Saddam's WMD programs, Robert Jervis of Columbia University, the chair of the CIA's Historical Review Panel, has written: "Most strikingly, no one proposed a view close to that we now believe to be true. This was a serious failure, but one that needs to be placed in context. No observers outside the government, including opponents of the war, proposed serious alternatives, and no one, including analysts in the Arab world, provided a description of Saddam's motives and behavior that was close to what we now think is correct. There is no reason to believe that any alternative would have been seen as highly credible had it been proposed, and indeed it is hard to argue that any alternative fit the available evidence better than the prevailing one."

"The fundamental reason for the intelligence failures in Iraq," Jervis continues, "was that the assumptions and inferences were reasonable, much more than the alternatives.... [T]he best-supported conclusion was that Saddam was actively pursuing all kinds of WMD, and probably had some on hand. The judgment should have been expressed with much less certainty, the limitations on direct evidence should have been stressed, and the grounds for reaching the assessments should have been explicated. But while it would be nice to believe that better analysis would have led to a fundamentally different conclusion, I do not think this is the case."

In the end, under United Nations resolutions, it was Saddam Hussein who had the burden of proof—the responsibility to demonstrate he had abandoned his WMD ambitions. And, in the end, the greatest intelligence failure was Saddam's own. After the war, the Deputy Prime Minister Tariq Aziz described Saddam Hussein as "very confident" that the US would never attack Iraq, because France and Russia—countries with close economic ties to the regime—would prevent such an invasion. Even after military operations began, according to Saddam's army chief of staff, "No Iraqi leader had believed Coalition forces would ever reach Baghdad." Saddam's intelligence was not only flawed, but delusional—and it led to actions that were suicidal.

Still, whatever the explanation for the absence of WMD stockpiles in Iraq, and however deserving Saddam Hussein was of his fate, by early 2004 a growing insurgency and intelligence failures were combining to hurt the president's standing with the American people, and America's credibility in the world. On a morning in February, the entire front page of the *Washington Post* was covered with dispiriting stories about Iraq, failed intelligence, and administration officials who had begun to distance themselves from the decision for war. The president was defiant and determined—but concerned that a few more press days like this would make his reelection difficult.

I respected his resolve—and agreed with his political judgment. The upcoming 2004 election would be difficult. I believed that we could surmount the failure to have found WMD, if only the occupation had gone smoothly. I believed that we could surmount the difficulties of occupation, if only we had found WMD. I did not see a path to reelection while the occupation remained difficult and we had failed to discover weapons stockpiles.

In this period, the White House was besieged by events. Through late 2003 and most of 2004, I cannot recall a week of sustained good news. But the president set a consistent tone of combative cheerfulness. And while the White House can be a place of considerable stress, it is never a place of boredom. In the midst of grave and troubling events, there is always some hint or reminder of the honor and enjoyment of serving the president.

In November 2003, President Bush headed to London for the first state visit (the most formal of diplomatic invitations) by an American president in British history. The political atmosphere we were entering was mixed. Prime Minister Tony Blair had faced his own intelligence investigations and a scandalous suicide in his cabinet. Yet it was the opposition Conservative Party that had thrown out its leader, and Blair remained the only large figure in British politics. The prime minister was a politician with Bill Clinton's skills—a spacious mind, a talent for extemporaneous speaking, and a winning, upbeat charm. But Blair also proved to have attributes that Clinton lacked—particularly conviction and political courage.

Blair believed that globalization was changing not only the nature of commerce, but the nature of international threats. In his view, distant problems—from genocide, to weapons of mass destruction, to global warming—would eventually prove dangerously uncontainable unless energetically confronted. This muscular foreign-policy liberalism made Prime Minister Blair a supporter of interventions in the Balkans to stop ethnic cleansing, in Sudan to halt genocide, and in Iraq to hold Saddam Hussein to account. As war approached, in frequent video conferences and phone calls, Blair and Bush developed a level of consultation and trust rivaled only by Churchill and Roosevelt in an earlier age.

We arrived at 11 p.m. London time at Heathrow Airport, with Prince Charles waiting for the president at the foot of the ramp. After taking Nighthawk helicopters to the back lawn of Buckingham Palace, we were escorted to our rooms in a wing given over to the visiting delegation. The palace is ornate and endless—room after room of massive antiques, heavy drapes, graceful arches, outsized beds, silver inkwells, fruit bowls, thick writing paper, gilded armoires, and oversized paintings of monarchs. An unamused George III watched over our staff office. A five-foot model of an Indian elephant stood guard outside the door of my room. After getting settled, the guests met in the Chinese dining room for hors d'oeuvres, and I sat with Condi Rice and Alma Powell (the wife of Secretary of State Powell), who talked of mutual friends in Birmingham, Alabama, where both had been raised. Buckingham Palace, it occurred to me, was a long way from the segregated Birmingham of their youth—but both graceful, confident women seemed perfectly suited to a royal setting. I returned to my room to find that Russell, the man appointed as my personal valet, had pressed all my clothes, shined my shoes, and neatly laid out my belongings in drawers and closets. This aspect of monarchism I could get used to.

The official arrival ceremony took place the next morning on the front grounds of the palace. Earlier, at Condi's instruction, I had given to David Manning, the British ambassador to the US, a draft of the major speech President Bush was scheduled to deliver. While waiting for the ceremony, I saw him hand the remarks to Foreign Secretary Jack Straw. Then Straw walked up to the podium and gave it to Blair, who put it in his breast pocket. The Queen and Prince Philip arrived first in a Bentley limousine; then the president and First Lady. Then row after row of black horses in perfect cadence, riders in armor, and a forty-one-gun salute. I had been part of a similar ceremony in Germany, with soldiers marching and bands playing. But when I heard "Deutschland, Deutschland Uber Alles," the hair rose on the back of my neck. Hearing "God Save the Queen" was like coming home.

The president's remarks, delivered later that day in the Royal Banqueting House at Whitehall Palace, were a success. The drama was high. The entire British press—more ruthless and acerbic than anything found in America—was rooting for the president to fall flat. The setting was odd—the same room where Charles I had been beheaded. But the speech itself was humorous and tough. It began by tracing the historical roots of some American character traits that many British find uncomfortable: "We're sometimes faulted for a naïve faith that liberty can change the world. If that's an error, it began with reading too much John Locke and Adam Smith. Americans have, on occasion, been called moralists who often speak in terms of right and wrong. That zeal has been inspired by examples on this island, by the tireless compassion of Lord Shaftesbury, the righteous courage of Wilberforce, and the firm determination of the Royal Navy over the decades to fight and end the trade in slaves. It's rightly said that Americans are a religious people. That's, in part, because the 'Good News' was translated by Tyndale, preached by Wesley, lived out in the example of William Booth." It was a message that combined flattery with an edge of defiance: we are who we are because of you.

The speech went on to set out three pillars of peace and security in the post-9/11 world: effective multilateral institutions; the willingness of free nations to restrain evil and aggression by force when necessary; and the expansion of freedom as the alternative to bitterness and terror. "Peoples of the Middle East," President Bush argued, "share a high civilization, a religion of personal responsibility, and a need for freedom as deep as our own. It is not realism to suppose that one-fifth of humanity is unsuited to liberty; it is pessimism and condescension, and we should have none of it." On Iraq the president was unapologetic: "The people have given us the duty to defend them. And that duty sometimes requires the violent restraint of violent men. In some cases, the measured use of force is all that protects us from a chaotic world ruled by force."

A headline in *The Independent* the next day read, "Where Was the Tongue-Tied Texan? This Was Fluent and Funny." A columnist in *The Times* wrote: "For a man who supposedly has difficulty with words, the Bush speech was brilliantly constructed, precisely calibrated to deflect criticism, restate the case for war, reinforce the alliance, and, coincidentally, kick off his presidential reelection campaign." This was one of the secret joys of speechwriting—stopping the president's critics in midsneer. Bush's foreign-policy approach—including both the "hard" elements of national power and the "soft" appeal of idealism and compassion—ran closely parallel to Blair's. The prime minister often received credit for the breadth of his vision; the president seldom did. But at least on that day in London, the critics were forced to take a second look.

That evening, our delegation put on formal dress—for the men, white tie and tails—and was escorted to a reception before the state dinner. I spent some time talking to Prime Minister Blair, who praised the Whitehall speech, and told me he had distributed an earlier Bush speech on democracy to his staff and cabinet as an example of the arguments they needed to make. Suitably charmed, I walked past the household guard into a lavish banquet room. I was seated next to Prince Michael of Kent, who bears a striking resemblance to Czar Nicholas II (a relative). The prince's background was so foreign and fascinating, he seemed like a character from a novel—godson of Franklin Roosevelt, fluent in Russian, a former Olympic bobsledder, rumored to wear a beard because of a disfiguring sledding accident. He also turned out to be kind and attentive, helping me through the complexities of forks and finger bowls. When the president passed my chair on his way to the head of the table, walking side by side with the Queen, he gave me one of his half winks—a statement that he could still see the absurdity in the midst of the splendor. The dinner was a blur of pageantry and alcohol—military uniforms in bright scarlet, gold plates glittering on the sideboard, bands playing show tunes, tapestries on the walls, royal thrones at the front of the room, matronly women in tiaras, champagne, then white wine, then sherry, then claret, then champagne again, then port. At the end of the dinner, bagpipers marched around the table to deafen the diners. Afterward, Prince Michael commented to me: "I like the sound of bagpipes … on a distant hill."

The next day, the tone of the visit suddenly changed. Terrorists in Istanbul had bombed British targets, killing more than twenty-five—an event that seemed timed to coincide with the state visit. Before a scheduled press conference with Bush and Blair, we entered the famous door of Number 10 Downing Street, which only opens from within. Blair's staff was in full crisis mode, scrambling to prepare their response to the attacks. I revised the president's opening statement in the staff office (which was once Prime Minister Thatcher's working office). Then I was escorted into Blair's small office, where he sat with the president. (On his desk, I noticed, was a picture of his family, surrounded by a frame that read: "I love Daddy.") After the president went over the draft aloud, we walked out the front door of Number 10 with hundreds of cameras clicking to the press conference in the Foreign Office Building. Blair, as usual, was strong and fluent. The president was less fluent, but resolved and heartfelt. Coming back to Number 10, I waited in one of the reception rooms as Bush and Blair held a closed meeting. I had my hand on a small writing desk with a red leather top. A member of Blair's staff informed me that this was the desk where Pitt had written out his ultimatum to Napoleon … where Asquith had written to Kaiser Wilhelm … where Chamberlain had written to Hitler.

That evening—the final evening of the visit—the Americans returned the hospitality of our hosts, entertaining the Queen in an intimate dinner at the American embassy. As we entered the dining room, each guest was greeted by the Queen and Prince Philip, along with President and Mrs. Bush. I was announced as the Honorable Michael Gerson. The president then introduced me to the Queen as "the man who wrote the speech I gave." This was met with a blank stare, and an awkward silence. Evidently, the elaborate traditions of royal protocol covered every contingency but this one. The Queen could not say anything; as a speechwriter, I was technically not supposed to exist. The moment was slightly humiliating—and the president seemed to enjoy it thoroughly.

Early in the 2004 election cycle, my political pessimism seemed to be confirmed. In January and February, the president had a sharp drop in his poll numbers on job approval, the economy, foreign policy, Iraq, and terrorism. Democrats were dominating television coverage with their own primary process. Our State of the Union address featured weak, uncreative policy, due to budget concerns and the internal triumph of conventional Republican thinking. The budget itself was unpopular and dreadfully out of balance. The Kay Report on Iraq weapons of mass destruction fed questions about the president's credibility. In every news cycle, the administration took a new beating, and the race narrowed until it was even.

But through the summer, the president gradually rebounded. The Democratic convention was flawed. It told Americans the one thing they already knew about John Kerry: that he had served honorably in Vietnam. And then the Swift Boat ads questioned the one thing Americans thought they knew. The authors of those ads—featuring disillusioned former Vietnam comrades of the senator—spent a few million dollars over a few months in a few states. But a remarkable 89 percent of Americans said they were familiar with the ads. And as the months went on, Senator Kerry himself—combining liberalism and hauteur in equal measure—did not wear well.

By the time of the Republican convention, the president was already regaining momentum. The preparations for that event involved some sobering reminders of 9/11. The president's homeland security advisor recommended that assistants to the president attending the convention keep their deputies in Washington, so that, in the event of a catastrophic terrorist attack, we would not all be killed at once. Andy Card worried about contingency plans in case the whole convention was disrupted or destroyed. By what procedure would the president be nominated?

Up in New York at the Waldorf Astoria, on the day of his convention speech, President Bush practiced in a small room on his floor of the hotel. The president was pleased with the speech's self-deprecation—the rhetorical jujitsu that attempts to turn weaknesses into strengths. "In the last four years, you and I have come to know each other. Even when we don't agree, at least you know what I believe and where I stand. You may have noticed I have a few flaws, too. People sometimes have to correct my English. I knew I had a problem when Arnold Schwarzenegger started doing it. Some folks look at me and see a certain swagger, which in Texas is called 'walking.' Now and then I come across as a little too blunt—and for that we can all thank the white-haired lady sitting right up there"—a reference to his mother.

But the emotional heart of the speech came when talking about the sacrifices of the last few years. I was determined that these remarks include, not only our best case for the war in Iraq, but a direct recognition of its human costs. In the room at the Waldorf, the president read over the words on the teleprompter: "I've learned firsthand that ordering Americans into battle is the hardest decision, even when it is right. I've returned the salutes of wounded soldiers, some with a very tough road ahead, who say they were just doing their job. I've held the children of the fallen, who are told their dad or mom is a hero, but would rather just have their mom or dad. I've met with the wives and husbands who have received a folded flag, and said a final good-bye to a soldier they loved."

At this point in the practice session, Condi Rice and Karen Hughes were in tears, and the president became too emotional to continue. Trying to compose himself, he turned to me and asked, "Is this necessary?" I responded, "Mr. President, we need to do this." In a suddenly biting tone, he answered, "*We* don't need to do this. *I* have to do this." That evening, when he delivered the lines, there were tears among the delegates all over the floor of the convention. But the president had just the right level of emotion—a break in his voice, but not a breakdown.

Despite ongoing violence in Iraq, the president pressed a strong case for reelection. His actions had led to the liberation of more than fifty million people in Afghanistan and Iraq. Ten million Afghan citizens had registered to vote in an election set for October. Iraq had regained its sovereignty, had a new prime minister and national council, and national elections were scheduled for January. The American economy—despite Democratic depictions of it as the second coming of the Great Depression—was fundamentally strong.

The president was a likable, persuasive, and underestimated campaigner. He had a close, continuing relationship with religious voters, who in the next months turned out in large numbers at every event. And I believe Americans continued to support President Bush because he had deeply and emotionally connected with them at least half a dozen times—in moments after 9/11, in his ultimatum to the Taliban, in the showdown with Saddam Hussein, in his Thanksgiving visit to Iraq—moments when Americans said to themselves: "I am glad he is my president." Other presidents, like President Carter or the first President Bush, had few or none of those moments.

As the election approached, Senator Kerry and his party placed all their money on one number of the roulette wheel: Iraq is Vietnam. All nuance and responsibility were abandoned. Iraq became the "wrong war, at the wrong place, at the wrong time." And this was an effective political move. Senator Kerry's previous vacillations on the war had pleased no one. By contrast, the message that "Bush lied and people died" rallied Democrats. It also politicized the foreign-policy debate and sapped public support for the war. The polls tightened once again. Not long before Election Day, I saw Karl Rove in the hallway of the second floor of the West Wing and asked, "How do you feel?" He responded, "I feel good . . . and nervous as hell. This is going to be close."

On the day of the election, after a frantic final campaign swing, we were returning to Washington on Air Force One. Karl was playing cards with the president in the conference room—when he won a hand, the president joked, "How dare you win on a day when I am so vulnerable?" As we returned in vans to the White House, the tracking numbers coming in by Blackberry were disturbing. Everything depended on Florida and Ohio, and we were behind in both states. I went home to change clothes and spoke by phone with Dan Bartlett: he wanted me to send him the draft concession statement. My wife, Dawn, began to sob on the couch in our living room. But by the time I got back to the White House, Karl had detected methodological problems in the exit polls, and began a heroic phone campaign with media figures to convince them the election wasn't over. Late that evening a Bush victory was clear—but the networks refused to call it, because they were twice shy from the burning they took in 2000.

The next morning, Dan, Karen, Karl, and I sat with the president, discussing a number of topics in a distracted fashion. In the middle of the conversation, Secretary Rumsfeld came in to congratulate the president, shaking our hands one by one—a visit that had the appearance of a job interview. After he left, President Bush said he was going over to the Residence to get some exercise. At that moment, his assistant Ashley called in, "Senator Kerry on the line." The president and the senator had a cordial five-minute conversation. As he got off the phone, his eyes filled with tears—tears of relief that another election crisis had been avoided. He hugged each of us in turn, and hugged Andy when he came into the Oval Office. Then he headed down the short hall to the vice president's office. The president shook Vice President Cheney's hand and said: "I know you aren't the hugging kind."

•   •   •

In December after the election, I urged the president to replace Sec-retary Rumsfeld. I had great respect for the secretary of defense, who had proven relentless in modernizing the military, and creative in the tactics that had quickly liberated Afghanistan and Iraq. But I felt that initial mistakes in the Iraqi occupation had compromised his standing as a spokesman for the administration. The president, I believed, would not get credit for progress on the ground in Iraq as long as Secretary Rumsfeld remained in charge. And I thought that Senator Joseph Lieberman would make a fine new secretary of defense. Lieberman had shown his courage as a strong and lonely supporter of the Iraq War in the Democratic Party. His selection, as a former Democratic vice presidential candidate, would be a powerful symbol of national unity.

My rather presumptuous advice was not taken. A variety of person-nel changes are considered at the beginning of any new presidential term. But the vice president made a strong case to retain Secretary Rumsfeld, arguing: Do you really want someone to learn this job in the middle of a war?

There had been a disturbing slowness in the American response to the insurgency in Iraq. While many individual units had impro-vised heroically, it had taken eighteen months to put a more effec-tive counterinsurgency strategy in place.

Some of this problem was located in Washington. Decision making on military strategy took place out of my sight. But that complicated process between the Department of Defense, the National Security Council, and the State Department clearly was not nimble or efficient. There was too much deference to the Defense Department's strategies and views, even as those strategies grew less and less plausible. There seemed to be little accountability for poor performance. And no one in the system seemed empowered to force the reexamination of flawed assumptions, and to bring the president new options.

Other problems were found in the theater of war itself. Our task in Iraq was complicated by Iran and Syria, whose governments were actively feeding instability within Iraq. Al-Qaeda, under the skilled and ruthless direction of al-Zarqawi, probed and prodded sectarian hatred with the bombing of mosques and markets. And America was unable to achieve what the experts call "intelligence dominance"; we lacked a clear picture of the role and reach of former regime elements and various terrorist groups, and knew little about Iran's murky relationship with Shia militias. This meant that Coalition forces were often fighting in near-blind conditions.

But progress on the political front in Iraq had tremendous momentum. The elections on January 30, 2005, were a triumph of Iraqi democracy, and a personal triumph for the president. Many in the administration wanted to postpone them, fearing chaos and thousands of casualties. The president insisted the elections go forward, and was vindicated by a largely peaceful, inspiring vote. These elections bound the Shia majority to the new government, while an open hand was extended to the Sunnis, who participated in subsequent elections in progressively larger numbers. In October 2005, an Iraqi constitution was approved by 79 percent of voters—the most liberal constitution in the Arab world. In December, a permanent national assembly was elected, with minimal violence and broad participation.

These were unprecedented events in the history of the Middle East, revealing a tenacious commitment to democracy among the Iraqi people. And these accomplishments contributed to the second theory of the Iraq War: a belief that political progress, and the training of the Iraqi military and police, would eventually result in greater security and thus allow American troops to be withdrawn. A Sunni stake in the political process, the argument went, would drain the insurgency of its anger and resentment, which was fueling much of the violence. And a stronger Iraqi military would be able to deal with a lower level of conflict.

So the main priorities at the Defense Department were to lower the profile of American troops and increase the training of Iraqi forces. Secretary Rumsfeld, General Abizaid, and General Casey were determined to avoid long-term Iraqi dependence, and felt that additional American soldiers and Marines would only feed that dependence. The Coalition needed to take off the "training wheels" and encourage the Iraqis to defeat their own insurgency.

This strategy was reinforced by an unfortunate fact: The American military—particularly the army—was stretched as thin as rice paper. Following the 9/11 attacks, the size of the army had not been significantly increased. Secretary Rumsfeld's approach to military transformation put an emphasis on mobility and lethality instead of mass. But an occupation requires manpower, and military leaders feared that a larger commitment in Iraq could result in the "breaking" of the army—a rapid decline in morale and preparedness.

The second theory of the Iraq War was credible—and wrong, or at least premature. Even as political progress was made, the security situation grew progressively worse. Disorder in Baghdad began to undermine the credibility of the new government. The successful elections actually masked growing security problems and delayed necessary adjustments. Every card that was played—the transfer of sovereignty, the capture of Saddam, the elections, the constitution, the death of al-Zarqawi—failed to quell the violence. And this succession of false summits eventually disillusioned a growing number of Americans, who had their hopes raised and disappointed too many times.

On February 22, 2006, al-Qaeda terrorists blew up the al-Askari shrine, one of the holiest sites of Shia Islam. Sectarian violence in Baghdad had been growing for months, and the mosque bombing, after a pause, dramatically accelerated it. Shia militias grew and fragmented, taking brutal revenge on innocent Sunnis instead of al-Qaeda terrorists, and making parts of the capital ungovernable. What had been a very difficult but containable problem—al-Qaeda in Iraq and the Sunni insurgency—was transforming itself into something even more difficult, with mutual Sunni-Shia violence and death squads as the toxic new ingredients. For years, in cruel acts of terrorism, al-Qaeda had been throwing matches on the tinder of Iraqi sectarian resentments. Eventually the fire took, and the mixed neighborhoods of Baghdad were engulfed by the flames. We had thought that political progress would lead to security. We found that security was necessary for any political progress to be sustained.

It was a military failure that provoked a major rethinking of the strategy. In June 2006, American and Iraqi forces set to out reestablish order in Baghdad in an effort called "Operation Together Forward." The intention was to clear out neighborhoods of militias and insurgents, hold the ground that had been cleared, and begin the process of rebuilding. But most Iraqi troops did not even show up, and neighborhoods that America cleared could not be held, because there were not enough soldiers. "Clear, hold, and build" turned into a demoralizing setback. In Operation Together Forward, America did not have the minimal number of troops necessary for success. As at other key moments in the Iraq war, the resources were short of the need.

In mid-September, the president ordered a bottom-up review of America's Iraq strategy. The initial response from the leadership team at the Department of Defense was business as usual, leading to a testy confrontation between the president and his generals at a Pentagon briefing. His patience had finally reached its end. In November, Secretary Rumsfeld was replaced. In January 2007, as much of official Washington counseled retreat and troop reductions, President Bush announced instead a surge in troops, a new military strategy, and a new general, David Petraeus, to implement it. As the author of the army's manual on the topic, Petraeus had literally written the book on counterinsurgency tactics. He set out to regain control of disputed parts of Baghdad, consolidate those gains with additional troops, and build long-term relationships and trust with neighborhood leaders—all the elements of a classic counterinsurgency approach.

This was the third theory of the Iraq war: to secure the people of Baghdad for the first time since the liberation, and allow the government to build its strength and legitimacy in an atmosphere of security. The change in strategy was needed—and came at least a year late. Was the surge in troops large enough to be decisive? Would Americans have the patience to support a third theory and war strategy?

Whatever the eventual outcome of the Iraq war—a precipitous, politically driven withdrawal, a gradual counterinsurgency victory, or something in between—it is necessary to begin drawing some lessons. The first is unavoidable: Regime change is the most difficult of foreign-policy options, the most fraught with unintended consequences, and the least suited to the American style of war. Regime removal, it turns out, is relatively easy, given our country's unrivaled military capabilities. But regime removal is different from regime change, which may require a massive and costly effort of nation building—especially when a society has been debilitated by decades of totalitarian rule. For nearly thirty years, Saddam Hussein instilled terror and distrust, fed divisions of clan and tribe, and encouraged the fears of the Sunni minority. Wounds so deep heal slowly and gradually, and only in an atmosphere of security and order—an atmosphere the Coalition did not initially provide.

Throughout most of my White House experience, I intuitively sided with Secretary Donald Rumsfeld's combative confidence against Secretary Colin Powell's caution and diplomacy. But it is now clear to me that, despite its indisputable utility on today's battlefield, the Rumsfeld Doctrine, with its stress on light and flexible high-tech military power, is less well suited to an occupation like Iraq than are certain elements of the Powell Doctrine—especially the need for clear goals and overwhelming force. Defeating an insurgency is possible (a fact proven in Malaysia and El Salvador); and sometimes it is necessary. But this kind of counterinsurgency campaign cannot be conducted quickly or on the cheap. For years, lower-level officers had made the case that when American troops in Iraq came into an area and stayed, there was relative calm. But for years there were not enough troops to make that strategy work on a sufficient scale in Baghdad.

Another lesson concerns the power of dramatic acts of violence in a media age. Al-Zarqawi's strategy in Iraq, in the end—even after his own end—was successful. Al-Qaeda was not responsible for most of the attacks in Iraq, but it authored the most spectacular and bloody ones— the destruction of mosques, the carnage at busy markets. And this had two effects. It created images of hopeless chaos in the American media, undermining public support for the war. Even more destructively, the attacks fed sectarian divisions within Iraq at the expense of democratic aspirations. The attraction of freedom is powerful. But hatred is not without its appeal, either, especially in the absence of order. A small group of ruthless men proved capable of fanning that hatred through spectacular acts of murder.

This is the definition of asymmetrical warfare: the car bomb instead of the tank, the assassination instead of the pitched battle, the suicide bomber instead of the strategic bomber. Conducting this kind of warfare does not require large numbers or great resources—just cruelty and patience. And in such a war, the victory of the democratic side depends as much on moral and mental attributes as it does on military capabilities. Not long before I left the White House, the president put the situation to me bluntly: "If the definition of success is no bombings on TV, America is in trouble. If the definition of success is steady progress in Iraq toward self-sufficiency, we can win." This explains President Bush's emphasis on public resolve. "The most important thing to know," he continued, "is that I'm not going to waver." Resolve is not a substitute for effectiveness and competence in the War on Terror—but effectiveness and competence cannot prevail without it.

That, for us, may be the most brutal fact of a brutal age. Either Americans (and Iraqis and Indonesians and Indians and the citizens of Western Europe) will react with fortitude and patience to inevitable bombings on TV—or they will lose the War on Terror, with the surrender ceremony taking place first in their own minds.

A final lesson concerns the doctrine of preemption, and has to do with the importance of good intelligence. Here we had two case studies, not just one. In the lead-up to Iraq, American intelligence services (like those of many nations) overestimated Saddam's WMD capabilities. But days after Saddam was captured in December 2003, Libya announced the destruction of its WMD. Muammar Qadhafi provided America and Great Britain full documentation of his chemical, biological, ballistic missile, and nuclear programs. In many ways, these programs were more advanced than we had thought. In other words, while Saddam's WMD programs had been overestimated, Qadhafi's had been underestimated.

Qadhafi eventually turned over massive amounts of information and equipment, the latter of which was moved to a facility in Tennessee for analysis. Libya and Iraq serve as equal and opposite warnings: America does not want to be surprised by threats that are smaller than we imagined—or greater than we imagined. It should be possible to penetrate dictatorships and police states like Iraq, Libya, or Iran. According to intelligence experts, this is an easier task today than getting information from the tight leadership circles of the Soviet Union or communist China. The intelligence reorganization of the last few years has been helpful. There is now a single intelligence advisor—the director of national intelligence, or DNI—who can survey dozens of intelligence databases and provide the president with a single briefing. But integration among the agencies remains weak. American intelligence agencies are still recovering from the irresponsible budgetary assault of the Congress in the 1990s. The next president will need to continue long-term improvements in American intelligence capabilities—or wander blind-folded, at night, in a minefield of global danger.

At the same time, there is also danger in learning the *wrong* lessons from Iraq—or in overlearning the lessons of caution. Some claim the American project in Iraq was doomed from the beginning, because Iraqis and Arabs more broadly are culturally incapable of sustaining democracy. That is a familiar historical charge, made in other periods, against Catholics in Southern Europe, Hindus and Muslims in India, Eastern Orthodox in Eastern Europe, and Confucian cultures across Asia. All of these groups experienced difficult days in their democratic transitions—moments when the skeptics seemed to be vindicated. Did Indian democracy look to be successful when more than a million people died by violence during the partition process in the later 1940s? But in all of these cases, betting against the advance of democracy was a poor wager.

It may be possible that the Arab world is the great exception to this trend of history; but if so, Iraq does not prove it. Americans who first entered Iraq did not report an inevitable sectarian conflict. To the contrary, the Shia were remarkably patient during the first two years after the liberation. Iraqis of every background, including most Sunnis, were pleased that Saddam was gone and were generally inclined to withhold judgment about the occupation. There was little resentment at the size of the occupation force, and great hope that the arrival of the Americans would improve the lives of the Iraqi people. Nor were the successive elections an illusion. They were real achievements. Iraqis voted under considerable threat, in percentages greater than do Western democracies—advances that should not be forgotten or denigrated.

Given these events, an imperious contempt for the Shia—a belief that barbarians will always be barbarians—is neither fair nor helpful. Iraqi patience and goodwill were not lacking; rather, they were squandered when the Coalition failed to provide security and basic services. Sectarian conflict was not preordained—it intensified when many of the Shia lost confidence in the ability of the Coalition and Iraqi army to defend them and turned for protection and revenge to militias and death squads. Iraq does not demonstrate that democracy is impossible in the Arab world; it demonstrates that founding a new democracy is difficult in a nation overrun by militias and insurgents.

This is not to say that support for democracy in the Arab world always requires immediate elections. Such elections in Saudi Arabia, for example, would likely result in a government more oppressive and dangerous than the current one. But in Iraq there was no alternative to elections. After the invasion and liberation—undertaken, it bears repeating, primarily for reasons of national security—the president was not about to install a potential Shia dictator in place of the old Sunni dictator. That kind of cynical power game would likely have facilitated a massive Shia retribution and perhaps even genocide against the Sunnis. Democracy is necessary in Iraq precisely because it is the only political system that eventually can tame sectarian tensions, giving the Shia majority the influence it deserves, while guaranteeing the rights and representation of the Sunni minority.

But democracy in Iraq certainly has enemies—jihadists, Baathist holdouts, and religious militias—who happen to be some of the worst criminals on the global stage. We have been led by history to a simple choice: do we stand with the flawed democrats of Iraq, or abandon them to overthrow and death? Some foreign-policy realists argue that such considerations of honor mean little in international affairs. But this national commitment is more than a matter of chivalry. If America abandons Muslim leaders and soldiers who are risking their lives to fight Islamic radicalism and terror—in Iraq, Afghanistan, and elsewhere—the War on Terror cannot be won.

Another false lesson is found in the assertion that the Iraq War has actually been creating the terrorist threat we seek to fight—stirring up a hornet's nest of understandable grievances in the Arab world. In fact, radical Islamist networks have never lacked for historical provocations. When bin Laden proclaimed his 1998 fatwa justifying the murder of

Americans, he used the excuse of President Clinton's sanctions and air strikes against Iraq—what he called a policy of "continuing aggression against the Iraqi people." He talked of the "devastation" caused by "horrible massacres" of the 1991 Gulf War. All this took place *before* the invasion of Iraq was even contemplated—and it was enough to result in the murder of nearly three thousand Americans on 9/11. Islamic radicals will seize on any excuse in their campaign of recruitment and incitement. If it were not Iraq, it would be the latest "crime" of Israel, or the situation in East Timor, or cartoons in a Dutch newspaper, or statements by the pope. The well of outrage is bottomless. The list of demands—from the overthrow of moderate Arab governments to the reconquest of Spain—is endless.

America is not responsible for the existence of Islamist ideology. Yet the shifting prospect of American success or failure in the Iraq War does have an effect on the recruitment of radicals. All "pan movements"—political ideologies that claim historical inevitability—expand or contract based on morale. Bin Laden talks of how the Arab world is attracted to the "strong horse"—the victor, the evident winner—and there is truth in that claim. In an ideological struggle, perception matters greatly, and outcomes matter most. Israel's perceived defeat in Lebanon in 1982 helped produce a generation of terrorists, convinced that armed struggle could humble their enemy. If America were really to retreat in humiliation from Iraq, Islamist radicals would trumpet their victory from North Africa to the islands of the Philippines ... increase their recruitment of the angry and misguided ... and expand the size and boldness of their attacks.

Perhaps the most dangerous and self-destructive lesson that might be drawn from Iraq is a hyper-caution indistinguishable from paralysis. In a backlash to the Iraq War, some Democrats seem to argue that any future American action or intervention will require both certainty as to the validity of our intelligence and international unanimity. The evidence on weapons of mass destruction must always be conclusive, or else it must always be mocked and dismissed. The United Nations must always grant its blessing and legitimacy. Were America to accept these ground rules, we would become a spectator in world events. The demand for intelligence certainty would allow flickering threats to become raging fires before any action were taken to extinguish them. The demand for international unanimity would make interventions to prevent genocide or ethnic cleansing nearly impossible. America acted in the former Yugoslavia under President Clinton without UN support, and may need to do the same in other places in the future. At some point, caution becomes demoralization, and humility becomes humiliation.

Errors in Iraq do not alter a fundamental reality: the axis of evil—the deadly nexus among outlaw regimes, weapons of mass destruction, and terrorist networks—is alive and well. Iran in particular has pressed ahead with its nuclear program ... remains the world's leading state-sponsor of terrorism ... arms and trains terrorist groups attacking Israel ... and is assembling a regional alliance (including Syria, Hezbollah, and proxies in Afghanistan and Iraq) against America. The Iranian government is actively feeding the violence in Iraq, intending thereby to keep America occupied and the Iraqi government weak and divided. Iran has a regime without moderates. In the summer of 2006, the Ayatollah Khamenei sent a letter to the Australian parliament reading, in part: "How long should the Islamic world tolerate the existence of the scheming and evil Zionist regime? How long should the Islamic government allow oppressive and arrogant America a free hand in this part of the world? The American regime must expect a hard slap on the face and the crushing fist of the Muslim nation because of its support for the crimes of the Zionist criminals." President Ahmadinejad of Iran is an apocalyptic fanatic who celebrates martyrdom and who views conflict with America and Israel as the fulfillment of prophecy. He is also unlikely to be swayed by the authority of the United Nations, having told a summit of terrorist leaders in Tehran: "They can pass resolutions until they are blue in the face."

Resisting the dangerous ambitions of Iran is a cause that should unite foreign policy idealists and realists. An Iranian bomb would give the ideology of radical Islam (at least the Shia variety) something it has previously lacked: a great power base. And this base—with its own internal power centers gathered around the president, the ayatollahs, and the Revolutionary Guard—is one of the most unstable and unpredictable regimes in the world. A nuclear Iran could be a source of weapons for terrorist groups—perhaps provided secretly, without fingerprints, to deliver a genocidal death blow against Israel. A nuclearizing Iran has already created an incentive for other nations in the region—particularly traditional rivals like Saudi Arabia, Egypt, and Turkey—to go nuclear, as well, and quickly. Saudi Arabia, once it became a nuclear power, could well fall victim to its own Islamist revolution, creating the prospect of a radical Sunni nuclear threat in addition to the Shia one in Tehran. Along this path of proliferation, we could witness the nuclearization of sectarian rivalries in the Middle East. This would be a strategic nightmare for America and the rest of the world.

The Iraq War has complicated American efforts to deal with Iran, leaving our troops overextended and vulnerable to Iranian escalation. Progressively tighter economic sanctions on Tehran are worth trying, though it is hard to imagine they will fundamentally alter Iranian behavior. Air strikes against hardened and deeply buried nuclear facilities may not succeed—or succeed in delaying the Iranian program only briefly. There is no obvious or easy solution to the Iranian crisis. But some kind of action may eventually be necessary in Iran, or some other unpredicted place, even in the absence of UN support and intelligence certainty. In the aftermath of Iraq, such action is likely to be deeply controversial.

Many Americans are feeling tired, or fed up. The War on Terror has now gone on longer than the period from Pearl Harbor to the Japanese surrender in World War II. Many Americans feel they deserve a break, a respite, from the responsibilities of history. But history, unfortunately, is unconcerned with our weariness—indifferent to our exhaustion. And the hardest duties may lie ahead. The mortal threats of our time may require new commitments, new sacrifice, and new courage. If the lesson drawn from Iraq is that the world is too complex and uncontrollable for America to act decisively in its own interests, then the American decline will have already begun—and there will be no peace or respite or safety on our long retreat.

The debate over Iraq has become a battle of historical analogies. Is this conflict like Korea—a hard slog, but necessary to a broader ideological struggle? Or is it like Vietnam—a wasted effort, for an uncertain goal? Democrats have seized on the Vietnam analogy, and found it to be politically potent, at least for the moment. But it is important to extract all of Vietnam's bitter lessons, not just the few that politicians prefer.

Vietnam offers a political lesson for Democrats. The Democratic Party eventually won the argument on withdrawal from Vietnam and the abandonment of our allies. But Democrats, at least at the presidential level, spent the next two decades attempting to escape the political taint of McGovernism—an enduring impression of foreign-policy weakness. President Clinton in particular took pains to distance himself from the legacy of war protests, attacks on the military, and "Come Home, America." But with Iraq, McGovernism has come back among Democrats—not only at the vicious and conspiratorial fringes, but at the party's center. At every recent stage of the Iraq conflict, some elected Democrats downplayed achievements, emphasized setbacks, and showed more real animus against President Bush than toward Saddam or al-Zarqawi. After the January 2005 Iraqi elections, Senator John Kerry commented, "It is hard to say that something is legitimate when whole portions of the country can't vote and doesn't [didn't] vote." After the capture of Saddam Hussein, Howard Dean said it had not "made America safer." Representative Jim McDermott told an interviewer that American forces could have captured Saddam, "a long time ago if they wanted." After al-Zarqawi was killed, Representative Pete Stark said, "This is just to cover Bush's [rear]." Many prominent Democrats seemed incapable of cheering for the home team—the American military—just because George Bush was temporarily its coach.

Braced by their midterm congressional victories in 2006, the Democratic congressional leadership quickly supported a cutoff of all funding for American troops in Iraq on a date certain in 2008. This removed all pretense from a policy of unconditional withdrawal. And this action took place just as a new military campaign was beginning under General Petraeus, leaving the impression of a party anxious to seal American defeat before it slips through their fingers.

It cannot be good politics, in the long term, to repeat every Democratic mistake of the 1970s. Here Vietnam provides another lesson—an example of the moral consequences when national commitments are broken. At the end of the Vietnam War, the Democratic Congress cut off funding from our allies in South Vietnam and Cambodia, resulting in the quick overthrow of both governments. Diplomatic messages were then sent by us to top-level Cambodian leaders, to assure them they would be evacuated. Most, however, chose to stay. According to Henry Kissinger, the former Cambodian Prime Minister Sirik Matak sent a handwritten response: "I thank you for your letter and for your offer to transport me toward freedom. I cannot, alas, leave in such a cowardly fashion. As for you, and in particular for your great country, I never believed that you would have the sentiment of abandoning a people which has chosen liberty. You have refused us your protection, and we can do nothing about it. You leave, and my wish is that you and your country will find happiness under this sky. But, mark it well, that if I shall die here on the spot and in my country that I love, it is no matter, because we all are born and must die. I have only committed this mistake of believing in you [Americans]." Matak, Kissinger adds in his memoirs, was shot in the stomach and left to die when the Khmer Rouge took power. Eventually between one and two million people were murdered in the Cambodian genocide. Peace for America—however sincerely desired—does not always mean peace for others.

Nor, as we learned in September 2001, does it necessarily mean peace for America, either. That is one key way in which Iraq is unlike Vietnam. When the communists took power in Vietnam, they had no intention of boarding planes and attacking the American mainland—but that is exactly the intention of some of our current enemies. In the backlash against the Vietnam War, America could afford to retreat from many global commitments for nearly a decade, until Ronald Reagan gave the Cold War an infusion of his confidence and idealism. In our time, a decade of retreat—a decade of denial and pleasing hopes, a decade of terrorist plotting and pursuit of technology, a decade of unchecked nuclear proliferation—could result in catastrophe beyond imagining.

Chapter 8

Democracy, Darfur, and Disease

A cabinet meeting was scheduled for the day after Senator Kerry's concession call in November 2004. It was a cheerful event for the cabinet secretaries who would not be looking for other employment, an event tinted by nostalgia for me, because I expected it to be my last. I had been nearly six years on the job in Austin and at the White House—through an election crisis, 9/11, Afghanistan, Iraq, and another bitter election—and felt I was nearing the end of my quota of contribution. I began to ask the question, as most long-term White House staffers eventually do: will I have the energy and intensity required for the next crisis? I found myself impatient with the repetitive ceremonial events on the president's schedule ("not *another* turkey pardon!") and less patient than usual with ridiculous speech edits from my colleagues. In moments of self-examination, I could see my temperament warping to the shape of the White House—snappish, accustomed to deference, resentful of minor slights. I knew the time was coming for me to leave.

I always enjoyed cabinet meetings, not for the overly crafted prayer that began each session, or for the scripted and generally uninteresting presentations, but for the room itself. John McConnell, Matt Scully, and I had once made a pilgrimage to the cabinet room on the anniversary of Franklin Roosevelt's death, to stand in the spot, before the fireplace, where Vice President Truman had taken the oath of office. The dull proceedings of the cabinet meeting encourage the mind to wander to the busts of Washington and Franklin, the portraits of Jefferson and Eisenhower—all of whom seem watchful and demanding. They act like the icons of Eastern Orthodoxy—not merely as pictures, but as a presence—a democratic communion of the saints.

Following this cabinet meeting, the president asked me to stay. "I know you are frustrated, but will you write my inaugural?" he said with a typically disconcerting bluntness. Turning down a direct request from the president, especially with George Washington looking on, was beyond my ability. "I want this to be the freedom speech," he continued. He was looking for a summary of everything that had come before, and a fully formed vision of the Bush foreign policy. "And pretty soon I want to sit down and talk about your future," he concluded.

I began my typical process of examining past inaugurals, reading academic articles on freedom and liberty, looking for appropriate historical references, outlining and re-outlining. But on December 17, 2004, something not so typical intervened. Up at a little after 5 a.m. at my home in Alexandria, I felt intense heartburn … a numbness in my hands … then a cold sweat … and soon I was on the floor, unable to get up. After an ambulance ride, doctors inserted two stents to open up narrowed arteries. I was told it had been a mild heart attack, on the back side of the heart. Dr. Tubb—the president's Air Force physician, who is a part-time counselor and full-time saint—was at the hospital almost immediately to comfort my wife and take care of details. He made sure I was checked in under an assumed name, John Alexandria, to avoid press inquiries. The precaution turned out to be unnecessary. Later I found out, adding insult to incapacity, that no journalists had cared enough to call.

A heart attack at age forty is like a cold shower of mortality—an announcement that middle age has arrived and intends to stay for a while. For me, it also involved a glimpse of grace. I am a Christian believer, but not a naturally religious person. My soul (assuming there is such a thing) is normally weighted by coldness and doubt. But strapped to the operating table, I felt an overwhelming sense of peace and gratitude that seemed to fill all the space normally taken by worry. I remember singing to myself an old hymn that came suddenly to mind: "I need Thee / Oh, I need Thee / Every hour I need Thee / Oh, bless me now my Savior / I come to Thee." A feeling of peace arrived like an unexpected, undeserved gift—and it provided me with a hint and a hope that death without fear may well be possible. Through most of my days, faith feels distinctly unreal and distant. On that day, faith was as real as rock and water and the unseen air. What should have been a time of fear was a time of clarity: I am a creature of dust and bile and pitiful vanity, somehow loved by the God of the universe. I deserve nothing. I have gained everything. I expect to meet my Savior, face to face.

After a few days in intensive care, hooked up to IVs and heart monitors, I came home. Familiar things and places seemed newly wonderful—then normal once again. At Christmas dinner, my son Nicholas lost a front tooth, and his toothless smile brought me more joy than I can possibly express. But time passes in a current so strong that joy and pain are quickly lost, and never recovered, until, at the end, when a final Joy recalls all our joys, and all our pains are given a meaning, so we would never change or trade them. In this life, at least, routine quickly replaces wonder, even if that routine is filled with miracles.

During my two weeks of recovery at home, the president called several times. Between the lines of his good wishes, I could hear his questions about how the inaugural was coming. "I'm not calling about the inaugural," he assured me, "I'm calling about the guy who is writing the inaugural." Soon I was back at the White House, working with my colleague John McConnell on the speech. January 20, 2005—the beginning of the president's second term—was a deadline that could not be negotiated.

On that cold and overcast day, I sat in the stands on the West Front of the Capitol, high up toward the Senate side. The president's tone, as he began the speech, was sober and measured—he was clearly taking care to articulate each word and idea. The events of 9/11 were the context for the entire speech, but references to the courage and falling buildings of that day had ripened, over three years, into clichés. So the president set the historical stage with spare and minimal scenery. "For half a century, America defended our own freedom by standing watch on distant borders. After the shipwreck of communism came years of relative quiet, years of repose, years of sabbatical—and then there came a day of fire." The reference to 9/11 took eight words.

Then President Bush offered an interpretation of those events—an argument that America is vulnerable to the disorders and hatreds of societies in the Middle East. "For as long as whole regions of the world simmer in resentment and tyranny—prone to ideologies that feed hatred and excuse murder—violence will gather, and multiply in destructive power, and cross the most defended borders, and raise a mortal threat." What is the long-term solution to this threat? "There is only one force of history that can break the reign of hatred and resentment, and expose the pretensions of tyrants, and reward the hopes of the decent and tolerant, and that is the force of human freedom." In his inaugural, John F. Kennedy had promised that America would "bear any burden, pay any price" to "ensure the survival and success of liberty." President Bush, playing off this formulation, argued, "The survival of liberty in our land increasingly depends on the success of liberty in other lands. The best hope for peace in our world is the expansion of freedom in all the world."

For months, I had searched for a strong, single-sentence description of the goals of the Bush Doctrine. During this process, Pete Wehner (at this point the head of an internal White House think tank called the Office of Strategic Initiatives) and I invited several historians and foreign-policy experts to the White House for a wide-ranging policy discussion. Between comments on Iran and Iraq, Professor John Gaddis of Yale University—one of the most distinguished foreign-policy theorists of our time—suggested that the president "throw an anchor into the future" with a large objective: the end of tyranny by some date certain. I thought that putting a timeline to the goal was odd, but the general idea intrigued me. The objective was bold, but limited—not the universal triumph of democracy, but the end of ruthless oppression. Other than this suggestion, Professor Gaddis deserves no credit or blame for the speech itself. He proposed no language and saw no draft. I brought the idea to the president, who embraced it. In the end, the inaugural threw forward this weighty anchor: "So it is the policy of the United States to seek and support the growth of democratic movements and institutions in every nation and culture, with the ultimate goal of ending tyranny in our world."

In the speech, this goal is immediately and carefully qualified. It is "not primarily the task of arms" ... freedom "by its nature" is chosen, not imposed ... the institutions that arise in other lands will be "very different from our own" ... the goal is not immediate, but "the concentrated work of generations." The president pledged to aid the work of democratic reformers, but also to engage regimes (such as Saudi Arabia and Egypt) with "long habits of control": "Start on this journey of progress and justice," he urged them, "and America will walk at your side." The task, the speech insists, is difficult. But liberty moves forward on the strength of two advantages—the influence of America and the nature of the human person. "We have confidence because freedom is the permanent hope of mankind, the hunger in dark places, the longing of the soul. When our founders declared a new order for the ages; when soldiers died in wave upon wave for a union based on liberty; when citizens marched in peaceful outrage under the banner 'Freedom Now'—they were acting on an ancient hope that is meant to be fulfilled. History has an ebb and flow of justice, but history also has a visible direction, set by liberty and the Author of Liberty."

President Bush's first inaugural had referred to liberty as "a seed upon the wind." This January 2005 speech, provoked by "a day of fire," set out a more forceful image. "By our efforts, we have lit a fire, as well—a fire in the minds of men. It warms those who feel its power, it burns those who fight its progress, and one day this untamed fire of freedom will reach the darkest corners of our world."

Seated on the podium at the Capitol in a huddle of coats, facing down the Washington Mall toward the Lincoln Memorial, the historical ghosts seem so near they brush your skin. There is Lincoln, just eleven days before his death, watched by his assassin in the inaugural stand, wondering if "every drop of blood drawn with the lash shall be paid by another drawn with the sword." There is Martin Luther King Jr., under Lincoln's gaze, proclaiming: "We have also come to this hallowed spot to remind America of the fierce urgency of *now*. This is no time to engage in the luxury of cooling off or to take the tranquilizing drug of gradualism. *Now* is the time to make real the promises of democracy." Both men were courageous and eloquent. But above all they were great clarifiers. They were willing to follow the logic of liberty to its end. If the Declaration of Independence is not a myth and a lie and a fraud, it is true for everyone. That truth is never convenient. It often upsets a false stability. Affirming that truth may provoke the bitterness of violent men. The triumph of that truth may be preceded by decades of defeat and disappointment, when cynicism seems to all the world like realism. But the truth of human dignity and equality always and eventually emerges, with a sudden splendor. Always. Followed to its logical conclusion, the inalienable right of all men to be free implies and requires the end of tyranny in our world. A distant goal, a difficult goal—but an American goal.

Speaking at Independence Hall in Philadelphia in 1861, Lincoln drew out the logic of the Declaration in this way: "I have often inquired of myself, what great principle or idea it was that kept this Confederacy so long together. It was not the mere matter of the separation of the colonies from the mother land; but something in that Declaration giving liberty, not alone to the people of this country, but hope to the world for all future time. It was that which gave promise that in due time the weights should be lifted from the shoulders of all men, and that *all* should have an equal chance. This is the sentiment embodied in that Declaration of Independence."

As I made my way back through the crowds from the Capitol to the White House, Deputy National Security Advisor Steve Hadley called my cell phone. He reported that some embassies had already called, wondering what the speech meant for them. The reaction of the world's dictators was, understandably, critical. The Chinese *People's Daily* called the speech "morally conceited and militarily aggressive." Kim Jong-Il denounced the United States as "a wrecker of democracy as it ruthlessly infringes upon the sovereignty of other countries." The *Iranian Times* accused the president of "belligerent, unilateralist policies." The president of Belarus, Europe's last dictator, commented that Bush's notion of freedom was "soaked in blood and smelling of oil."

Some American conservatives chose to join this rather poor company. They accused the president of "mission inebriation"; called Bush the "Jacobin in Chief"; and concluded, "If Bush means it literally, then we have an extremist in the White House." But this, in its own way, was also understandable. Some strains of American conservatism are deeply suspicious of the role of abstract ideals like liberty or freedom in foreign (and domestic) policy. Some conservatives fear that a global role in promoting those values creates a Leviathan government at home. Some are convinced that American liberty, based on ancient British institutions and Christian cultural habits, is unique and unexportable. Some assert the absolute priority of cultural norms over philosophical abstractions like the Declaration of Independence, which they devalue as a document without legal standing. This is a long and distinguished tradition. But it is manifestly not the tradition of Lincoln or King—or Bush. And the clarity of the president's second inaugural exposed those divisions.

In some ways, the president's second inaugural was radical—but not uniquely radical in presidential history. President John F. Kennedy argued, "The 'magic power' on our side is the desire of every person to be free." He said: "It is because I believe our system is more in keeping with the fundamentals of human nature that I believe we are ultimately going to be successful." "These various elements in our foreign policy," Kennedy proclaimed, "lead to a single goal—the goal of a peaceful world of free and independent states." A world of free states is another way of saying the end of tyranny.

That goal was also familiar to President Ronald Reagan. Speaking in 1982 at Westminster in London, he said, "We must be staunch in our conviction that freedom is not the sole prerogative of a lucky few, but the inalienable and universal right of all human beings.... Democracy already flourishes in countries with very different cultures and historical experiences. It would be cultural condescension, or worse, to say that any people prefer dictatorship to democracy." In 1983, Reagan added: "I believe that communism is another sad, bizarre chapter in human history whose last pages even now are being written. I believe this because the source of our strength in the quest for human freedom is not material, but spiritual. And because it knows no limitation, it must terrify and ultimately triumph over those who would enslave their fellow man." Despite historical attempts to domesticate President Reagan—to muddy his moral clarity—this is a radical argument: the quest for human freedom "knows no limitation" and will "ultimately triumph" over tyranny.

Behind this language of idealism—rooted, in every case, in the Declaration of Independence—there is a consistent strain of American foreign policy that reaches from Roosevelt, to Truman, to Kennedy, to Reagan, to Bush. These presidents, while differing in policy and practice, believed that the United States benefits, in the long run, from the growth of a liberal international order—an order characterized by democracy, free trade, economic progress and development, and good government. Dictators like Hitler or Stalin (or Kim Jong-Il or Saddam Hussein) who use violence against their people are much more likely, in this view, to use violence against their neighbors. Democracies are more likely to confine their rivalries to the arenas of culture and trade. The American interest advances when freedom advances. And unlike the realpolitik power games of the past, the American interest is not purchased at the expense of others, because all nations can share in the benefits of liberty.

A few have attempted to overturn this consensus. In 1969, Henry Kissinger summarized the animating spirit of the Nixon foreign policy: "We will judge other countries, including communist countries, on the basis of their actions, not on the basis of their domestic ideologies." But both President Carter and President Reagan consciously and publicly rejected this approach. Reagan, in particular, was convinced that the domestic ideology of a country—if it is rooted in oppression and the will to power—ultimately *determines* its actions in the world. And President Clinton—while often hesitant and inconsistent in practice—affirmed this same general approach, defining a policy of "democratic enlargement."

The Bush foreign policy did depart from precedent in one large and dramatic way. Shocked into action by terrorist murder, which was spawned in a region characterized by brutal tyranny, President Bush decided to apply democratic internationalism in the Middle East. No previous president had consistently tried.

I think Prime Minister Blair's analysis of the second inaugural comes closest to the mark: "President Bush's inauguration speech last week marks a consistent evolution of US policy. He spoke of America's mission to bring freedom in place of tyranny to the world. Leave aside for a moment the odd insistence by some commentators that such a plea is evidence of a 'neo-conservative' grip on Washington—I thought progressives were all in favour of freedom rather than tyranny. The underlying features of the speech seem to me to be these. America accepts that terrorism cannot be defeated by military might alone. The more people live under democracy, with human liberty intact, the less inclined they or their states will be to indulge terrorism or to engage it in. This may be open to debate—though personally I agree with it—but it emphatically puts defeating the causes of terrorism alongside defeating the terrorists. Secondly, by its very nature, such a mission cannot be accomplished alone. It is the very antithesis of isolationism; the very essence of international engagement.... And it is based on enlightened self-interest. Freedom is good in itself. But it is also the best ultimate guarantee that human beings will live in sympathy with each other. The hard head has led to the warm heart."

When the president finally talked to me about my own future, I found his offer difficult to refuse. I was to hire a new head of speechwriting, releasing me from the daily tyranny of small presidential events, and allowing me to focus on larger projects. (This prayer was answered in the form of Bill McGurn, a brilliant writer and a principled man who had spent years at the *Wall Street Journal*.) As Assistant to the President for Policy and Strategic Planning, I was to be an advocate for the president's enthusiasms, which I tended to share. I did not expect the job to be easy—and I was not disappointed.

I quickly found that working on the human-rights and democracy agenda was both inspiring and frustrating. On the inspiring side, the president had a consistent interest in the lives and stories of dissidents. In June 2005, President Bush met in the Oval Office with a North Korean defector named Kang Chol-Hwan. Bush had read his terrifying memoir, *The Aquariums of Pyongyang,* which detailed a level of massive, organized brutality unequaled since the gulags. Kang told the president, in halting English, "When I heard you had read my book, I was convinced that God is alive." "When I escaped," he said, "my purpose was to disclose the gruesome reality. But the international community wasn't interested." South Korea in particular, he argued, consistently downplayed the human-rights issue, seeking to avoid confrontation. The president responded that raising the human-rights issue was essential. Tyrants, he argued, want us to focus on the weapons, not on the people, but that he would continue to focus on the people. Kang Chol-Hwan left the Oval Office knowing he had an ally.

I also had the opportunity to introduce the president to Simon Deng, a former slave from Sudan, taken captive as a teenager. He sat next to the president in the Roosevelt Room, during a meeting on the crisis in Darfur. At first, Deng wanted to talk only about Sudan policy—he was reluctant to tell his story. But the president drew him out. "I am here in this beautiful building," Deng finally said, before his voice choked with emotion, and he had trouble continuing. "I am here in this beautiful building, thank God, and I was once given as a gift." Gaining in confidence, Deng added, alluding to his own story, "Only a few slaves from Sudan have voted for you twice." Deng had some intense ritual scarification across his forehead. But I remember thinking: *If the Republican Party stands for anyone, it is and must be for people like this.* Deng supported the president because the president stood for liberty and human rights—because he didn't view him and others like him as benighted and primitive foreigners, incapable of freedom.

Detailing the advances and setbacks of the human-rights and democracy agenda would take a book in itself. But the period from late 2004 to the middle of 2005 was a time of intense promise. Decisions by the president had led to the liberation of over fifty million people who had suffered under the grinding boot of two of the worst regimes on earth. In both Afghanistan and Iraq, their progress toward self-government was rocky and contested, but undeniable. Iraq in particular had not missed a single deadline in its democratic transformation. And what Thomas Jefferson had called the "contagion of liberty" seemed to be at a particularly infectious stage. First the Rose Revolution in Georgia ... then the Orange Revolution in Ukraine ... then Palestinian presidential elections ... then the Cedar Revolution in

Lebanon ... then the Tulip Revolution in Kyrgyzstan. The street demonstrations in Lebanon's Martyr's Square—which swelled to at least 800,000 people—eventually forced the retreat of occupying Syrian troops. Political reforms moved forward in some of the Gulf State monarchies. Morocco instituted an innovative family law giving new rights to women, children, and minorities. President Mubarak accepted the principle of multiparty presidential elections for the first time in Egypt's long history.

In the midst of these hopeful events, Lebanese Druze leader Walid Jumblatt remarked that the January 30, 2005, Iraqi elections had torn down the Middle East's "Berlin Wall" and midwifed "a new Arab world." The French newspaper *Le Figaro* reluctantly asked, "And if Bush was Right?" In June 2005, Henry Kissinger surveyed these "extraordinary advances in democracy" and wrote: "This welcome trend was partly triggered by President Bush's Middle East policy and accelerated by his second inaugural address, which elevated the progress of freedom in the world to the defining objective of American foreign policy." At the end of the year, Freedom House reported: "The global picture thus suggests that 2005 was one of the most successful years for freedom since Freedom House began measuring world freedom in 1972." Some creative and destructive power had been shaken loose.

In May 2005, I sat in Freedom Square in the ancient Caucasus nation of Georgia—Christian in history, but vaguely Middle Eastern in architecture and culture. Over 150,000 people had gathered to hear President Bush—more people than had participated in the protests of the Rose Revolution that had overthrown their dictator a year earlier. In introducing Bush, President Shakashvilli said: "I had the opportunity to listen to your second inaugural speech. I remember your words: 'All who live in tyranny and hopelessness can know: the United Sates will not ignore your oppression or excuse your oppressors. When you stand for your liberty, we will stand with you.' That evening my feeling was that you were addressing me personally and our people, you were talking about *our* freedom and success, were defending *our* democracy." At the end of the ceremony, the loudspeakers along the square began the Georgian national anthem, which had been banned during the Soviet era. But the broadcast system quickly broke down. In the silence, the crowd began to sing the song *a cappella*, softly at first, then with enthusiastic pride. Afterward, the First Lady of Georgia told the president, "This is typical of Georgia. Out of chaos, something beautiful."

Swiftly, maybe inevitably, this democratic progress inspired a backlash. The growing violence in Iraq called into question the ability of elections to overcome sectarian differences, and dictators in the region used the chaos to press their self-interested case against the dangers of freedom. In the Palestinian territories, legislative elections brought the terrorist group Hamas to power, as the Muslim Brotherhood gained political traction in Egypt, raising the prospect that elections might empower anti-American forces in the Middle East. The increased nuclear assertiveness of Iran led the Bush administration to seek closer ties with Sunni powers like Egypt and Saudi Arabia in an effort of containment, making it more awkward to press those regimes for political reform. And not long after the delivery of the second inaugural, a major internal shift took place within the administration: Condi Rice left the White House to become secretary of state. There is no finer representative of our country abroad—tireless, tough, charming, unflappable. But as the center of gravity of policy and decision making moved to the State Department, it also empowered that agency's regional bureaus—career diplomats who (with some notable exceptions) did not share the president's foreign-policy perspective. All attempts to raise human rights and democracy in China, North Korea, Egypt, or Saudi Arabia became trapped in a thousand sticky strands of objections and cautions—until the web became almost impenetrable.

The treatment of Egypt was, for me, the most frustrating case study. That country, in many ways, is the defining test of the democracy agenda. Along with Baghdad and Damascus, Cairo is one of the great cultural centers of the Arab world. By population, Egypt outweighs all its competitors—there are more schoolchildren in Cairo than there are people in Jordan. Egypt has a history of liberal institutions, including fine universities, a healthy civil society, and strong, independent judges— existing elements of a democratic culture. And as one of the largest recipients of American aid in the world, Egypt is more subject to American leverage than is, say, Saudi Arabia.

In 2002, Egypt's President Hosni Mubarak had imprisoned Saad Eddin Ibrahim, a brilliant, elegant democratic reformer. The American response was forceful. After the administration threatened to cut off over 100 million dollars in economic aid, Ibrahim was released. In the summer of 2005, I traveled with Condi to Cairo, where we met another dissident, Ayman Nour, who had courageously chosen to run against Mubarak in the upcoming presidential election. But he was deeply pessimistic. The door of elections, he said, is "not an open door; it is a revolving door. It will end up with one conclusion—a monologue, not a dialogue. The law is unclear and unfair." At the end of the meeting, Condi assured him, "We're watching." After the election, Nour was arrested and sentenced to five years in prison—perhaps a death sentence for a diabetic in fragile health. Mubarak set off a wave of repression in which protesters, including women, were brutally beaten. But the American response was less than forceful—mainly the ritual protests of diplomacy. America watched, and did little. Something had shifted, which I protested with little effect.

As the democracy agenda sputtered, a portion of the foreign-policy establishment seemed relieved, even happy, that idealism was being discredited (in their view) by events ... that the more realistic effort to engage the dictators could resume in earnest ... and that history was returning to its old and familiar grooves. It is an odd reaction for American foreign-policy thinkers to take consolation from receding democratic momentum in the world. One would think sadness and disappointment more appropriate. But there seemed to be more than sufficient comfort in the belief that Bush had been wrong after all.

In fact, the cynicism of the present is no more justified than over-confidence and euphoria would have been early in 2005. The tides of history shift quickly, and the moods of the moment are an unreliable guide to the events of the future. The promotion of democracy in other lands, it is safe to say, will be at least as difficult as the achievement of democracy in our own—a process that consumed decades of incremental progress, bloody conflict, and consistent courage. Democratic regression is possible. Elections can sometimes bring illiberal forces to power—as we saw in Germany in the 1930s, and nearly saw in close elections across Europe during the early days of the Cold War that would have brought communists to office. Elections are often the beginning of a democratic consolidation, not the end—their success or failure is measured by the eventual strength of democratic institutions such as political parties and independent courts. These facts are not new discoveries, nor does the recognition of obstacles discredit the democratic movements of the last century. The fact that elections can turn out poorly does not invalidate self-government. The fact that democracy can express the darker impulses of a culture does not prove the worthlessness of human freedom. Perfection, thank God, is not a prerequisite for idealism.

The events of the last few years offer encouragement as well as warning. During the long decades that America actively propped up "favorable" Middle Eastern dictators in the interests of stability (and, understandably, to counter Soviet influence in the region), there was almost no democratic progress. In five years of President Bush's "forward strategy of freedom in the Middle East," there was more democratic progress than in the previous fifty years combined. That is not likely to be a coincidence.

Two questions require answers: Is democratic progress in the Islamic world possible? And: Is it necessary?

The first question, at one level, is absurd. A majority of the world's Muslims already live in democratic societies from India and Indonesia and Turkey, to Mali and Senegal, to the United States and the European Union. That does not suggest a creed inalterably incompatible with pluralism. The question becomes more pertinent in considering the Arab world, comprising about one-fifth of Muslims. The twenty-two governments of the Arab Middle East are overwhelmingly characterized by despotic rule. But those who believe these tyrants and military dictators are permanent and inevitable expressions of Arab culture must ignore the fact that they are a relatively recent phenomenon. Their totalitarian models of government were transplants from Nazism and communism; they did not grow from the soil of Islam. As Professor Bernard Lewis and others have pointed out, Islam sets a series of traditional limits on the power of the ruler. He should govern in consultation with other elements of society and avoid arbitrary decisions. He should respect private property. While Islam has no tradition of secular law—the law of the Koran is seen as complete and sufficient—the Islamic ruler is not above the law. Like every culture, Islam contains elements that are conducive to pluralism and limited government, and elements that are not. And as in every society before them, including our own, Islamic and Arab societies will make progress by strengthening the first elements at the expense of the second.

Cultural pessimists must also ignore the fact that America has found heroic Muslim allies in the fight against Islamic extremism. The Kurds in Iraq and the Northern Alliance in Afghanistan proved themselves tough and courageous. Reformers like Amina Lemrini in Morocco and Ghada Jamsheer in Bahrain push for the rights of women at great personal risk. Soldiers in Afghanistan and Iraq are currently risking and losing their lives in a struggle against assorted terrorists, jihadists, and rejectionists. These efforts may not, in the end, be enough—but they deserve more and better than our contempt.

Is democratic progress necessary in the Arab world? It is, and for the most urgent of reasons. The status quo of tyranny and stagnation is not sustainable. Change is coming to the Middle East whether we prefer it or not—and America has a stake in the form that it takes.

Tagging along with Secretary Rice on a visit to Saudi Arabia in 2005, I attended a dinner with the Saudi royal family at one of their many palaces. Crown Prince Abdullah (later the King) welcomed Condi with a grave formality. He is clearly a pious man, whose piety, however, includes a deep hatred for Israel—he spent much of his time recounting Israeli crimes. Soon we were ushered into a large banqueting hall. The Saudis cannot be accused of understatement. There was gold filigree on the ceiling, massive crystal candelabras, attendants with pistols and bandoliers, hundreds of dishes set out on a buffet, including a whole roasted lamb with head attached. At one side of the massive room ran the long banqueting table. In the center lay an elaborate pool. At the far end a seating area was flanked by a bank of forty televisions tuned to a variety of cable offerings (one television, I remember, showed Richard Perle being interviewed). The lounge area was reached from the dining area by walking through a large transparent tube laid through a massive aquarium filled with tropical fish and circling sharks. I could not tell whether the choice of ornamental wildlife was intended to be menacing or not. The setting resembled nothing in my experience—except, perhaps, the cinematic lair of a James Bond villain.

All this held a certain exotic appeal—like Buckingham Palace without taste, restraint, or beauty. It symbolized, to me, a historical reality. The Saudi ruling class remains in power only because of compressed plant material under the soil of their country—oil wealth, amounting to 60 percent of the world's reserves, which has also preserved an outdated aristocracy like an insect in amber. It is a parasitic elite that produces nothing, contributes little, and consumes on a massive scale—sometimes spending hundreds of millions of dollars on jet-setting vacations when the desert grows too hot. Meanwhile, the water in Riyadh is unsafe to drink ... few Saudis study science or engineering ... most manual labor is done by imported foreigners ... Islamic extremism is ignored or condoned or quietly subsidized ... and a pampered few maintain their power through the secret police and a universal welfare system that is

indistinguishable from bribery. To visit Saudi Arabia is to visit a caricature of pre-revolutionary France, a society in which any reasonable man
would be a rebel.

On the same trip, our delegation met with Egypt's President
Mubarak at Sharm el-Sheikh, a resort city in the Sinai Peninsula.
Mubarak, in his eighties, is one of the great wily survivors of Middle
Eastern politics. He has a Marlon Brando manner—large, vague, ponderous—and a switchblade-sharp mind. In the habit of some older
people, he kept the reception room so hot that I began to feel faint, and
to ponder whether losing consciousness might actually make a unique
contribution to our relations. But Mubarak's long monologue, a fascinating tour of the current complexities of the Middle East, awakened
my attention. He dropped names of world leaders from the first President Bush (who was coming to meet him in a few months) to Shimon
Peres (who was coming that day for lunch). Israel's Prime Minister
Sharon, he said, was the only man who could implement the road map
toward peace with the Palestinians. He complained about the Iranians,
who had named a unit of their military after the man who murdered
the Egyptian hero Anwar Sadat. Iraq, he argued, needed a strong
leader—"but fair" (like himself, presumably). And he assured us that
democracy in that country would not work.

Mubarak was impressive in his Nixonian breadth of mind. Equally
Nixonian was his failure, at any point in his tour, to mention any consideration other than power. He is a realist's realist. In part, that realism
has led him on occasion to take a constructive role in the Middle East
peace process and the War on Terror. In part, it is what has led him to
destroy any liberal opposition … engage in a self-serving bargain with
Islamic radicals … and work for the dynastic succession of his son. In
addition, Egypt's state-controlled media are a reliable and creative source
of anti-American propaganda, rife with claims that the US has carried
out all the terrorism in Iraq, just as we authored the 9/11 attacks, just as
we are intending to invade Sudan, convert the Sudanese to Christianity,
and steal their oil.

It is impossible to imagine either of these models of Middle East-ern government—spoiled royalty or exhausted autocracy—as the wave of the future. This is a region with some of the highest birth-rates and some of the lowest literacy levels in the world. Since 1980, the population of the Muslim Near East has doubled, while its share of global investment has fallen by half, and its share of world trade by two-thirds. Governments in the region have proved incapable of reversing these trends—incapable of any accomplishment save the maintenance of their own power. Vast economic inequality, cultural stagnation, and boiling resentment are making that power increasingly fragile. Those who bet on the durability of the current order in the Middle East are not "realists"; they are in denial. And the only serious alternatives to that order are, on the one hand, the disciplined and ruthless forces of radical Islam and, on the other hand, the scattered forces of democracy and reform.

In fact, many of these regimes have chosen a survival strategy that seems designed to ensure Islamist revolution. As their many failures have become undeniable, they have taken baby steps of reform—allowing more economic and cultural openness—while keeping a monopoly on political power. This has encouraged all legitimate discontent and oppo-sition to gather in the only healthy institutional alternative to the state: the radical mosque. By undermining and destroying a third political alternative—political parties committed to pluralism—Middle Eastern regimes are actively empowering their worst enemies. Under these cir-cumstances, immediate, national elections are not always advisable. In a free choice between corrupt autocrats and radical Islamist "reformers," the latter are likely to win. But even if elections are not always the answer, political reform is still the key. Societies like Egypt need legal political parties, freedom of the press, freedom of association and assem-bly—the institutions and rights that eventually will allow citizens to make a non-Islamist transition to a more hopeful and prosperous society. Promoting this kind of broad political change—not just elections—should be the focus of American policy.

The Middle East will tend toward extremism, or it will tend toward freedom. America does not control the outcome of that contest, but we have a direct interest in the success of one side, and we should do all we can to advance it. Our goal is to move regimes toward political pluralism, without destructive destabilization. This is not a reckless undertaking; it is an unavoidable one. It calls for steady purpose, not mood swings of elation and despair. But there must be a sense of urgency. The question is not: are we pushing for reform too early? A different question hangs over America and the world: are we pushing for reform too late?

Another human-rights issue in which the president was deeply engaged was the genocide in the Darfur region of Sudan. When Bush took office, that nation had seen seventeen years of bloodletting, during a civil war between north and south that eventually cost over two million lives. Securing a peace treaty to end this war was one of the great diplomatic achievements of President Bush's first term. But as this historic agreement was being negotiated, a new conflict was breaking out in Sudan's west. In early 2003, rebel groups in Darfur launched a series of attacks on government garrisons. The regime of Omar Hassan al-Bashir in Khartoum (an Islamist government that had once sheltered Osama bin Laden) responded by bombing villages and recruiting and arming Arab nomadic tribesmen (known as the Janjaweed) to fight a brutal proxy war against the rebels. These mounted, irregular militias began systematically burning and destroying agrarian villages, ethnically cleansing whole regions, and using systematic rape as a tool of humiliation and intimidation. Soon nearly half a million people were dead from fighting, famine, and disease, and over two million men, women, and children had been forced into displaced-persons camps, completely dependent on international food aid, and subject to rape and murder whenever they ventured beyond the gates. In 2004, the Bush administration declared this to be a genocide, and the African Union (a regional organization of African governments) sent a small military force to observe and report on the situation.

By 2005, the situation in Darfur had stabilized somewhat, but mainly because there were few villages left to destroy. The Janjaweed still roamed and raped with impunity. The government of Sudan felt few consequences for sponsoring the first genocide of the twenty-first century. And American policy was stuck and stagnant. Deputy Secretary of State Robert Zoellick, the brilliant and prickly former trade representative, was in charge of our Sudan policy. When I expressed an interest in traveling to the region in November to review our approach, Bob called me to his elegant office at the State Department, reminded me of my place in things (I had none), and treated me to a long and detailed lecture on the politics of Darfur. Bob viewed the problem as a tribal civil war, conducted over limited resources, in which traditions of "reciprocity" led to a cycle of violence. He was convinced that the regime in Khartoum had made a "strategic choice" to seek greater integration and trade with the world. And though al-Bashir and his colleagues were often lured into tactical choices that "don't fit their strategic design," only negotiations could pull them back to a better course. Frustration, he continued, could lead to the proposal of simplistic solutions, such as a United Nations peacekeeping force. Troops are not the "magic bullet"—a phrase that is usually used by someone who doesn't want such ammunition in the arsenal at all. He ended with this advice: "You can't solve all the problems of the world"—a sentiment that seemed odd coming from someone charged by the president with solving this one particular problem.

This was foreign-policy "realism" in a very cramped nutshell. Zoellick argued that the president should not raise his profile on Darfur because no good outcome was likely—while expressing confidence in the power of diplomacy and engagement to win concessions from the regime in Khartoum. In theory, foreign-policy realism is supposed to take power and interest seriously as the main givens of world politics. In practice, realism often amounts to a trust in the magical power of negotiations with dictators in Khartoum, or Tehran, or Damascus. As it happened, President al-Bashir of Sudan was a master at those negotiations—making minor concessions, stepping back from them, renegotiating previous negotiations—until years had passed without anything changing on the ground. And as far as I could tell, the regime felt very little outside pressure to change its ways. Sudan was a major source of oil for China, which often provided diplomatic protection in the UN Security Council. It was an importer of Russian arms. The regime cultivated Islamist solidarity with Arab governments. All of these relationships acted as shields to protect Khartoum from international pressure.

What I witnessed in Sudan that November only deepened my concerns. We were to meet al-Bashir at the rebuilt presidential palace where the British imperial hero, Gordon of Khartoum, had been killed in an Islamist uprising. Guards in starched white uniforms, with AK-47s and bayonets, stood at the entrance. We walked under massive elephant tusks, with machine-gun emplacements pointed toward those who entered, and were escorted by pushy security people to the presidential reception chamber, with its vaguely Arab columns and modular office furniture. President al-Bashir—black hair, black shirt, and black slacks—shook our hands in turn, and I felt the strange, icy electricity of contact with a mass murderer. Zoellick gave a long and learned opening statement, which the Sudanese president accepted with resigned patience. In his own remarks, al-Bashir was not only unrepentant, but aggressive. "You are not going to the source of the problem. The issue there is tribal conflict, with tribal factions. Even divisions within the rebels. There would be no violence if the rebels respected the cease-fire. The rebels have looted the Arab tribes." He said that his government was conducting "legitimate defensive operations," pressed for the lifting of American sanctions, and hinted he wanted to be invited as a guest to the United States. It was not the statement of a leader who felt any pressure or fear.

Darfur itself is one of the lonely places of the world—reddish soil and reddish dust … an occasional stand of trees near dry streams and lakes … low hills with light green grass, bluish green shrubs, and scattered cattle … round huts with pointed roofs. Moving along the dirt roads, we were protected by African Union troops, Kenyans, and Namibians. We passed donkey carts and women in bright wraps of green, blue, and vivid orange—a colorful, human protest against the bleak landscape. In the white tents of an African Union military base, we were given an extended military briefing. Janjaweed operated throughout the area, we were told. The rebels extorted taxes from the business community. Bandits attacked food convoys, because "it is easier to harvest a truck than to harvest a field." And behind all the chaos, there was "some hidden agenda" that promoted tribal dissension and violence. Our briefer—a brisk Rwandan officer—concluded this grim overview by saying: "But we will not be discouraged. As the Bible says, 'No one who puts his hand to the plow and turns back is fit for service in the Kingdom of God.'" After the briefing ended, I asked another officer about the reference to the "hidden agenda." He answered me with exasperation: "Obviously the hidden agenda is the government in Khartoum. They promote division, and the rebels are playing into their hands with all their infighting. The government wants chaos."

Later that day we boarded an AU helicopter, built by the Soviet Union in its heyday but now dangerously shabby and smelling of fuel inside the cabin. We landed in an open field, and walked to a village named Shek En Nil—150 housing compounds, all empty, a few burned into charred rings. Weeks before, Darfur rebels had taken control of the town in a surprise attack that forced the Sudanese garrison to run. The government counterattacked with helicopter gunships, forcing the rebels to move out. Then the regime directed its Janjaweed allies to move into the village on camels and horseback. They looted Shek En Nil and burned sixteen houses. Eighteen hundred people were forced into the camps—all from the Zaghawa tribe associated with the rebels. It was a miniature version of the entire Darfur crisis. What had begun as a counterinsurgency operation became—through a cruel and disproportionate overreaction—an act of ethnic cleansing.

I left Sudan convinced that the pillars of American policy were crumbling. The conditions in the camps were not desperate, but they were fragile. (The Kalma camp we visited had been harassed by fifty Janjaweed horsemen the day before we arrived.) The African Union force in Darfur was well-intentioned but overwhelmed—without secure communications, sufficient mobility or firepower, or even a mandate to protect civilians. The "strategic choice" of the regime in Khartoum was clear enough to me: it was actively cooperating with the Janjaweed, blocking the visas of aid workers, undermining the work of the African Union, and encouraging tribal conflict. This crisis was more than a tribal civil war. The overreaction of the government to the rebels was so massive and brutal it amounted to genocide. Yet, because there was no perfect solution to the security situation, America ended up doing little, except for massively aiding the victims. I was convinced that America needed to give immediate military aid to the AU forces ... increase military pressure on the government (perhaps with a no-fly zone that would ground the regime's aircraft in Darfur) ... and push for an eventual transition to a capable United Nations military force at least twice the size of the AU mission. This might not be a "magic bullet," I figured, but it would likely save some lives, limit Khartoum's options of brutality, and maybe create a more favorable atmosphere for negotiations.

I reported these recommendations to the president upon my return. He was favorable to a UN transition and committed to stronger action, and this renewed urgency was communicated to the national security staff. By February, America was working toward a Security Council vote on a UN force for Darfur. But the Department of Defense was largely uncooperative—resisting even a few US military observers in the military planning process. And the Office of Management and Budget, by underfunding our broader commitment to UN peacekeeping operations, was complicating the task of passing a Security Council resolution. The president's effort to address the crisis was not only being complicated by the Chinese or the French; it was being complicated by the Department of Defense and OMB.

Frustrated and angry, I sent the president a few articles from Sudan activists harshly accusing the administration of timidity on the Darfur crisis. After reading the articles, the president took vivid exception to much of the criticism. But he informed me he intended to act. In the next day or two, the president spoke to the secretary general of NATO, to Chancellor Merkel of Germany, and to President Chirac of France, making the case for a stronger NATO effort in Darfur. Because his own administration had been passive, the president began to take charge himself.

A few days later, the president was in Florida for a town-hall meeting. After a general question from the audience on Africa, he veered off to announce his support for doubling the number of troops in Darfur in a UN force, and called for a broader NATO role—which became front-page news in the *New York Times* and the *Washington Post*. That afternoon I saw Bob Zoellick on West Executive Avenue, the street between the West Wing and the Old Executive Office Building. He snapped to me, "Why didn't he just say we should triple the troops?"— which would have been fine with me.

With consistent presidential pressure, the administration put into place the elements of a more effective approach. Bob eventually engaged in a heroic, marathon negotiation that resulted in the Darfur Peace Agreement (DPA), signed by the government and one of the main rebel groups. The DPA did not actually bring peace, but it cleared the way for the United Nations Security Council to pass a resolution authorizing a peacekeeping force of 22,000 for Darfur.

Yet this conflict remains a case study in the limits of presidential power. President Bush intervened, again and again, to push the process toward action. But the options for US unilateral action are indeed limited—it would be difficult and dangerous to place thousands of American boots on the ground in the middle of a Muslim country, ruled by a regime that feeds Islamist hatred. And the Department of Defense—stretched by a world of exhausting commitments—remains deeply reluctant to even consider less intrusive military options, such as a no-fly zone. NATO, paralyzed by internal squabbling about its own mission and future, has failed to take a more muscular role in Darfur. The United Nations military-planning process moves with ponderous inefficiency. For those who insist that America must be more multilateral in its foreign policy, welcome to your world. The response to the crisis in Darfur has been a model of multilateralism—but international institutions such as the UN and NATO are not designed for urgency.

As for America, we face our own moral challenge. In our country, memories of the Holocaust are so strong, preserved by its aging survivors and a museum on the Washington Mall. Yet timely action against genocide—in Cambodia or Iraq or Rwanda—is so rare. It is a contradiction we must eventually confront.

While the issues of democracy and Darfur brought occasional frustration, the issues of development and disease brought a consistent infusion of purpose and progress. If historians prove fairer than journalists, the president eventually will be credited with a series of bold humanitarian accomplishments. In particular, he sponsored the largest percentage increases in foreign assistance since the Marshall Plan—larger percentage increases than any of our G–8 partners. Since 2000, US official development assistance has more than doubled from $10 billion to more than $22 billion in 2006. Some of this spending has gone to nation building in Afghanistan and Iraq, but much has been devoted to a series of initiatives on health, women's empowerment, and economic reform. Development assistance for sub-Saharan Africa rose to $5.6 billion in 2006—five times the level of 2000. With little attention or credit, President Bush has overseen the most creative period of thinking on global development since John F. Kennedy's New Frontier.

Some of the impetus came from a clear-eyed consideration of American interests following 9/11. Poverty cannot be called the direct cause of terrorism—many terrorist leaders (like bin Laden) and their recruits come from wealthier backgrounds. But poverty contributes to instability and civil conflict in many parts of Africa, Asia, and South America—and terrorist groups often exploit conflict zones for recruitment and training. Poor and weak governments have little capacity to control their own territory or borders, and lawless regions attract terrorists as an abandoned house in a rough neighborhood attracts crack dealers. Failed states and ungoverned regions do not merely export terrorism; they act as incubators for drug trafficking (like Colombia), human trafficking (like the Balkans), refugees (like Sudan), and pandemics (like AIDS and new threats like the avian flu). A world of misery is a world of danger. We have also found that persistent poverty undermines the freedom agenda, because it allows populist demagogues like Hugo Chavez in Venezuela to harness resentment at the expense of democracy. For freedom to take deep root in any nation, its economic benefits must reach broader sectors of society than a small, globalized elite.

But we have good reason to believe that foreign assistance, under the right circumstances, can be effective, particularly when it encourages economic reforms that attract greater trade and investment. As conservatives point out, many countries with large flows of foreign aid remain economically stagnant, with our generosity doing little more than propping up corrupt regimes. Poorly governed countries, unsurprisingly, make poor use of aid. Sometimes emergency humanitarian assistance is required even for people in such regimes—starvation is not just a punishment for living in a poorly governed country. But in countries with good policies—with low inflation; the rule of law; low trade barriers; effective, honest bureaucracies—aid can work well and be of genuine assistance. Through the Millennium Challenge Account, the Bush administration has channeled substantial new development aid to countries that are committed to good government and increased spending on health and education. The administration has encouraged open trade, the quickest path for any nation out of desperate poverty. And it has worked for improvements in health that make all other progress possible.

Many of these efforts have been focused on Africa, for a variety of reasons. Africa is an increasingly strategic continent, with large reserves of oil and brushfires of conflict with radical Islam raging across its center. American resources and sympathy are drawn to the severest needs—and in parts of Africa the needs are very severe. America has long and complicated ties of history to the African continent, and historic injustice imposes continuing duties. But the ties between America and Africa are also being strengthened by a relatively new historical trend—the movement of the center of gravity of world Christianity to the developing south.

In 1900, about 80 percent of the world's Christians lived in Europe and America. Today, about 60 percent live in the developing world. There are now more evangelical Christians in Brazil and Nigeria together than there are in the United States. There are now more Presbyterians in Ghana than in Scotland. There are now nearly four times more Anglicans in the Archdiocese of Kampala than there are members of the entire American Episcopal Church. American religious leaders such as Rick Warren are encouraging ties between American congregations and their counterparts in Africa. Over one and a half million Americans now take short-term foreign mission trips each year, and often return with an awakened awareness of the struggles and dignity of their not-so-distant Christian brothers and sisters in the developing world. Christians who had previously focused only on abortion and family issues now lobby for debt relief and against sex trafficking, for religious liberty and in support of the battle against HIV/AIDS. Conservative Christianity, for the first time, is becoming a force that pushes the American government toward internationalism and greater global engagement.

At the White House—in one of the most bitter periods of partisan-ship in modern political history—I saw the development of some odd and encouraging alliances. On Sudan, I worked closely with tradition-ally liberal human-rights organizations, as well as evangelical groups. On HIV/AIDS, I found common purpose with homosexual-rights advocates as well as Catholic non-profit organizations. I organized con-structive lunches on development issues between the president and Bill Gates—strangely, they had never met—and between Bush and Bono, the lead singer of U–2. The president had a strong predisposition to dis-like celebrity activists—he had generally found them self-serving and poorly informed—but he was charmed, much against his will, by Bono's animated Irish storytelling, his deep knowledge of development, and his evident sincerity. After the lunch, the president's reaction to me—"He seems like a really good guy"—was as superlative as Bush could get about a rock star in Bulgari sunglasses.

The first time I met Bono, over lunch at the Four Seasons, he talked about a visit he had taken to the campus of Wheaton College (the Christian school I attended). He had been surprised and impressed to see evangelicals on the leading edge of social justice. "It was not like the preachers on TV I'd seen while growing up," he told me. He still had problems with evangelicalism's off-putting religious intensity. Franklin Graham (Billy Graham's son), he reported, had turned to him every ten minutes on a long car trip and said: "But do you really accept Jesus Christ as your personal savior?" But he was impressed by Billy Graham's gentle spirit, and had traveled to North Carolina just to get his blessing. "I take blessings very seriously," he explained.

Our meeting took place just days before I left for my own first trip to Africa. As the lunch broke up, Bono told me: "You are going to meet people whose lives you are saving, and they won't even know it."

Quite apart from all the strategic and political reasons to help the poor and dying in foreign lands, Bono had identified the great emotional pull of these issues. In times of war, so many problems and choices confront us that even the noblest goals can become tainted by unintended results and unforeseen failures. Even when war is just and necessary, the passions unleashed by violence are never pure. But the choice to save an infant from malaria, or to rescue a mother from lingering death by AIDS, is not conflicted. Contributing to those decisions by the president was my best experience in government.

Malaria, taking nearly a million lives a year, is Africa's largest cause of funerals. And the caskets are mainly quite small, since over 80 percent of the dead are children under five years old. It is a problem that reveals nature at its most sinister. The female mosquito needs a meal of blood before laying her eggs. She is attracted to the moisture and warmth of the human body. As she extracts the blood with cutting probes, she injects an anticoagulant saliva to prevent the blood from clotting in her stomach—and a microscopic parasite called Plasmodium travels along with her saliva. The parasite periodically destroys millions of red blood cells in its new host, leading to fever and a total loss of energy. For the young and weak, the attacks are often fatal. Before I went to Africa, I visited the National Institutes of Health in Bethesda, Maryland, to see an infected red blood cell—bumpy with small, sticky nodes—under the electron microscope. On the African continent in early 2005, I saw the result: primitive wards, open to the elements, filled with lethargic patients receiving outdated, ineffective treatments ... a beautiful and polite sixteen-year-old AIDS orphan, taking care of her three brothers and sisters, her hand burning with fever when I shook it ... and a mother carrying her own baby home through the gates of the hospital, dead in a small sack held to her chest, the loneliest sight I have ever seen. The health ministers I met in Namibia, Mozambique, and other countries view this disease as their greatest challenge, draining productivity and destroying tourism.

But with new Artemisian-based drugs, malaria is treatable. And with old and proven methods—bed nets and indoor insecticide spraying—malaria is preventable. The suffering of this disease is not only tragic, it is unnecessary. And that transforms the situation from a tragedy into a scandal.

Previous American efforts to fight malaria in Africa had been scattered and ineffective—the scale was never broad enough to defeat the wily and persistent mosquito. So upon my return to Washington, I began to work with a bright young NSC staffer named John Simon on a new malaria initiative. The G–8 Summit in Gleneagles, Scotland, hosted by Prime Minister Blair, was still about four months down the road. But I knew Blair was intending to make Africa a focus of the meeting—and that, eventually, the president would need to bring some proposal of his own to the table. The President's Malaria Initiative (as we named it) was designed to cut malaria deaths in half in fifteen African countries, by increasing indoor spraying, providing more treated bed nets, and getting effective drugs to the victims. I began to sell the president on the details of the proposal. He was generally attracted to policy ideas that were result-oriented and morally urgent—and this was no exception.

The initiative was internally controversial. In a Situation Room policy meeting in June of 2005, some objected to the cost—over a billion dollars—and feared that Congress might make other cuts to cover the expense. But the group agreed to present the proposal to the president in policy time the next day. That Oval Office meeting was attended by the vice president, Treasury Secretary Snow, Secretary Rice, Andy Card, Karl Rove, Josh Bolten, and several others. I knew that some of this group intended to argue strenuously against the malaria initiative, and I had prepared my arguments carefully. But when the meeting moved on to the section of the briefing book marked "Proposals," the president leafed through distractedly and, coming to this one, said, "I've talked to Mike about that; I approve it." That night, I went out to dinner with my family, and tried to explain to my two boys what had happened at the office that day—that hundreds of thousands of children were going to live, because the president has a good heart. But I just started sobbing, leaving my sons to be embarrassed, once again, by their strange and sentimental father.

The greatest humanitarian challenge of the early twenty-first century is HIV/AIDS—and here the solutions are not nearly as obvious as malaria. The mosquito is indifferent to human morality. AIDS raises the deepest questions of sexuality, culture, and economic inequality. Just minutes from the beaches and open-air restaurants of Cape Town, there is a slum of about twenty thousand people who migrated from rural areas of the Eastern Cape. They are overwhelmingly young (I saw no one over fifty), sexually active, and about 27 to 30 percent are HIV positive. Because of the extreme poverty, men with jobs—taxi drivers, postmen, bus drivers—gain enormous sexual power, providing young girls with clothing, bus rides, and other favors in exchange for sex. "There is a lot of sex for cell-phone air time," I was told by Pastor John, who ministers in the community. And this kind of transactional sex is often rough and unprotected, increasing the transmission of HIV to young women. Some of the corrugated-roof houses have been turned into makeshift bars called "shabins," where it is possible to buy grain alcohol in small plastic bags for a few pennies, and the services of a prostitute for a dollar. "With alcohol," Pastor John observed, "there is no condom use." The migrants in this slum return to the Eastern Cape for Easter, Christmas—and to be buried. When they sense the end is near, they board a bus for home, so their families do not have to pay for the cost of transporting their bodies.

Pastor John's ministry, called Living Hope, is focusing on reaching children aged four to sixteen, trying "to give them the prevention lifestyle." Every weekday there is a children's club, with Bible lessons, crafts, a meal, and prayer. Among children eleven to sixteen years old (the average age of sexual debut is around thirteen), about 11 percent are HIV positive. About 10 percent of the girls report sexual coercion. "You have to go to younger age groups, before they make sexual choices," Pastor John explained. "We are going to see if we can go beyond awareness to prevention. There is plenty of awareness in the community, but it hasn't affected behavior."

"It is a huge challenge," he continued, "How do you teach abstinence to children who live in a small shack, and see their mom and her boyfriends having sex all the time?" In the American context, Pastor John's theology would be seen as fundamentalist. But the severity of the crisis he faces has left him anything but rigid. "With eleven-year-old children we teach abstinence. When we deal with sex workers, we give out condoms. We deal with people where they are."

This is a good summary of the African approach to AIDS prevention, called "ABC"—which stands for abstinence, be faithful, and condom use. It is typical of American cultural self-centeredness that we attempt to impose our own culture-war debates on Africa. The *New York Times* and liberal activists allege that the Bush administration has cut off condoms to the continent in some kind of religious plot—when the number of condoms distributed by the United States to focus countries in Africa increased by more than 70 percent in four years. Liberal groups also try to downplay the importance of "A" and "B"—but Africans find both to be vital. Delaying the onset of sexual activity in young people is essential to the success of AIDS prevention. And in countries like Uganda, one of the main problems is "multiple concurrent partners"—most often men who betray their wives with many sexual partners at the same time. In this case, "be faithful" is a feminist issue, because male infidelity can be a death sentence for women.

On the other side, some American religious conservatives think condoms do nothing but encourage promiscuity. This is equally absurd. One of the main problems in Africa is "discordant couples," in which one partner is HIV positive and one is negative. In this case, condoms are essential: can we really expect abstinence *within* marriage? And everywhere I visited in Africa, I found that condoms were essential to successful AIDS prevention among older teens. In South Africa, I asked the head of a Christian abstinence program in high schools, "What do you do if you know that a seventeen-year-old you are counseling is having risky sex?" He replied, "We give her a condom—her life is at stake." The closer you get to the problems of Africa, the more abstract and irrelevant the culture-war debates of America appear.

This combination of explicit sex education, idealism about human potential, and realism about human nature has had some successes. In Uganda—where there are more people living with AIDS than have the disease in the whole of the United States—the prevalence of AIDS used to be at 19 or 20 percent; now it appears to have plateaued around 7 percent. Kenya has seen a decline in concurrent sexual partners, an older sexual debut for children (especially among girls), a decline in polygamous marriage, higher condom use during casual sex, a rapid decline in sexually transmitted diseases (which are associated with HIV infection), and increased secondary abstinence in youth—meaning that some children and teens are stopping sexual activity after they have begun. And behind all these advances in Kenya is the shock treatment that comes from tragic example—over 75 percent of Kenyans know someone living with AIDS, or someone who has died from it.

But the greatest change of the last several years has been the growing availability of AIDS drugs. AIDS in Africa is surrounded by a dense cloud of stigma, which discourages AIDS testing, and leads to brutal discrimination against AIDS victims. But the availability of treatment has begun to disperse that cloud. At a clinic in Addis Ababa, Ethiopia, I was asked by the staff if I wanted to talk to one of the patients they served. I expected to meet someone who had received a negative result. To my chagrin, I was introduced to a young woman, maybe twenty-two years old, who was still waiting for the results of her AIDS test. Speaking through an interpreter, I told her I wouldn't disturb her. She responded, "A few years ago, I would never have talked to a foreigner about AIDS. But now I know that even if I'm positive, it isn't a death sentence. Three of my friends have already been tested, and I need to know."

There are still many challenges when it comes to treatment. In parts of Africa with strong medical infrastructure, AIDS treatment has scaled up quickly. But in many places that infrastructure is nonexistent—the nation of Mozambique, for example, has just five hundred doctors for a population of nearly twenty million people. That's one doctor for every forty thousand Mozambican citizens. Most of the continent has an urgent need for more community health workers, to provide treatment support and other services. Men, unwilling to admit need and weakness, still tend to receive treatment very late. The treatment itself awakens the appetite, and nutrition, in many parts of Africa, remains a challenge. Opportunistic infections such as tuberculosis, closely associated with AIDS, are rampant.

But for all the difficulties, AIDS treatment in Africa remains a modern miracle—the closest I will ever come to seeing the wonders of healing that are spoken of in the New Testament. I met a six-year-old girl in Namibia who was born with HIV, to parents who were both HIV positive. Her mother gave her the name Haunapawa, which means, in the local language, "The world doesn't have any good in it"—a heavy burden for a shy little girl. Before her treatment, she had been repeatedly hospitalized for pneumonia and other infections. But when I met her, she was entirely healthy—and because of that little life, the world has more good in it. I met a sweet and beautiful young woman—living in a shack, with newspapers on the walls and linoleum on the floor—whose legs had once been covered with carcinoma as a result of her AIDS. "I was dying," she told me quietly. "Everyone told me I would die. But now I can walk. Now I can dance."

And I visited a Sisters of Charity orphanage in Addis—an outpost of bright and cheerful order in the sprawling chaos of that city. The sisters care for four hundred orphans, all of whom are HIV positive. Some lost both parents to AIDS. Others were abandoned. Walking through the dorms, I saw hundreds of neat little beds. Covering one wall of the last dorm room was a large mural of Jesus and the children. Each of the six or seven portraits in the mural was of a child who had died at the orphanage. The other children, the sister said, "still come in to talk and play with them." Many of these children, she added, have an "easy death." One three-year-old boy called for her in the middle of the night, thanked her for everything she had done for him, and told her that he would die before morning. Others have a harder time. "They tell me, 'Sister, why can't you come with me where I am going? Why do I have to go alone?'"

Up until a few years ago, every single child at that orphanage died before the age of seven, or eight, or nine. Now, because of AIDS drugs, nearly every child lives, and the sisters have begun planning for job training when the orphans reach age sixteen.

This is an honest-to-God miracle of science, repeated in hundreds of thousands of cases across Africa—and Americans should be proud of the part they have taken in it. But even more impressive than the science is the people it benefits. In a dirty, urban slum of Kampala, Uganda—naked babies with uncontested flies, garbage in the streets—I visited the home of a man named Moses. He invited me into his single room, the size of a closet, with a single bed and two old chairs. Moses had started AIDS treatment a year before—he showed me his pink "adherence book," with careful checks for each day that he took his medicine. He talked about the terrible side effects he felt at first—some type of growth on his "private parts"; about how it took several months to feel better; about how he is now strong enough to play soccer. Now Moses gives lectures in local schools on living a "life of purpose"— there are charts propped against the wall reading "love your neighbor," "pray daily," "take care of your body." At the end of our talk, he said simply: "I am a Christian. Will you pray with me?" And he began to sing a praise song I didn't know: "May the Sprit of the Lord come down.... May the power of the Lord come down.... May the healing of the Lord come down." Then a simple prayer for God's blessing. Suppressing tears, I hugged him and told him he was my brother—and he is my brother, my brother Moses, in the worst slum I have ever seen, in the middle of Africa, in the unseen Kingdom of God.

Over time at the White House, I gained a slightly dismissive reputation as a bit of an eccentric. Playing the moral card on human rights, genocide, or disease can only be done so many times before the returns begin to diminish. By 2006, I was not an easy colleague to work with. I was increasingly irritated by the budgetary limits that made creative policy initiatives so rare … frustrated by conservative indifference to humanitarian issues on the Hill … angry at the inability of liberal opinion to concede the president had done anything good … disturbed by policy shifts within the administration … and keenly aware of my own limitations as an advocate. And perhaps I was just tired, which sometimes happens in government.

But tiredness is not identical to cynicism. It is true, as the foreign-policy realists assert, that America's immediate interests are not always identical to our highest ideals. Sometimes we must hold the hand of flawed regimes, for fear of finding something worse. You can't, it turns out, solve all the problems of the world. But there seems to be something uniquely American about trying. And the most unforgivable sins of our history—from slavery, to segregation, to indifference in face of the genocide—have come, not because we pursued our ideals too vigorously, but because we did not pursue them vigorously enough.

In the end, America is idealistic because it is the creation of an ideal—and this has led toward engagement in the world because that ideal is universal. Whatever its costs and failures and unavoidable compromises, American idealism is ultimately a national strength.

In 2005, a friend visited a remote clinic in Zambia. She found that some people who had come to the facility—sick with AIDS—had walked for days in the hope of treatment. When asked why they had come, one Zambian woman responded, "Because we heard the Americans are going to help us." That is a familiar refrain in history. In Nazi-occupied Europe ... in the gulags of the Soviet Union ... there were many who said, "We heard the Americans are going to help us." That is what America has been, and should always be.

Chapter 9

The Eternal Realities

At various stages of my life, like many idealists of a serious turn of mind, I have dabbled in despair. And at those moments, the noble pessimism of traditional conservatism has seemed especially attractive. Its belief that societies are organisms instead of machines, and that attempts to engineer them through politics are like grafting machinery onto a flower. Its tragic sense that the West is in terminal moral decline, but remains beautiful even in the twilight. Its assertion that wisdom is not found in rational reflection or moral absolutes, but rather in history, in lived experience—and that history, with its abundant precedents of pain, is all but immune to our aspirations.

In *Murder in the Cathedral,* T. S. Eliot's Archbishop Thomas Becket summarizes this view of history: "Only the fool, fixed in his folly, may think / He can turn the wheel on which he turns." The forces of history cannot be controlled, because we are controlled by them. And most people, as the chorus in the play reminds us, want no part in a heroism that disturbs their peace: "O Thomas our Lord, leave us and leave us be, in our humble and tarnished frame of existence, leave us; do not ask us / To stand to the doom on the house, to doom on the Archbishop, to doom on the world."

Yet the story of Thomas Becket is ultimately the story of religious defiance of tradition and royalty—a defiance that results in Becket's martyrdom by agents of the King. Faith adds some additional, uncompromising element to our humble and tarnished frame of existence—an element of heroism and hope. In Eliot's earliest, pencil-written notes for the play, he says that Becket's assigned role is to hold "to the Law of God above the Law of Man." And so, before his death, Becket proclaims: "I have had a tremour of blessing, a wink of heaven, a whisper, / And I would no longer be denied; all things / Proceed to a joyful consummation."

The poet T. S. Eliot, one of the great traditionalists and royalists of the twentieth century, begins his "Choruses From 'The Rock'" with this conservative lament: "The cycles of Heaven in twenty centuries / Bring us farther from God and nearer to the Dust." But like many religious people, Eliot finds himself ambushed by hope—led by the twitching string of divine purpose toward a vision of "Light / Light / The visible reminder of Invisible Light." Near the end of this poem, he concludes, "Our age is an age of moderate virtue / And of moderate vice / When men will not lay down the Cross / Because they will never assume it. / Yet nothing is impossible, nothing, / To men of faith and conviction."

My skepticism and pessimism have been confounded by my heroes—by men and women of faith and conviction who taught that loving your neighbor is inconsistent with enslaving them; who rescued children, by the power of law, from the nightmare factories of the industrial revolution; who found that the long tradition of segregation created ten thousand petty tyrants; who opposed tyranny abroad as vigorously as treason, because every man is the child of a King. History does teach that human evil is durable, and that social reform is easier to start than to finish well. But history also teaches that some organic social arrangements can become rotten; that it is not "social engineering" to rescue a human life from oppression, it is justice; that societies are capable of renewal because every individual is capable of redemption; that history without reference to moral absolutes can become a hell of permanent, unchallenged slavery. Traditional conservatism may celebrate a weary virtue, but history, in case after case, is only moved by an eager purity.

Given the gallery of heroes in the previous pages—from abolitionists like William Lloyd Garrison, to progressives like William Jennings Bryan, to religious reformers like Martin Luther King Jr. and Pope John Paul II—it is fair to ask: in what sense is this approach of mine conservative?

Honesty requires the recognition that many conservatives, in other times, have been hostile to religiously motivated reform. The abolition of the British slave trade around the turn of the nineteenth century provides an example. That effort was led by William Wilberforce, a witty, eloquent, conservative member of parliament whose Christian faith led to a moral revulsion at slavery so intense and physical it nearly destroyed his health. For two years, Wilberforce and his allies collected evidence about the horrors of British slave ships and the brutality of the West Indian sugar plantations, and proposed bill after bill to abolish the profitable trade in slaves. In Parliament, Wilberforce argued, "There is a principle above every thing that is political.... [W]hen I reflect on the command which says, 'Thou shalt do no murder,' believing the authority to be divine, how can I dare to set up any reasonings of my own against it? And ... when we think of eternity, and of the future consequences of all human conduct, what is there in this life that should make any man contradict the dictates of his conscience, the principles of justice, the laws of religion, and of God?"

Yet many of the heroes of British conservatism were inalterably opposed to abolition. The Duke of Wellington protested the "frenzy" of the abolition movement and warned that religious reformers would not stop "until they have accomplished their ends, which are the destruction of the Church and Negro emancipation." The British

Revolutionary War hero, Lord Tarleton, was so committed to preserving the trade that he campaigned on the stump under a flag showing an African in chains. Lord Nelson said, "I was bred in the good old school and taught to appreciate the value of our West Indian possessions ... and neither in the field nor the senate shall their just rights be infringed, while I have an arm to fight in their defense or a tongue to launch my voice against the damnable doctrine of Wilberforce and his hypocritical allies."

A century and a half later, conservative reaction to the American civil-rights movement was, to be charitable, mixed. Conservative writers such as James J. Kilpatrick (who later renounced race hatred) trotted out an appalling cultural condescension to undermine claims of equality. "The Negro race, as a race, is in fact an inferior race," Kilpatrick claimed, in a column his editor refused to run. "Within the frame of reference of a Negroid civilization, a mud hut may be a masterpiece; a tribal council may be a marvel of social organization; a carved image may have a primitive purity all its own. Well and good. But the mud hut ought not to be equated with Monticello, or jungle rule with Periclean Athens, or Phallic dolls with Elgin marbles. When the Negro today proclaims or demands his 'equality,' he is talking of equality within the terms of Western civilization. And what, pray, has he contributed to it?" An odd question, particularly since the movement of African Americans to secure their rights—with arguments rooted in Holy Scripture and the Declaration—helped define the meaning of equality in Western civilization. And that is a monument that surpasses the Elgin marbles.

Traditional conservatives have often believed that appealing to abstract rights and moral principles is like smoking in the magazine where gunpowder is kept—a possible source of radical, sudden, and destructive change. And this led conservatives of the eighteenth and nineteenth centuries to oppose, not only the secular rationalism of the French Revolution, but the irrepressible moralism of Methodism—John Wesley's evangelical revolt against the coldness and complacency of the Church of England. "Conservatives," argues the scholar Robert Nisbet, "have for the most part believed in the Divine much as all educated people believe in gravity or the spherical shape of the earth— firmly but not ecstatically. The hatred of 'enthusiasm' in the Dissenters and in the Wesleyans in the nineteenth century in England by most Anglicans was shared in full by just about all conservatives. Religion is acceptable: it is indeed a good thing provided it is not made the base of the intrusion of personal beliefs into the public policy of the nation." In that case, Wesleyan "intrusion" into public policy eventually took the form of concern about the working conditions of the urban poor, and moral opposition to slavery. (John Wesley sent a note from his deathbed to William Wilberforce reading: "Unless God has raised you up for this very thing [the abolition of the slave trade], you will be worn out by the opposition of men and devils; but if God be for you, who can be against you?") Conservatives have sometimes preferred a tame and domesticated religion, which is prone, according to Nisbet, to believe that "sufficient due to God was being rendered through ritual and liturgy." This leaves little room for the possibility that a living God might make current demands.

President Bush's religious convictions have come under similar suspicion from the right. Professor Jeffrey Hart of Dartmouth notes with dismay that Bush has "brought religion into politics in a way unknown to recent memory." He calls that influence "populist and radical." And he wonders: "What exactly was conservative about this form of religious expression, with its roots in the camp revivals?"

There is no doubt that men and women streaming out of those camp revivals have occasionally overturned the conservative social order in America. The First Great Awakening, led by George Whitefield in the 1730s, promoted the doctrines of individual conscience and liberty that added momentum to the American Revolution, sending many traditional conservatives fleeing for Canada. The Second Great Awakening, which flamed a century later, created the moral constituency for abolition, and the political constituency for Lincoln's election. The Third Great Awakening, at the end of the nineteenth century and the beginning of the twentieth, led to a Social Gospel that confronted the excesses of the industrial revolution with soup kitchens, homes for unwed mothers, and progressive laws.

It is possible to maintain a principled, conservative opposition to all these works of religious "enthusiasm"—to long for a Confederate States of America where eight-year-old boys are gainfully employed as chimney sweeps—but few conservatives actually do. Even though the conservative habit of mind once opposed most of these changes, they are now accepted by American conservatives as moral progress. And this highlights an unavoidable fact: conservatism assumes and depends upon an objective measure of right and wrong that skepticism does not produce. Without a firm moral conviction that independence is superior to servitude, and that freedom is superior to slavery, and that the weak deserve special care and protection, the ideology of conservatism is radically incomplete. In the absence of elevating ideals, it can become pessimistic and unambitious—a morally indifferent preference for the status quo. When conservatism is separated from moral convictions rooted in reason and faith—when it becomes skeptical, materialistic, and merely commercial—conservatism becomes cold at its core, and sometimes helps to perpetuate great evils.

This is the reason that one great conservative tradition is the tradition of modifying the term itself. The conservatism of Wilberforce must somehow be distinguished from the conservatism of Wellington. Randolph Churchill and his allies tried "Tory Democracy" to indicate a more modern and inclusive conservatism. We have seen, at various times, Progressive Conservatism, and Neo-Conservatism, and National Greatness Conservatism, and Reaganism. I had much to do with promoting the idea of Compassionate Conservatism—an attempt to distinguish a Catholic-influenced, conservatism-of-the-common-good from its libertarian rival. But in the middle of a global War on Terror, that term now seems too narrow. What we require is a conservatism committed to the defense of human dignity at home, and the promotion of human rights abroad ... a conservatism that responds to attacks on American ideals with confidence in those ideals ... a conservatism of restless reform, and idealism, and moral conviction ... what might be called a Heroic Conservatism.

It is often claimed that conservatism is not an ideology—but America happens to have an ideology, defined by a specific, philosophic claim: "We hold these truths to be self-evident, that all men are created equal, that they are endowed by their Creator with certain inalienable rights, that among these are life, liberty and the pursuit of happiness." The most basic definition of Heroic Conservatism is this: it is that form of conservatism that takes the Declaration of Independence seriously, for us and for all who bear the Divine image. And that, it turns out, is more controversial than it might at first appear.

For thousands of years, the greatest thinkers of the West have wrestled with a fundamental question: in what sense, if any, are we equal as human beings, when we are so obviously unequal in intelligence, ambition, and moral character? Inequality is the plain evidence of our senses. Some philosophies and ideologies—such as racism and fascism—assume those appearances are correct, and that societies should be organized accordingly, with superior human beings (however that group is defined) in charge. The Jewish tradition, in contrast, asserts the radical equality of having a single, common ancestor, "so that no one can say to his fellow," according to the Midrash, "my father was greater than yours." Christianity brought this Jewish tradition to the world, adding an equality of abject spiritual need—a teaching, affirmed by Puritans and Pilgrims, that "the ground is level at the foot of the cross." And the Enlightenment of the eighteenth century asserted an equality of rights rooted in nature—a belief that no human being can be ruled without their consent.

The American Founders, in various forms and degrees, held to all these philosophies of equality, traced to nature and to nature's God. They grandly summarized these beliefs in the Declaration of Independence—then they proceeded to accommodate political reality by writing a Constitution that recognized the existence of slavery. Nearly all of the Founders were morally uncomfortable with slavery. Most believed the institution was unstable, because human beings, when put in a position of servitude, will eventually revolt. But the cost of union was compromise on the principle of human equality. America got a government, but the deepest meaning of the country was left unresolved. And the tension would only build.

Early in the nineteenth century, about one in seven residents of America was owned by another. To justify that state of affairs, the ideology of racism began to harden. Slavery was no longer defended in the South as a temporary evil, but as a permanent good. Quack scientific theories were employed to argue that Africans were incapable of freedom. Yet slave masters still feared that a desire for freedom would result in slave uprisings. So oppressive laws were passed to prevent the education of slaves and the free association of African Americans. And Southern politicians, the better to defend the interests of slave holders, pushed to guarantee slavery in new American territories. Both sides—pro- and anti-slavery—appealed, with some justification, to the text of the Constitution. Only one side, however, was in revolt against the Declaration of Independence. The great debate that led to the Civil War began—not only on the meaning and status of the Declaration, but on the role of morality and religion in politics. And the voices of that debate still speak to our time.

One side of this controversy was taken by Senator John Calhoun of South Carolina—the intense, logical, humorless defender of Southern culture, who could never compose a love poem, it was said, because every line he wrote began "whereas." Calhoun was a conservative traditionalist—he believed that the organic culture of the South, including slavery, should not be undermined by the imposition of abstract rational or moral principles, which would only lead to "anarchy, poverty, misery and wretchedness." History had chosen who should rule and who should serve. Thus "the most false and dangerous of all political errors," he said, is the proposition that "all men are born free and equal." "We now begin to experience," Calhoun said, "the danger of admitting so great an error to have a place in the declaration of our independence." Calhoun's respect for history and culture led to a kind of conservative multiculturalism: no one could morally "judge" the culture of the South, especially according to the glittering generalities of the Declaration of Independence.

Another side in the argument was taken by Senator Stephen Douglas, Lincoln's political rival. Though short in stature, Douglas managed a formidable presence, with an impressive voice and a graceful manner at the podium. He used his skills to defend "popular sovereignty," which he defined bluntly: "We must allow the people to decide for themselves what is good or evil." Douglas believed that each state and territory should determine the status of slavery within its borders. "I care more for the great principle of self-government," he said, "the right of the people to rule, than I do for all the Negroes in Christendom." The majority would determine morality.

Abraham Lincoln, as scholar Harry Jaffa and others have detailed, proclaimed a fundamentally different view. He was a realistic politician—no friend of radical, immediate abolition—but he believed that America was defined by something higher than tradition or majority rule. "I should like to know," he said, "if taking this old Declaration of Independence, which declares all men are equal upon principle, and making exceptions to it, where will it stop. If one man says it does not mean a negro, why not say it does not mean some other man? If the Declaration is not the truth, let us get the statute book, in which we find it and tear it out! Who is so bold to do it! If it is not true let us tear it out! Let us stick to it then, let us stand firmly by it." Against Calhoun, he insisted that the claims of the American Founding are universal and unqualified—including "Negroes," "foreigners," and "Catholics." Against Douglas, he insisted that some things are always wrong, even if a majority thinks they are right. "That is the issue that will continue in this country when these poor tongues of Judge Douglas and myself shall be silent. It is the eternal struggle between these two principles—right and wrong—throughout the world." Slavery, he said, is a "vast moral evil." The doctrine of human equality found in the Declaration, in contrast, is the "father of all moral principle [among] us."

Lincoln not only rejected slavery, he rejected relativism—the belief that moral standards change from culture to culture, or shift with public opinion. And he rooted his moral beliefs in two great traditions: the Enlightenment views of the Founders, and the teachings of religion. Early in his career, most of Lincoln's arguments against slavery would have been familiar to Jefferson or Washington. Men are neither gods nor animals—they are human, and can rule each other only by consent. It is absurd to think that a slightly lighter skin color creates the right to rule. Slavery is stolen labor, a form of theft.

But as the Civil War progressed, and casualties began to pile up behind stone walls and in peach orchards, these commonsense, natural-law arguments did not seem so compelling. "When I think of the sacrifice yet to be offered," Lincoln said, "and the hearts and homes yet to be made desolate before this dreadful war is over, my heart is like lead within me, and I feel at times like hiding in a deep darkness." What cause could possibly justify so much blood and mourning? Cold and rational arguments about "consent" and natural rights could not motivate personal sacrifice on such a scale. And so, in the great speeches of his last two years, Lincoln (who was not an orthodox Christian himself) turned increasingly to the language of religion. In his second inaugural, he quoted the words of Jesus—"woe unto the world because of offenses"—arguing that the "offense" of slavery was the reason for the punishment of "a living God" on the whole country. And the removal of this offense, he believed, was necessary for the healing and redemption of the nation itself.

One newspaper at the time complained that Lincoln's second inaugural raised issues about the separation of church and state. Another editorialized, "The President's theology smacks of the dark ages." Lincoln, the paper argued, had abandoned "all pretense of statesmanship ... by taking refuge in piety." This kind of controversy seems to be the fate of all moral principle expressed in public affairs.

Lincoln and his appeal to moral principle have remained controversial among some traditional conservatives. The conservative scholar Wilmore Kendall accused Lincoln of zealotry—of being prepared to cause a war rather than concede his moral point. And this zealotry raised, for Kendall, the prospect of imitators—an "endless series of Abraham Lincolns, each persuaded that he is superior in wisdom and virtue to the Fathers." Another scholar, M. E. Bradford, has accused Lincoln of operating by an impulse like that of the Puritans, "authorized from on high to reform the world in imitation of themselves." Echoes of these accusations can be heard in some criticisms of President Bush, including by conservatives.

Traditional conservatism attempts to rally moral law and religion to its side, but often in a subordinate position to culture and tradition. This tendency has been challenged over the last few decades by three movements that have changed the nature of conservatism itself. The philosopher Leo Strauss, and his influential disciples, reasserted that tradition was not enough in politics; that it was possible and necessary to discern right and wrong through the exercise of human reason. Roman Catholic thinkers revived a belief in natural law—the conviction that a God-ordained moral law could be uncovered by the human mind. And reform-minded evangelicals joined the conservative coalition, after a long political retreat, contributing a moral vision rooted in faith. Each of these movements found common ground in the ideals of the

Declaration of Independence, with its assertion of self-evident moral truths. And these groups were eventually the natural constituencies of the Bush presidency—a coalition of moralists who believe in liberty.

There are many points of overlap between this heroic conservatism—this Lincoln and Declaration of Independence conservatism—and traditional conservatism. Both recognize that true freedom is found in fulfilling our nature as moral beings. We are designed and intended for the noble commitments of family, community, and patriotism—and undermining those duties leaves individuals scattered, lonely, and more susceptible to the false order of totalitarianism. Like all true conservatives, I believe that a free society depends on strong traditional institutions that teach character—the moral habits that make the exercise of freedom something more than anarchy and license. Like all true conservatives, I believe in limited government, because fallen human beings cannot be trusted with absolute power, and because most of the best and highest things of life—faith and art and family—are not and should not be political at all, and are only sullied by contact with power.

But there is at least one great difference between heroic and traditional conservatism. Taking the Declaration of Independence seriously introduces into conservatism a radical belief in the rights of every individual, and a conviction that government must act, when appropriate, to secure those rights when they are assaulted by oppression, poverty, and disease. When a fifteen-year-old girl in the inner city lives in an atmosphere of squalor and daily abuse ... when a Down syndrome fetus is casually killed as a life not worthy to be lived ... when an infant in Africa grows burning hot, then cold with death from the lack of malaria pills that cost a few dollars ... when a dissident lives in an airless prison, wondering if anyone in the world cares about his life or knows his name ... these are not unfortunate facts of history; they are violations of God's intended order. And solutions that are within our grasp are within our duty.

This kind of heroic conservatism is not a rigid application of Lincoln's political philosophy, although there is much good in it. It is broader: a conservatism elevated by a radical concern for human rights and dignity. That passion can come (as it came for many of the Founders) from a rational reflection on the order of nature. But in America today, this passion mainly comes from religious faith, in all its pleasing variety. And the radicalism of faith should not be underestimated, particularly in the case of Christianity. It is revealing that a young Jewish girl, trying to express the historical impact of the Advent, used these words: "He has scattered the proud in the imagination of their hearts. He has put down the mighty from their thrones, and exalted the lowly. He has filled the hungry with good things, and the rich He has sent away empty." Her Son was eventually killed as a threat to the Roman political order, and the Romans found, over time, that their suspicions were correct, because the Christian faith challenged and subverted their culture and tradition in fundamental ways. "In view of what he plainly said," argued H. G. Wells, "is it any wonder that all who were rich and prosperous felt a horror of strange things, a swimming of their world at his teaching? ... He was like some terrible moral huntsman digging mankind out of the smug burrows in which they had lived hitherto. In the white blaze of this kingdom of his there was to be no property, no privilege, no pride and no precedence; no motive indeed and no reward but love. Is it any wonder that men were dazzled and blinded and cried out against him?"

Some conservatives may talk of Christianity as a source of ritual and stability and order. G. K. Chesterton, like many others, found something else: "The grinding power of the plain words of the Gospel story is like the power of millstones; and those who can read them simply enough will feel as if rocks had been rolled upon them."

When the Rev. Martin Luther King Jr. was accused of extremism by members of the white clergy, at first he was offended. But then, according to his *Letter from the Birmingham Jail*, "I gradually gained a measure of satisfaction from the label. Was not Jesus an extremist for love: 'Love your enemies, bless them that curse you, do good to them that hate you, and pray for them which despitefully use you and perse- cute you.' Was not Amos an extremist for justice: 'Let justice roll down like water and righteousness like an ever-flowing stream.' Was not Paul an extremist for the Christian Gospel: 'I bear in my body the marks of the Lord Jesus.' Was not Martin Luther an extremist: 'Here I stand; I cannot do otherwise, so help me God.' And John Bunyan: 'I will stay in jail to the end of my days before I make a butchery of my conscience.' And Abraham Lincoln: 'This nation cannot survive half slave and half free.' And Thomas Jefferson: 'We hold these truths to be self-evident, that all men are created equal....' So the question is not whether we will be extremists but what kind of extremists we will be. Will we be extremists for hate or for love? Will we be extremists for the preserva- tion of injustice or for the extension of justice? In that dramatic scene on Calvary's hill three men were crucified. We must never forget that all three were crucified for the same crime—the crime of extremism. Two were extremists for immorality ... the other, Jesus Christ, was an extremist for love, truth and goodness.... Perhaps the South, the nation and the world are in dire need of creative extremists."

This is different from a right-wing extremism that seeks to reim- pose a vanished past ... or a left-wing extremism that pursues utopia at any human cost. It is, instead, a vision of human dignity that stands in perpetual challenge to a fallen world. And a world without that ideal- ism would be more fallen still.

For people influenced by Christianity, and other faiths that deal in moral absolutes, the preservation of tradition cannot be enough. Tra- ditional conservatism has a piece missing—a piece that is shaped like conscience. And conscience sometimes leads to abolition and civil- rights marches and overturned tables in the temple courtyard. There has always been a creative tension between the conservative defense of the existing order and the universal moral ideals of religion. That tension is important to conservatism's success and vitality—because a moral vision has often been necessary to save conservatism from its worst instincts.

It is precisely this religiously informed moral vision—which has acted as a foundation for human rights and liberty in American history—that is now attacked as an enemy of human liberty. On the faculties of elite universities, few would accept the existence of a moral truth that applies in all cultures. The idea of "nature" as a source of human rights is seen as absurd, because "nature" is merely a "social construct." And religious moralism, in particular, is viewed as a dangerous and backward source of repression and intolerance. Relativism rules—except when it comes to apartheid in South Africa, or genocide in Darfur, or repression in Burma. On these issues, moral judgment and the derided philosophy of the American Founding suddenly return.

And thank goodness they do. The hypocrisy of modern liberalism is actually a sign of moral health. Students and faculty may claim that the Declaration is a dead text written by dead white males, but their conscience testifies against their words. Every cry for justice assumes an objective standard of justice. Every defense of human rights requires the existence of right and wrong. In cases like these, the moral instincts of modern liberalism prove far more admirable than its beliefs. If relativists were not hypocrites, they would be monsters.

Some types of traditional conservatism offer a different kind of skepticism: not relativism but historicism—the belief that truth is found in tradition, or in the working out of some historical process, instead of in philosophic abstractions like the Declaration. This kind of skepticism is impatient with moralism and dismissive of all grand ideals and schemes of reform. But a systematic skepticism cannot answer the question: which traditions are worth preserving, and which should be overturned? Certainly historical traditions concerning the family, manners, and military honor deserve our respect, because the human race is often wise, while the individual is often foolish. But few human traditions were more deeply rooted in history than human slavery. And what about the long Western tradition of contempt for and violence against Jews? Without moral rules, there can be no moral means of discriminating among traditions.

Historicism also involves a false view of history itself. Skeptical conservatives assert, for example, that we should respect the American constitutional order, yet have no need of a moral law that stands above it. But the people who created that constitutional order were revolutionaries prepared to offer up their lives, their fortunes, and their sacred honor for a burning moral and philosophic vision. It always falls to conservatives to consolidate the work of idealists. But that consolidation should not involve an attack on idealism itself—the only thing that creates a social order worth conserving.

Both relativism and historicism make the same claim: that human rights do not need a philosophic basis, a moral foundation. Those rights can simply be assumed. The late philosopher Richard Rorty claimed: "A liberal society is badly served by an attempt to supply it with philosophic foundations. For the attempts to supply such foundations presupposes a natural order of topics which is prior to, and overrides the results of, encounters between old and new vocabularies." Stripped of academic jargon, Rorty was arguing that free societies should not be constrained or limited by truth or morality. But then why should people in free societies respect the rights of others? None of the modern answers makes much sense. Some argue that the instinct to cooperate is imprinted by evolution. But why should I obey that biological instinct above the equally (or more) powerful instinct to take whatever I want? Why should I choose to follow the instinct of benevolence instead of a radical will to power? Some argue that we should respect the rights of others for prudential reasons—to avoid punishment. But, in fact, many people get away with violating the rights of others.

In the end, the ideas of justice and tolerance require at least one absolute truth: a belief in human dignity. That belief can be rooted in religion or in philosophy, but the breadth and firmness of that moral belief determines much about the justice and humanity of any society. A belief in human dignity is undermined by skepticism. It is strengthened by a broad public recognition of its importance to the common good. A respect for human rights cannot be assumed among the young; it must be taught. A nation fortunate enough to have a widespread belief in human rights and dignity should maintain that belief.

It is useful, in this debate, to stare into the abyss: What if the Declaration of Independence—along with its assumption of the existence of moral truth—is not true? What if the skeptics of left and right are correct?

First, it becomes impossible to motivate, or even to measure, social progress. Without a belief in right and wrong … without a firm conception of better and worse … without a vision of how things ought to be … we do not even know what progress might look like. Without a moral ideal that stands in contrast to the evils of this world, suffering becomes a fact to be accepted, instead of a flaw to be remedied. How does systematic doubt and skepticism motivate a medical missionary, or an AIDS activist, or a democratic reformer? How does world-weariness lead a soldier to volunteer for battle, or cause a rescuer to risk her life saving Jews in the Holocaust, or lead a dissident to stand in front of a tank? Sometimes skepticism can lead to a kind of stoic courage—an unblinking acceptance of fate. But it is usually moral conviction—a vision of justice—that leads to reforming zeal.

Second, if human rights and dignity have no basis or foundation, the only reliable guide to human behavior is the desire for power. As C. S. Lewis notes: "When all that says 'it is good' has been debunked, what says 'I want' remains." Apart from a broadly shared moral code, human wants are unlimited and unrestrained. And that amounts, in the end, to the rule of the strong—the rule of those who can seek their wants and impose their will most effectively.

One well-known leader of the twentieth century made this case clearly: "Everything I have said and done in these last years is relativism by intuition—if relativism signifies contempt for fixed categories and men who claim to be bearers of an objective, immortal truth—then there is nothing more relativist than fascistic attitudes and activity. From the fact that all ideologies are of equal value, that all ideologies are mere fictions, the modern relativist infers that everybody has the right to create for himself his own ideology and to attempt to enforce it with all the energy of which he is capable."

That quote comes from Benito Mussolini. And it demonstrates another point by Lewis: "I am very doubtful whether history shows us one example of a man who, having stepped outside traditional morality and attained power, has used that power benevolently." All the mass murderers of the last century, from Hitler to Stalin to Mao, were driven by a type of radical freedom—a freedom from morality and religion, a freedom of the radical will to power. Whenever government power becomes untethered from the moral truths embodied in the Declaration, it is carried in a strong current toward oppression. "A dogmatic belief in objective value," concludes Lewis, "is necessary to the very idea of a rule which is not tyranny or an obedience which is not slavery."

The Holocaust Memorial Museum on the Mall in Washington preserves the artifacts of history's greatest crime—a room full of shoes, removed by the trembling hands of people entering a Nazi prison camp ... the innocent drawings of children murdered in batches by modern, efficient, civilized adults ... a tower of pictures of smiling men, women, and children from a single Lithuanian village, every one executed in a matter of days, the pictures all that remains of their lives and loves and hopes. The museum is a reminder that evil is not a myth; it is as real as barbed wire and empty shoes. Around the museum, etched in the walls, are quotes from the Torah—"I have set before you life and death; choose life"—along with statements by Holocaust survivors and American presidents. But the quote right above the entrance of the museum is not from scripture or a Holocaust witness. It reads: "We hold these truths to be self-evident, that all men are created equal, that they are endowed by their Creator with certain inalienable rights, that among these are life, liberty and the pursuit of happiness." The Declaration of Independence was given this place of prominence because it is, for all time, the negation of Nazism ... the check on willful, lawless power ... the definition of an idealism that makes us human.

And what if that Declaration is actually true? Robert Frost put the question this way:

> *That's a hard mystery of Jefferson's.*
> *What did he mean? Of course the easy way*
> *Is to decide it simply isn't true.*
> *It may not be. I heard a fellow say so.*
> *But never mind, the Welshman got it planted*
> *Where it will trouble us a thousand years.*
> *Each age will have to reconsider it.*

If the Declaration is true, how should it trouble us? Most modern and mainstream American conservatives are not skeptical about the existence of the moral law. They respect the Declaration, and believe in religious values. But many are deeply skeptical about the ability of government to pursue those ideals. Theirs is a world-weary conservatism, moved to protect what they value from action by others, not to act in the service of humanity. Since, in this view, all policy is crippled by unintended consequences, since government is a blunt and ineffective instrument, the best course of action is generally inaction. Conservatives should stand athwart history and yell stop. Don't just stand there; do nothing.

This pessimism about policy, as I've argued earlier, is unjustified. On issues from welfare to crime to education, pessimism and inaction have led to injustice. Muscular action, based on conservative principles, has led to progress, sometimes dramatic progress. Energetic, conservative reform has proved stronger than supposedly unchangeable cultural habits. A limited government does not need to be a laissez-faire or lethargic government.

But the main problem with this practical skepticism is that it doesn't take the ideal of human equality and dignity seriously enough. The Declaration of Independence was not intended as an unreachable ideal, but as a guide to political action, and its application led to a rebellion against colonialism, a civil war, and a continuing revolution in human affairs. The religious belief in universal human dignity is not a heavenly goal; it is a demand for earthly justice. It makes little difference in the world if someone is skeptical about these moral ideals, or if they affirm them without consequence or effect. Those who do not feel the urgency of these ideals have not examined them closely enough.

What if every human being we meet, and every prisoner in maximum security, and every hungry child in a distant land, and every unwed mother, and everyone with a severe disability, and everyone we love, and everyone we hate, is actually the reflected image of his or her Creator, the most precious thing we will ever touch or see in this life? How should we live and act, given this amazing, exhausting reality?

The primary implications are personal. When solutions are within our power, we are called to show compassion and generosity toward our neighbor. We are required to treat others with civility, even when our differences are unbridgeable, because we should respect the image of God we see in one another. We should be tolerant of human frailty and failure, because those also are universal.

Yet there are political implications of this belief, as well. If human dignity is universal, we must care for and act on behalf of a drowning humanity. If the Declaration is true, then oppression should always offend us. Sometimes that oppression comes from centralized power, in societies ruled through fear. But acts of injustice are not only performed by a national government. Sometimes a national government must oppose oppression at other levels of government—like when federal troops were necessary to enforce desegregation in some American states. And sometimes a belief in human dignity requires the government to take the side of individuals against powerful, *im*personal forces that assault their dignity—Social Security to prevent hunger in old age, Medicaid to treat sickness in poor children, laws to ensure safe working conditions, AIDS drugs for the dying.

Because politics can protect the weak in the cause of justice, it can be a noble profession. And because the oppression of the weak is an offense against the image of God, politics is an urgent calling. Every generation is required to ask, what are the great moral objects of *our* time—the goals that are worth *our* sacrifice? What are the ideals that should gather movements? What are the movements that could transform America and the world?

I don't claim to have an authoritative list of these great moral objects. But a few are unavoidable.

America is called to confront a new totalitarian threat to human liberty— the political ideology of radical Islam, given form and power in outlaw regimes and terrorist networks.

Opposing that threat is a daily, hand-to-hand battle, involving police forces, intelligence operatives, and military assets in dozens of countries—a battle in which a single mistake can be catastrophic. The gap between the frightening reality of this war and the indifference of the public and political class is wide and dangerous. In government, this struggle was the daily context of our work—the sum of our fears, the measure of our success. Among the public, and in our political debate, concern about this threat is slight, and sometimes dismissive. Eventually, President Bush's legacy on this issue will be clear: while others turned away, he took this threat seriously every day.

He also chose to confront the root cause of terrorism: a political culture of violence, conspiracy theories, and resentment in the Middle East. He set out to change that culture with a set of ideals that have fostered peace and contented prosperity in every other human culture: human rights, social freedom, and self-government. This is, without doubt, ambitious—ambitious enough to guarantee failures along the way. But as America found in the twentieth century, sometimes there is no alternative to ambition. The implementation of this vision is difficult. Current efforts can be justly criticized. The proper mix of public confrontation, quiet persuasion, support for dissidents, and economic incentives for reform can be debated. But no one has proposed a serious alternative to President Bush's vision. Certainly, retreat from the Middle East … the base abandonment of our allies … the anxious cultivation of dictators from a position of weakness … a surrender to the nuclear ambitions of the worst regimes in the world … an eager, panting defeatism … is not likely to increase America's influence or its safety.

Once again, the Declaration of Independence is central to a great American debate. Are some destined for tyranny, or are all designed for freedom? We know that the advance of freedom is not always easy or orderly. Sometimes it comes like a wildfire that leaps across barriers and borders. Sometimes it works through erosion, like water on a stone. It is never a gift; it is always won with sacrifice. Gains can be squandered. Promising leaders can regress. But realism about these difficulties is different from a pessimism that condemns whole regions and races to perpetual oppression.

In the 1980s, the French thinker Jean-François Revel wrote an influential book called *How Democracies Perish*. The first sentence read: "Perhaps in history democracy will have been an accident, a brief parenthesis which comes to a close before our very eyes." Revel argued that democracies were self-hating, inwardly oriented, lacking in courage and patience. "Communism is a better machine for world conquest than democracy, and this is what will decide the final outcome of the struggle."

Six years later, Soviet communism was dead and global democracy reached an unimagined peak of influence.

Pessimism is once again the order of the day. We cannot know where democracy in the Middle East and other disputed places will stand six years from now. No force of historical inevitability guarantees our success. Progress, as always, depends on human choices and human courage. But we do know that democracy has some inherent advantages. Freedom is the design of human nature. It is the source of human creativity—the catalyst for advances in science and art. It is the reason for the wealth of nations. It results, over time, in more prosperous, united, and peaceful countries. No one should underestimate the "soft power" advantages of the Declaration of Independence. So let us stick to it then; let us stand firmly by it.

America is called by our interests and our values to promote development and fight disease in the world. And the greatest challenge lies on the continent of Africa. Africa is not a hopeless basket case—not a "dark continent" in need of pity and colonial concern. Economies on that continent are now better managed ... inflation is lower ... foreign investment is up. Sixteen African countries have had economic growth rates in excess of 4.5 percent for over a decade.

But this progress only highlights some harsher realities. Half of all people in sub-Saharan Africa still live on less than a dollar a day. The mega-slums of Kinshasa, Lagos, and Nairobi combine anarchy, disease, lawlessness, and squalor. Clinics I have visited in those slums close at night for fear of crime, and the pregnant women they serve pray to deliver their babies during the day. Human waste is often disposed of in paper bags, thrown over any convenient fence. Together, the diseases of AIDS and malaria take the lives of more people in Africa every month than died in the 2004 tsunami in the Pacific; the tidal wave of disease in Africa comes as regularly as the tides. A whole continent is burying its teachers, doctors, nurses, civil servants, fathers, and mothers. AIDS has left over twelve million orphans across

Africa—the lucky live with relatives; the unfortunate care for each other.

America's commitment to Africa has dramatically increased in the last few years, though this remains largely unnoticed among Americans. A poll in 2006 found that 22 percent of Americans thought that the Bush administration had *decreased* funding for HIV/AIDS in developing countries ... 23 percent thought it had remained the same ... 14 percent said it had increased somewhat ... and 3 percent, *3 percent*, thought that aid had more than doubled—the correct answer.

Yet, by the measure of our wealth, and by the measure of the need, these contributions remain pathetic. About 1.4 percent of the federal budget is devoted to development and diplomacy—like the widow's mite from the billionaire.

Global health is an area where opportunities create responsibilities, and indifference creates casualties. A decade ago, treatment for an individual case of AIDS cost about $10,000 a year; today, it runs about $140. Treatment for tuberculosis costs about $10 and has an 80 percent success rate. Effective malaria treatments cost about $2, and bed nets run about $5 or $10. Building a health-care infrastructure to deliver these treatments is a challenge, but the Emergency Plan for AIDS Relief has demonstrated it is not impossible. In the case of all these diseases, lives are lost each day because America is not more generous. Dramatically increasing that generosity is a cause that could unite liberals and moral conservatives—and would be remembered as one of the great humanitarian accomplishments of American history.

Another issue where America has much to offer is women's empowerment. Across Africa it is clear that no element of the ABC approach to AIDS prevention—abstinence, be faithful, use condoms—works when women have no power in a relationship. One extraordinary, resilient woman I met in Nairobi told me she had been raped four times, starting at age seven. Her father responded to the first rape by telling her it was her fault. Now, while struggling with terrible emotional scars, she works to pass stronger laws against rape in Kenya. Across Africa, women who report rapes are ignored by prosecutors, and even victimized again by police. A strong women's empowerment agenda would help establish rape investigation units in Africa, increase the number of prosecutors focused on this issue, and encourage the creation of family courts. Even a few high-profile rape prosecutions can have a strong deterrent effect and send an important social signal. More broadly, America should encourage the education of girls—which provides an alternative to the sex trade—and the ownership by women of small businesses. Societies where the sexes are more equal in power are ultimately more just and healthy. Encouraging that equality is a natural role for America.

America is called to heal the divisions caused by poverty and racial inequality. If you read through all of the past presidential inaugurals, as I have done, it is clear that the story of America is largely the story of race, from the internal contradictions of our Founding, to the debates that led to the Civil War, to the failure of Reconstruction and the reassertion of white supremacy, to the civil-rights movement. And that story has not ended. A legacy of inequality and oppression remains. It is true that most of the poor in America are white; and most African Americans are not poor. But the most durable, concentrated, and desperate poverty is found in parts of the South—as Katrina revealed—and in the inner cities. African Americans are three times more likely to live in extreme poverty than are whites.

This separate nation of intense poverty—bypassed by highways, avoided by the prudent, hidden behind sound barriers—is different from the one most of us inhabit. These are communities of pregnant teens, and young men on probation, and neglected toddlers, and 1.3 million children who must visit their fathers in prison. For many, gangs seem like the only source of belonging, sex seems like the only source of affection, drugs seem a reasonable form of escape from circumstances most of us would not tolerate for an hour. These young people have every incentive to live for the moment, few reasons to plan for the future, and good reason to doubt the promise of America. A number of these men and women beat the odds, but those odds are scandalously stacked against them—and our goal should be to change those odds in their favor.

No war against poverty is likely to liberate millions at once. Government cannot drop miracle-working bureaucrats into these communities like paratroopers. But the situation is not hopeless—and the pose of hopelessness is a convenient excuse for indifference. Government can work to fortify local institutions that encourage ambition, shape character, and reclaim discarded lives. As I've argued, we should strengthen the institutions of rescue—charities, often based in churches, which treat addiction, house the homeless, and provide job training. Anti-religious bigotry against these charities, which denies them needed support, has the effect of hurting the most vulnerable Americans.

We should strengthen the institutions of social mobility. Many inner-city public schools are dangerous, disorderly, and failing at their most basic educational mission. Charter schools do a better job. Inner-city Catholic schools are better still, but are closing in many places for lack of resources. There is no reason—other than ideological stubbornness and self-interested teachers' unions—that low-income parents with children in failing public schools should not be given vouchers to enable them to attend functioning private and religious schools.

Another source of social mobility is savings. Though disparities in earnings between whites and African Americans have narrowed over the years, the disparities of wealth remain dramatic. The median net worth of white and Asian Americans in 2004 was $142,700. The median net worth of African Americans was $20,400. The racial divide in America is widest when it comes to wealth. States and cities across America are experimenting with proposals that encourage and match the savings of the poor—savings that, over time, can turn into the down payment on a home, or seed money for a small business. In the lead-up to the

2004 State of the Union, I argued for a KidSave program that would set up tax-free savings accounts for every poor child at birth—and subsidize those accounts with a few thousand dollars. Over decades, through compound interest, these accounts could provide significant help in retirement, and begin to equalize the wealth gap in America. The Kid-Save proposal made its way into several drafts of the speech—until it was killed by the concerted effort of our economic team, who objected to "free money" for the poor.

We should also strengthen the transmission of values to the young, particularly through the provision of mentors. Mentoring at-risk children—even for just a few hours a week—has proven results in decreasing violence and increasing graduation rates. Many disadvantaged children, it turns out, begin to thrive when one caring adult shows them love and commitment. And it should not surprise us that children need love as much as they need food and air. Professor John DiIulio of the University of Pennsylvania estimates that guaranteeing a mentor to every black male under ten years old whose parent or guardian requests one would cost about $3 billion a year—less than a tenth of what we spend on state prisons alone. And it would make at least a portion of those cells unnecessary.

America is called to ensure that science and technology serve the cause of human dignity instead of unraveling it. From one perspective, this challenge isn't new, because eugenics—the use of science to weed out flawed humans—is not new. At the end of his life, William Jennings Bryan—the Democratic presidential candidate, secretary of state, and evangelical moralist—undertook a failed campaign against Darwinism, which subjected him to the ridicule of history. His scientific views were unsophisticated. But history has largely forgotten that Bryan's main concern was not biology, it was the political application of evolution—not Darwinism, but Social Darwinism. He feared that a society that worshiped strength and health would have little room for the weak. He feared that a "few supposedly superior intellects, self-appointed" would move along human evolution by directing "the mating and movements of the mass of mankind."

And Bryan feared these things with good reason. The textbook used by John Scopes, the substitute biology teacher in Tennessee—the book that provoked the Scopes Monkey Trial—was titled *A Civic Biology*. Note the name. The book singled out two feebleminded families with suspiciously ethnic names as "true parasites ... if such people were lower animals, we would probably kill them off to prevent them from spreading." The author went on to recommend confining such families—this was the "civic" part—in asylums to halt their reproduction.

But this kind of eugenics had many advocates in American history. H. L. Mencken, the anti-religious journalist who dubbed Bryan "the idol of Idiotdom," took a similarly muscular reading of Darwin. "There must be a complete surrender to the law of natural selection," he wrote. "The strong must grow stronger, and that they may do so, they must waste not strength in the vain task of trying to lift up the weak."

Elitism and eugenics are not required by the scientific theory of Darwinism, but they evolved from within it, and entered wide practice. In the early decades of the twentieth century, more than half of American states conducted involuntary, eugenic sterilizations—until the practice was discredited in the 1940s by more efficient eugenics movements abroad, which put mentally disabled children, epileptics, and other "useless eaters" into gas chambers and ovens.

The advance of medical science in our time is hopeful and morally positive. But, with our growing technological power to build more perfect humans, the temptations and debates of eugenics have returned. Genetic screening and prenatal genetic diagnosis allow doctors to remove imperfections from dwarfism to Down syndrome. But the method of ending these conditions is to end the lives of those afflicted by them. And what was once an option is becoming a presumption. "Soon it will be a sin of parents," argues British geneticist Robert Edwards, "to have a child that carries the heavy burden of genetic disease." A sin. Which leaves disabled children who escape the net of screening—the result of parental sin—to be born into a new form of bastardy. Progress toward human perfection has the perverse effect of making imperfection more obvious, and more intolerable. And the social message is clearly sent: this is no world to be weak in.

It will be essential over the next few decades for Americans who remain committed to the proposition that all men are created equal to stand against a degraded science that ends flawed lives in the cause of public health and social advancement. Those who benefit from this cruel "progress" are strident. Those who suffer and die are quiet—and someone must speak in their behalf, and in their cause.

These challenges—from the promotion of liberty, to the defeat of disease, to racial equality, to the protection of the weak—are varied. But they reflect a unifying commitment: an active moral and political concern for the value and dignity of human life. In Lincoln's words, "Nothing stamped with the Divine image and likeness was sent into the world to be trodden on, or degraded, and imbruted by its fellows."

For many (but not all), this conviction is rooted in religion—a belief in "the Divine image and likeness." But that does not make it a "private" belief, because the defense of human dignity is the purpose of law, and the highest goal of politics.

I am convinced that this vision is broadly shared—by Catholics, who seek the common good ... by Jews, who know the consequences when human dignity is denied ... by evangelicals, who are awakening to the broader, humanitarian demands of their faith ... by mainline Protestant Christians, who have carried the cause of justice for so long ... by Americans of every background who insist on taking American ideals seriously. It is, perhaps, the fate of such morally driven people to feel like ideological misfits in both political parties. Where does someone belong who is pro-life *and* pro-poor? Someone who supports the traditional family *and* increased spending to fight AIDS? Someone who is passionate about the rights of handicapped children in America *and* the lives of displaced children in Darfur? I know that I have often felt homeless in the traditional camps of American politics.

But there is an American tradition where these moral concerns find a home—the tradition of abolitionists and religious reformers, of Catholic conscience and natural rights, of Lincoln and the Declaration. And that tradition, as we've seen, counts amazing achievements of conscience. Idealists are sometimes challenged with the question: how can a movement starting with a few committed people change history? On the testimony of history, the answer is simple: That is the only way it is ever changed.

There is no transforming power in cynicism and skepticism. They leave men and women captive to doubt, and useless to God and their neighbor. But there is influence in conviction and faith—and they are needed in our time. We are called to a struggle against a new totalitarian ideology that must be opposed with courage and patience. We are called to heal the sick around the world, and bring hope to hopeless places. We are called to heal the divisions of race that still scar our country. Courage and idealism are urgently needed in the cause of human dignity. These are heroic times—they require a heroic conservatism.

Since the 1980s, the Republican Party has been at least a temporary home for people like me because of its openness to religious influence and its unapologetic assertion of American ideals. But in the current backlash against the failures of the Bush era, some Republican voices demand a complete ideological housecleaning. Don't like the outcome in Iraq? Then jettison the goal of promoting democracy that has united American foreign policy since Roosevelt. Don't like the budget deficit? Then abandon the ideals of compassion and social justice that have guided religious people for thousands of years. This exaggerated reaction—if Bush is for it, it must be bad—is more of a tantrum than a serious political argument.

And this debate among Republicans has been revealing. In the anti-Bush backlash, the darker impulses of conservatism have become more assertive, more public, and more pronounced. It is not a pretty sight. A Republican Party that abandons dissidents and allies in the cause of "realism" ... that attacks the treatment of disease as budgetary waste ... that is unmoved by the struggles of poor children ... that elevates autonomy and choice above the rights of the weak ...will not earn or deserve the support of moral and religious voters. And with their departure, the politics of the Republican Party would consist mainly of commercial interest and libertarian selfishness—hardly a winning combination.

Conservatism without idealism and compassion is dead. Only a heroic conservatism can appeal to the conscience, inspire the nation, and change the world.

My own experience of politics turns out to be similar to that of others—a story of high hopes only partially fulfilled. Freedom, unsurprisingly, was not universal by the time I left government. Poverty was not abolished. Disease was not defeated. The Republican Party has returned to old habits of fratricide. The Bush administration, at its best, proclaimed and worked toward a heroic conservatism—but it did not embody it. In several areas—from AIDS to the stem-cell debate to the promotion of liberty—the president acted in admirable ways that did nothing to benefit him politically. But the vision of compassion and freedom that seemed so clear in speeches and in the president's mind was sometimes poorly implemented. And some who served in the administration did not share the vision at all.

So what do I conclude? One time-honored response is to condemn everyone and the world for failing to meet your own standards of purity and virtue—to blame colleagues and enemies for blocking the arrival of your own private millennium. But I have been high enough in government to know that most mistakes are only obvious in retro-spect … and that fate can leave all choices flawed … and that the best intentions, even when held by the president, are sometimes undermined in the alternating friction and inertia of administration. Governing is occasionally a response to the call of trumpets, and sometimes a chess game of move and countermove, but most often it is a scrambling effort to meet the challenge of sudden events, an effort undertaken with lim-ited time and information at one's disposal. Those who make that effort deserve close scrutiny, but also understanding.

Political involvement must be more than a series of infatuations, ending in the rage of disappointed love. That is not politics; it is high school. Causes such as human rights, freedom, and social justice are always contested and difficult. They advance against a headwind of interest and indifference. Progress is often measured in increments achieved by successive generations. Our duties are found in the pres-ent—our success may come beyond our allotted years. So politics is not a calling for the impatient or immature.

Many of the projects begun in the last few years—particularly the advance of freedom in the Middle East, the relief of disease and poverty abroad, and the promotion of faith-based solutions to human needs—are in their earliest stages. There have been unprecedented successes and undeniable failures—and neither are indicators of an inevitable future.

That future is uncertain, but not random, at least to people of faith. The central, clarifying insight of religion is simple: The events of our lives and our history either have an inner pull and purpose or they are merely one damn thing after another, the pointless accumulation of effort, failure, and decay. Either events gather into a story with a point—or they amount to a joke. In the Christian story, death and suffering and evil are real—real enough to pin an innocent man to a cross. And evil will never be finally eradicated this side of eternity. But history still has a direction, set by a God Who calls His flawed servants to a small part in a Great Story. And no act of compassion, no work of justice, no matter how hidden or hopeless, is ever useless or wasted. Every act and every life matters and counts, because they matter and count to the Author.

Why is this important to politics? Because persistence and sacrifice in a just cause requires hope—and hope is another contribution of faith.

In July 1944, a bomb exploded in Hitler's meeting room in a failed attempt at assassination. The Nazi terror that followed swept up many opponents of the regime, including a thirty-seven-year-old Jesuit priest named Alfred Delp. Delp was not implicated in the plot, but he had associated with members of the resistance. So he was imprisoned and hanged. Right before his execution, he told a chaplain: "In half an hour, I'll know more than you do."

While in prison, Delp wrote a sermon on the Advent—the Christian celebration of God's restless pursuit of mankind. "Oh, if it ever happens," he said, "that we forget the message and the promises; if all we know is the four walls and the prison windows of our gray days; if we can no longer hear the gentle step of the announcing angels; if our soul no longer is at once shaken and exalted by their whispered word—then it will be all over with us. We are living wasted time and are dead before they do us any harm.... Space is still filled with the noise of destruction and annihilation, the shouts of self-assurance and arrogance, the weeping of despair and helplessness. But just beyond the horizon the eternal realities stand silent in their age-old longing. There shines on us the first mild light of the radiant fulfillment to come. From afar sounds the first notes as pipes and singing boys, not yet discernible as a song or melody. It is all far off still, and only just announced and foretold. But it is happening. This is today. And tomorrow the angels will tell what has happened with loud rejoicing voices, and we shall know it and be glad, if we have believed and trusted in Advent."

In the last few years, we have heard the noise of destruction and the weeping of despair. In my own small story, I have seen reasons for frustration and discouragement. But I have also seen reasons for hope. I have seen a wounded nation rise to great purposes ... and millions of men and women draw their first free breath. I have seen the generosity of the poor in a burning pit mine ... and black death defeated in a young woman who loves to dance. I have prayed with Moses in his sad but promised land ... and held squirming orphans who, without the influence of America, would be images painted on a wall in the arms of Jesus. I have had a tremor of blessing, a wink of heaven, a whisper. And I believe in a fulfillment to come.

Index